The
EVERYTHING®
Resume Book

Dear Reader,

I've spent twenty-four years, half of my life so far, critiquing resumes. Each time I review a draft, I trust that the changes I make inspire new attitudes and actions. Resumes encapsulate the past, but they are also forecasters of the future. Beyond describing what you have already done, your resume targets the goals you will someday achieve.

This book is meant for all readers, regardless of age or experience. Thanks to my editor and the wonderful *Everything*® book format, all concepts should be easy to understand and to use. Most important is the concept that your resume is one integral factor of a comprehensive job-search. Without that understanding, you limit the potential your resume can have.

The EVERYTHING® Series

Editorial

Publishing Director	Gary M. Krebs
Managing Editor	Kate McBride
Copy Chief	Laura MacLaughlin
Acquisitions Editor	Eric Hall
Development Editor	Michael Paydos
Production Editor	Khrysti Nazzaro

Production

Production Director	Susan Beale
Production Manager	Michelle Roy Kelly
Series Designers	Daria Perreault
	Colleen Cunningham
Cover Design	Paul Beatrice
	Frank Rivera
Layout and Graphics	Colleen Cunningham
	Rachael Eiben
	Michelle Roy Kelly
	Daria Perreault
	Erin Ring
Series Cover Artist	Barry Littmann

Visit the entire Everything® Series at everything.com

THE
EVERYTHING®
RESUME BOOK

2ND EDITION

Great resumes
for every situation

Burton Jay Nadler

Adams Media Corporation
Avon, Massachusetts

Resumes document the past,
but children are the legacies we leave the future.

An Everything® Series Book.
Everything® is a registered trademark of Adams Media Corporation.

Published by Adams Media Corporation
57 Littlefield Street, Avon, MA 02322 U.S.A.
www.adamsmedia.com

ISBN: 1-58062-807-9
Printed in the United States of America.

J   I   H   G   F   E   D   C   B   A

Library of Congress Cataloging-in-Publication Data
Nadler, Burton Jay
The everything resume book / Burton Jay Nadler.– 2nd ed.
p.   cm.   (An everything series book)
Rev. ed. of: The everything resume book : great resumes
for every situation / by Steven Graber.
ISBN 1-58062-807-9
1. Résumés (Employment) I. Graber, Steven. Everything resume book.
II. Title. III. Series: Everything series.
HF5383 .N28 2003
650.14'2–dc21

2002153890

This publication is designed to provide accurate and authoritative information with regard to the subject matter covered. It is sold with the understanding that the publisher is not engaged in rendering legal, accounting, or other professional advice. If legal advice or other expert assistance is required, the services of a competent professional person should be sought.

—From a *Declaration of Principles* jointly adopted by a Committee of the American Bar Association and a Committee of Publishers and Associations

Many of the designations used by manufacturers and sellers to distinguish their products are claimed as trademarks. Where those designations appear in this book and Adams Media was aware of a trademark claim, the designations have been printed with initial capital letters.

This book is available at quantity discounts for bulk purchases.
For information, call 1-800-872-5627.

Contents

Resumes as Interview Preparation and Motivation Tools / 117

Resume Review and Critique / 135

What They Say about Your Resume / 159

Acknowledgments

Jordan, Justin, Sarah, Rachel, Leah, Haley, Logan, Robbie, Kelly, Landry, Taylor, Dani, Lexi, Lauren, Jordan, and Britt. You are legacies of family and friends. All of you, particularly the first two, fill those who love you with pride. Keep building emotional and behavioral resumes and attaining dreams.

One Spartan never had a written resume. Stories told by others varied in truth, tone, and content, but the accomplishments always came out the same. You are missed and not forgotten.

College and recruiting colleagues, students and alumni. You continue to teach me many lessons that I share through books like this one.

Top Ten Reasons to
Update Your Resume

1. You've been promoted!

2. With the shifts in the economy occurring on a weekly basis, you never know when you might get laid off.

3. Your boss's office is looking better and better . . .

4. You moved, got a new cell phone, got married, or had your contact information change in some way.

5. After ten winters totaling fifty feet of snow, you're thinking that a migration south might be a change for the better.

6. You are thinking about new career goals or a change in careers.

7. You just finished grad school or a special training program.

8. You just noticed that your current resume lists DOS as the only operating system you know.

9. You have a hunch that your office pen thefts will one day catch up to you.

10. You never know when you'll need to have it ready at a moment's notice . . .

Introduction

▶ THE PHRASE "It's time to get your resume together" sends shivers down many a spine, causing headaches as well as heartaches. Graduating from college, hunting for a new, more responsible position, and losing a job can all cause nervous perspiration and palpitations. It is possible, however, to be invigorated by a review of your achievements and to look forward to a challenging, rewarding future.

Resume writing and job hunting don't have to make you anxious. This book illustrates resume formats that clarify goals, simplify the job search, and speed up the interviewing process. Job seekers do not have to read the minds of their prospective employers to determine vaguely what "they" want. It's more important that the job-search documents—resumes, cover letters, and follow-up letters—project the sense that the job seeker knows him- or herself, including the skills and assets that make him or her the perfect candidate for the job.

The resume is a document that universally symbolizes the beginning of a job hunt. When used effectively, it should symbolize and support the beginning, middle, and end as well. *The Everything® Resume Book, 2nd Edition* is designed to do the same. Read and act upon the powerful ideas presented in this book to create the powerful page that will inspire and facilitate your effective job search.

History tells us that over the years, many people have used resumes to achieve many different ends. Palace favorites once carried documents marked by waxed impressions of royal signet rings to prove their power and status. Envoys and ambassadors to this day carry documents citing their status that allow them safe transport and immunity. Wealthy travelers were once able to present papers at banks throughout the civilized world to establish their identities and be assured immediate credit.

For centuries, we have used documents to confirm our identities, make introductions, and inspire others to see us as useful, valuable, and capable. Regardless of its origins, the resume can provide a powerful boost to your job hunt. E

Chapter 1

E Resume Writing and the Job Search

We all know the purpose of a resume—to help us get a job! But many job seekers don't see that all aspects of the job hunt are interrelated. Your career, education, and life lead to your resume; your resume inspires you to apply for certain jobs; your resume and application lead to job interviews; and one of those interviews, you hope, lands you a new job.

Resume Writing for Today's Job World

Nothing illustrates the importance of resume writing like the vast number of books written on the subject. Over the years, there have been almost as many suggestions for format, contents, and approaches as there are resume books in print.

Books published only a few years ago are already out of date. As technology changes, so do the concepts related to state-of-the-art resumes, the so-called "e-resumes." While books once detailed how to prepare a resume suitable for scanning, today's resumes are transmitted by e-mail or over the Web. That means less concern with formatting and more focus on keywords for online searches.

This book addresses traditional resumes as well as e-resumes. Samples like those included in these chapters should inspire you. Resume illustrations can often appear intimidating, as presentations of perfect job candidates. Don't worry! You aren't competing with these mythic people for jobs, but you can use their example to make your resume as dynamic as theirs.

Seeking Inspiration

One late-night search of an online book retailer's inventory returned over 600 titles on the search keyword "resume." You, too, have probably encountered the confusion of shelf after shelf of titles in the career section of your local bookstore. No matter how, where, or why you purchased this edition of *The Everything® Resume Book,* you have taken a solid first step out of that information quagmire. You are now ready for education as well as motivation.

The Old Approach: "Resumes Any Way"

For years, resume books have established and reinforced a "resumes any way" attitude. No matter the title, these books all espoused the same belief: "There is no one perfect resume." Ironically, even those authors who did promote the so-called "perfect" resume did little more than echo the others. Most, if not all, of those books focused on creating the resume that potential employers (the infamous "they") would want to see.

Readers were encouraged to assume the thoughts and preferences of their prospective employers. Energies and attitudes were focused on what "they"—meaning human resources professionals, managers, recruiters, and executives—wanted to see in job-search documents like resumes, cover letters, and other supporting material. The "resumes any way" approach covered too many bases and included long, often contradictory, laundry lists of what "they" wanted.

Such an approach has an obvious disadvantage. There's no way that you, the job hunter, can possibly know what "they" want to see in your resume. A far more sensible—and effective—approach is to focus on what you do know: yourself. A successful, effective resume presents you as a person who knows the job and has the skills and abilities to do that job better than anyone else. It's that simple!

Focus on Yourself

With the proper attitude, guidance, and communication tools, anyone can successfully look for a job. You don't have to be a hotshot Ivy League graduate. Whoever you are, and whatever you have done to date, you can develop a powerful resume that will help you achieve your career goals. As your resume will reveal, you are the best.

Simplified Steps to Job-Search Success

Great resumes are the beginning of job-search success! Through the process of resume writing, you will also be empowered to do the following:

1. Set and articulate professional goals.
2. Create or update a goal-directed resume.
3. Develop a "target list" of potential employers, and a "network" of advocates.
4. Respond to posted job openings.
5. Call first, then fax or e-mail and, finally, mail resumes, cover letters, and supporting materials.

6. Follow up, assess strategies, follow up, enhance competencies, then follow up again and again.
7. Interview using your resume for guidance.
8. Receive offers, and accept one.

Set and Articulate Professional Goals

Your resume does not have to set and state your lifelong goals. But it should express the aim of your immediate job search, and you should understand how these aims fit in to your long-term career plan. Pre-research (that is, research before job search) is the key to goal-setting, and that includes an inventory of your achievements and qualifications. A successful, goal-oriented resume projects focus and mirrors self-knowledge. The most powerful resumes make clear statements of the job hunter's objectives.

Pre-research, the time before putting your resume together when you investigate your chosen job field, is conducted using four techniques:

- Paper and pencil or eyes to screen (using printed and Web resources)
- Person to person (conducting information conversations)
- Exploration by academics (taking courses or seminars)
- Exploration by experience (including internships or special projects)

An objective like, "I'm looking for anything, anywhere," is not focused enough to be effective. As you create and update your resume, focus will become easier, and it will be easier to project the confidence you gain from self-assessment. Goal-setting often begins by assessing yourself (identifying your values, interests, and skills). Next comes research into careers, job functions, and academic options. When you write your resume and other job-search documents, you project the knowledge you've gained about yourself and your chosen field, creating a powerful self-presentation. The interview, at that point, is your opportunity to flesh out in person the image you've already created on paper.

The list on pages 3–4 spells out eight steps to a successful job search. You must be able to articulate your goals and qualifications in order to complete all eight (in other words, to get the job you want). Career counseling is available from a variety of sources that can help you with your self-assessment.

If you are a college student or graduate, your college career center may provide services to address your needs. There are also private counselors. Many career guidance books include "do-it-yourself" assessment exercises designed to help you find your chosen career. Some Web sites also provide assessment exercises. Appendix D lists valuable resources for undertaking this first critical step to job-search success.

One of the best and simplest ways of focusing your career goals is to read the trade magazines and other publications of a few industries. In as little as a few hours of reading, you can learn enough about job requirements and your own skill set to contribute to a powerful and clear statement of professional objectives.

ESSENTIAL

Looking in the mirror is self-reflection for some, but it's not the kind of assessment you need for job-search success. Don't confuse introspection with assessment or active exploration. Meditation rarely yields goal articulation, but reading a book or two might help. Printed and online resources also help. Reference librarians and Web search engines are excellent and underused resources.

Goal-Directed Resumes Your Way

Not coincidently, the steps for creating or updating your resume run parallel to the steps you take toward identifying and articulating your professional goals. In turn, a strong resume inspires you to write dynamic cover letters and follow-ups. This chapter prepares you to complete a fast, effective resume. (Chapter 7 provides more guidance and inspiration for quick resume writing.)

Develop a "Target List" of Potential Employers

Just as important as your resume is your target list of people, places, and organizations that might be potential employers. You develop this list starting with professional directories and other printed and online resources. (Online resources can provide a wealth of contact information, as detailed in Appendix D.) Your colleagues, friends, family, faculty, and fellow graduates can also help with pre-research, networking, and actual job-search efforts. When you ask around for assistance and job referrals, always include a copy of your resume with your request. This is a good way of projecting your potential and inspiring continued support from your advocates.

Once you've collected some names and numbers, it's time to pick up the phone. Telephone calls are your best way to confirm the proper contact people and, if possible, to clarify the nature of any jobs available. Keep updating your list, and maintain clear records of your contacts. Know whom you've talked to, when you talked, and what you talked about. Follow-up is critical, so you must always know the status of your interactions with those on your hit list.

QUESTION?

What is a job-search advocate?
Job-search advocates are those people who actively support your efforts to find your ideal job. They offer ongoing advice and regularly refer you to postings and, when possible, to prospective employers. Advocates are most often nurtured, not just found.

Talking to people is the best way to gather, analyze, and prioritize information regarding employment options and referrals. Initiate the networking process with a call or, more common today, an e-mail. When you "e-communicate," introduce yourself and state that you will soon follow up with a call. Always be courteous and clear about why you're getting in touch. You can ask for specific referrals or informal "information conversations." Conversations like these are a good way to learn about the careers of people in your chosen industry and to solicit their help in your job search. These contacts can act as advocates within their organizations, offering direct referrals and providing recommendations. They can also introduce you to associates in other companies, thus increasing the scope and power of your network.

Building Your Network

The purpose of networking is twofold. First, you want to know as much about your chosen field as possible. You network with as many people as you can in that field to get all of their input and points of view. Second, you want to become known in your chosen field. The more people you meet, the more your name and your qualifications become known. Networking is a powerful component of any successful job search.

Professional groups and online resources like field-focused Web sites or mailing lists are good ways to begin networking. Go slowly. Instead of introducing yourself right away as a job seeker, ask for a business card. Then, in follow-up communications, you can identify your career goals and ask for guidance. Once the person has responded to your request, share your resume as an effective way of presenting your goals and qualifications.

FACT

Successful job seekers often cite networking as one of the most important factors in their success. Most polls of experienced job candidates rank networking as a top tool. Even in this Internet age, person-to-person networking is still important, yet few do it well.

End each networking conversation by getting guidance on what you should do next, whom you should contact, and, of course, with a resounding "Thank you!" Keep communications current by dropping a line every now and then to keep your contact informed of your progress.

Finding Job Postings and Advertisements

Many people fool themselves into thinking they are conducting a comprehensive job search just because their resumes are uploaded onto a few headhunter Web sites. It's true that Web-based job postings are part of an effective job-search strategy. But answering these ads is a reactive effort—that is, a reaction, rather than an action—and that's just part of a comprehensive campaign. An effective job search must also include proactive strategies, including networking. In later chapters we detail some effective proactive strategies. We also identify potential Web and printed resources as well as related strategies.

ESSENTIAL

Comprehensive job-search campaigns include proactive as well as reactive strategies and resources. No matter how proactive you are, you should still be prepared to maximize your reactive efforts. Old-fashioned newspaper want ads are still a good source of information about potential jobs. Don't forget about postings printed in general and subject-specific periodicals. Professional newsletters and journals are too often ignored.

Call, Fax, or E-Mail, and (Finally) Mail Your Resume

Your goal is to inform as many people as possible about your goals. Keep the flow of communications persistent, but make sure they're appropriate, too. Here are some communications tips for strengthening your network and approaching others effectively:

- Don't ever wait to communicate! First, call to confirm your contact person. When possible, request detailed information regarding available positions and posting methods.
- If you are told not to contact someone directly, respect this request.
- Submit documentation as instructed, confident that it will be processed and forwarded appropriately.
- After making the initial call, fax, e-mail, or mail your resume. Attach a resume to your initial correspondence as well as follow-up e-mails, fax notes, and letters.

Don't worry about how your initial inquiries are interpreted. It's okay to ask for basic information. In fact, if you fail to take those courageous first steps, you will be unlikely to succeed at all. Typical first contacts might sound like the following.

"Hello. I would like to speak with the person in charge of hiring for your firm. Could you provide me with his/her name and title, then forward me to him/her? Thank you."

"Hello. My name is Chris Smith. I am interested in a position with your firm. I would like to fax or e-mail you a copy of my cover letter and resume. What is most convenient, and to whom should I address my inquiry? What is the fax number (or e-mail address) of the contact person? Also, are printed or online descriptions of opportunities available to review?"

The best way to view your job search is to think of it as a communication process. You initiate the communication reactively when you answer postings; you are proactive when you contact the people on your target list. Don't hesitate to communicate, and be polite and respectful when doing so.

FACT

A common mistake on resumes, especially in describing your work experience, is to write ". . . over three years experience in . . . ." "Years" as used in this statement is a type of possessive and must therefore include an apostrophe: ". . . over three years' experience in . . . ."

Follow Up, Follow Up, Follow Up

There is always an appropriate way to follow up. E-mail whenever possible. It's usually easier to be clear in writing, and you can send your message after hours, when you have time to clearly pose questions or convey your appreciation. Thank-you notes, faxed or e-mailed, are the most common form of follow-up. Continue to build your relationships with prospective employers, and reinforce your existing networking relationships via a well-crafted series of e-mails or phone calls.

Enthusiastic and upbeat questions and comments are obviously much more effective than impatient and demanding inquiries. Be sensitive and creative in your follow-up communications. Be persistent, but don't pester.

It's sometimes difficult to pick up the phone or compose yet another friendly follow-up e-mail. But remember that each follow-up effort increases your chances of reaching your goal and getting that job. Regularly assess the effectiveness of your follow-up efforts (did your follow-up lead to another conversation? a return letter? an interview?) and refocus if you need to.

Be polite and persistent. Always call to confirm whether materials were received. This gives you a chance to ask your contact what will happen next and when you should take your next step. You can ask whether you should communicate again within a designated time period. If the answer is "Be patient," don't make a pest of yourself by calling back anyway. However, others in your network—particularly your job-search advocates—can support you with calls or e-mails to a potential employer.

It is your responsibility to communicate effectively during your job search. Don't expect prospective employers to follow up with you, and don't expect your resume to get you in the door all on its own. Your resume is a crucial part of your job search, but it's follow-up that fuels a job-seeker's success.

ALERT!

"Phone-a-phobia" can be fatal. E-mail may be state of the art, but the telephone is still a powerful communication tool. In fact, it's essential to your job search. Decide what you will say before you call. Be sure to confirm receipt of previous letters, identify next steps, and politely request an interview. First interviews are often conducted by phone.

The Interview

Chapter 9 provides detailed preparation for interviews, with specific questions and answers. The first and most basic thing to remember about interviewing is to project confidence, whether the interview is in person or over the phone. To be confident, you need to be prepared.

Your resume is the focal point and foundation for interview preparation. Be confident in the abilities you describe in your resume and in your qualifications to perform the job. It is best to know as much as possible about the interview situation. Ask beforehand about how many people will be interviewing you and how long the interview is scheduled to take. Are there any materials your interviewers recommend you read before they talk to you? Inquire about proper attire. "Business casual" means pressed slacks, an ironed shirt, and a tie (with sport coat optional) for men, and slacks or skirt, ironed shirt, or sweater appropriate for women. Others are "business formal," with suits required for men and women.

ALERT!

In preparing for your interview, don't memorize answers to typical questions, and don't practice too much. Role-play is a good way to become familiar with topics and build confidence. Use your resume as a checklist, but be prepared to talk about other topics and concepts as well.

There are different types of interviews, and it is best to be prepared for any of them. In the "conversational" type, interviewers chat with candidates and ask fairly typical interview questions. Another type is the "behavioral" interview, in which you are asked about past achievements and about details regarding behaviors (and skills) that contributed to these undertakings. Behavioral interviewers typically ask, "What would you do in this situation?"

Occasionally, particularly for consulting firms, interviews are "case studies," in which interviewers ask you to analyze specific situations so they can see how you "think on your seat." Counseling professionals and network members can coach you here. Practice may not make perfect, but role-playing will build confidence.

Offers and Acceptance

You are going to get a job offer, and you will need the skills to analyze and appropriately respond to it. Remain focused. Salary data is available online (see resources in Appendix D) and in books. Here's where your network comes in really handy; ask around to see what kind of offer you should expect and how to negotiate, if necessary.

Once you accept an offer, stop your job search. Period. Do not take another offer and renege on the first one. If you need to know about an offer, conduct your research before you accept. With an offer in hand, it is much easier to call other prospective employers and talk about your chances of their offering you a position. Don't hesitate to make those calls if you think their input might help you make a good decision.

Psychological Barriers

For some, the idea of updating or creating a resume generates a counterproductive attitude. These negative beliefs include the following:

- I can't create a resume if I don't have anything to offer.
- Even the sample resumes look better than mine.
- I haven't done much, so I shouldn't update my resume.
- If I don't have an ideal job in mind, I can't create or update my resume.
- I don't know what employers want to see, so I can't start or finish my resume.
- I've heard they don't really read resumes, so why bother.
- It's not really the right time to look for a job, so I don't have to create or update my resume.

The search for the perfect resume and the ideal time to create or update one may last forever for those suffering from self-doubt and lack of focus. You know you need a resume to start and complete your job search. Ironically, if you delay your resume writing and subsequent job search, you also delay the ultimate positive reinforcement that comes with interviews and, yes, offers.

Some Excuses

The reasons and excuses for avoiding creating and updating a resume are too numerous to name. The following examples show how futile and pointless these excuses are in the face of such an important need, the need for a powerful resume.

- I can't find my old version, and I don
- I don't have enough money to pay f
  resume developers, so I'll wait.
- I can't seem to get it to one page, s
- I missed the deadline for that job ┌
  before I need to finish my resume.
- I don't know what employers wan
  my resume.

Resumes Created in a D

Even people who think of the job search as difficult and ⸍⸌⸗
anxiety must agree that it ends with success! You will attain your goals! It
all begins with a few easy steps. Chapter 2 describes the seven steps to a
successful resume, which are illustrated throughout this book (especially
in our sample resumes). Here's how you get your start:

1. Review some samples, including your old resumes and the examples
   in this book. Pay particular attention to those related to your goals.
2. Pick the approach that you want to model. Imitation is more than
   flattery. It is the best strategy in writing your resume.
3. Determine the format, content, and order of your resume. Will you
   use headlines? What entries will be presented within these categories?
   In what order will these sections appear?

FACT

Most experts agree that a job search takes at least three months.
Be surprised if it takes only a few weeks, and remain determined
and upbeat if it takes longer than the estimated three months.
Everything starts with the proper attitude. Eventually, all true job
searches end with success.

Next, if you have not already done so, identify your objectives and
target audiences. What is your job-search target? (This is not
necessarily your career goal.) Can you clearly and concisely articulate

s? If not, don't fret. Chapter 4 will take you through this step
inimal pain.

Once you've defined your goals, you can create a resume in one day.
ut your goals on paper, then list your relevant qualifications and
achievements. Examine your general qualifications, and present your
specific competencies and capabilities in terms of their importance. Once
you have a draft together, read it over with an eye to the person (you) it
represents. Your aim is to present yourself as qualified, knowledgeable,
and self-confident. By following these steps, you can create a resume in
just one day. Why not make it today?

No More Procrastination

Creating a resume is frustrating work, and it is easy to procrastinate.
At this early stage, though, you have already begun the journey toward
updating or creating a powerful resume. You will soon have "travel
papers" in hand for the voyage that will end with meaningful
employment.

By the time you finish this chapter and the next, you will know
what it takes to update or create a powerful resume and how to
fit your resume into a comprehensive job search.

Your Job-Search Foundation

Resume writing happens through a series of cognitive and behavioral
steps. These steps also form a foundation for your effective job-search
campaign. Each of the eight steps toward job-search success (the steps
outlined earlier in this chapter) depends on a powerful, goal-oriented
resume. The only way to write a focused, targeted resume is to set and
articulate your goals. For many people, goal articulation is the missing link
to resume writing and job search. Those seeking "anything, anywhere,"
often find "nothing, nowhere."

With focus, you will create or update goal-directed resumes—you can have more than one targeted resume, each reflecting a different goal. These are your tools for initial contact, follow-up, interview prep, and interviews themselves.

When you call first, then fax or e-mail, and, finally, mail your resumes to potential employers, you begin a communication process that includes your resume at every step. As you stop to follow up and assess your strategy, you refocus your job-search efforts. This includes updating your resume. Ultimately, when your efforts yield an interview, your resume will be your preparation tool. Throughout the process, your resume is your key communication device. It presents your past performance and your future potential. It is the reference point for potential employers to use in selecting you as a worthy job candidate.

ESSENTIAL

Here's a confidence-building exercise. Take out a piece of paper, or open a new file on your computer. At the top of the page, write your name, address, telephone number, and e-mail address. You've just started your resume.

After you ace the interview—using your resume as a powerful tool—and accept an offer, you might want to update your resume right away. No, you don't have to begin your next job search so soon. But entering your new position on your resume makes a bold, confident psychological statement. Your new resume will honestly and accurately reflect that you started that very day.

Chapter 2

Writing Your Resume

During the years that the "resumes any way" attitude prevailed, authors echoed the belief that "there is no one perfect resume." This mentality made it difficult for resume writers to find the focus necessary to present themselves successfully on paper. In our approach, where resumes are created "your way," we follow seven simple steps to creating successful resumes.

The Seven Key Steps to Writing a Resume

1. Review as many resume samples as you can. Look over old versions of your own resume, and ask friends and associates if they'd mind letting you take a look at theirs. This book includes many samples of many different resumes, designed for many different fields.

2. Analyze those resumes. Think about what makes them work. Effective elements might include things like format, content, and the order of information.

3. Identify your job objectives and your target audience. What field are you planning to enter? Be sure you know the proper terminology, the job functions that will make you valuable, and how to present yourself as a valuable candidate.

4. Perform an inventory of your qualifications and achievements. Knowing yourself and being confident in your abilities is key to creating a powerful resume.

5. Analyze your competencies and capabilities as they relate to your job goals and your chosen field. This is another aspect of the "know yourself" mantra. How do you see yourself contributing to this field?

6. Draft your resume, and critique it. Compare your draft to the samples you've analyzed and admired. How does it compare in terms of format, content, and order of information you've presented? Fix those elements you see can be stronger. Proofread it carefully, and after you're sure it's perfect, ask a friend to look it over.

7. Make plenty of copies, and distribute your resume whenever appropriate.

The Resume Your Way

If there is no perfect resume, how can you hope to create a document that all employers would want to see? The answer comes from a change in emphasis. Stop thinking about "resumes any way," designed to present yourself as you think "they" want to see you. Start writing resumes *your* way.

A good resume presents your past achievements as well as the assets and capabilities that qualify you for this new job. As you get better at communicating your qualifications, you will approach the job of writing your resume with confidence. The seven steps to success are good guidelines, and they should inspire confidence. But before you start writing, it is also a good idea to understand the different types of resumes and the purposes they serve. The following sections describe some traditional types and formats of resumes.

Chronological, Functional, and Combined Resumes

Chronological resumes present information in reverse chronological order, starting with the present and working backward. They traditionally use one-word "headers" to identify content sections. As you've read and heard again and again, they are no longer than one page in length.

Functional resumes present candidate skill sets and discussions independent from job descriptions, if those descriptions are included at all. Most resume guides recommend functional formats for "career changers" or for those who are "keeping their options open," while the chronological format is usually recommended for all others.

Combined resumes include a skill profile and present work history, educational background, and other content under typical headers and in reverse chronological order.

Targeted and Multipurpose Resumes

Recent resume guides use phrases like "targeted" and "multipurpose." Targeted resumes include a clear objective or description of professional goals. Multipurpose resumes are intended to be all things to all people, broadly presenting one's general job worthiness.

Combinations, Permutations, and Confusion

If we recall some basic math, we see that these five types of resumes give us six possible permutations in the resume equation. Knowing that your resume is in "a targeted and chronological format" doesn't make it a better job-search tool, nor you a better job seeker, but at least you know what to call it.

Chronological resumes present content in reverse chronological order, starting with the present then working backward. These one-page documents use one-word headers for content sections. Students and recent graduates usually list education first, and experience comes first for everyone else.

Some guides advise you to include all the schools you attended. Some suggest that you include only those schools where you were conferred a degree. Many books and articles emphatically suggest that you list courses, while as many others strongly urge you not to because "'they' know what someone with your major took." Some suggest that you present all scholarships and honors, no matter how small, because the longer the list, the more "they" will be impressed. Still others encourage you not to present all scholarships and honors. But when it comes to grades, everyone agrees: Only include good grades and averages!

Advice regarding experience is equally conflicted. Some say describe all jobs, no matter how small, in active terms, in hopes that some of those verbs will catch a prospective employer's eye. Others state with conviction that you should only include impressive jobs. Should you list volunteer and community service experience? Some say yes, but some say no; the same goes for personal interests. We (almost) reach consensus on the closing sentence: "References available upon request" should be your closer.

ALERT!

Amazingly, authors, resume counselors, and others continue to encourage functional resumes when almost all inquiries to prospective employers reveal that this format is ineffective and difficult to review. According to studies and polls, the pure functional resume format is the least preferred.

Functional resumes present and highlight skill sets independent from the jobs in which they were gained. In this resume type, skill listings come before all other content. The functional format is traditionally recommended for first-time job seekers as well as career changers with little or no specific focus. Skill summaries tend to be lengthy, presented with hope that some broadly chosen phrases might stick in the minds of readers and encourage interviews. In this model, it's employers, not the job seekers, who define the job being sought.

Combination resumes contain skill or qualification profiles, like the functional format, but they also incorporate the chronological format by presenting work history, educational background, and other content in reverse chronological order. These resumes often combine the conflicts described for the other types. "How can I create a resume for 'they,' anyway?" was the question that left many without an answer.

The Modern Resume Your Way

As you focus on your chosen career field and articulate your abilities, your resume writing and your job search will be inspired. A resume that projects "me and my goals" will strengthen the rest of your job search; it will also have an impact on the outcome. Keep your goals firmly in mind. Enhance the power and purpose of your resume. Plan and implement strategic actions.

Goal-setting is critical to all resume-writing and job-search efforts. While useful multipurpose documents abound, targeted resumes are the most powerful. Overall, goal development and articulation are the most crucial components of resume writing and your comprehensive job search.

State-of-the-Art Documents Focused on You

A resume that focuses upon you makes you the central figure in the resume-writing and job-search process. You must clarify and articulate your goals, on paper but also in person. If anyone asks how you created such an effective resume, you can take a page from Frank Sinatra and respond: "I did it my way!"

Our first sample resume (shown in **FIGURE 1-1**) is an adaptation of the "Harvard Business School Resume." For generations, this was the required format for graduates of this prestigious school of business, and it illustrates a frequently copied and generally effective resume.

The Harvard Business School format is appropriate for investment banking and consulting positions. However, no single resume format is specifically required by any particular field. The samples presented in this book are aimed for many popular fields. It's up to you, the job seeker, to establish your targets and create or update the formats you deem appropriate.

Sample Resume: Harvard Business School Format

FIGURE 1-1

CHRIS SMITH

100 Main Street, Apartment 1 • Hometown, NY 00000
csmith@company.com • (555) 555-1234

education

1995–1997   HARVARD GRADUATE SCHOOL OF BUSINESS   BOSTON, MA
Candidate for Master in Business Administration degree, June 1997.
Vice President of Marketing Club. Codirector of Marketing Project. Outreach 1996
Volunteer Program. Tutor first-year students.

1987–1990   CORNELL UNIVERSITY   ITHACA, NY
Bachelor of Arts degree, double major in American Civilization and French,
May 1990. Studied international relations and political science in Paris at
L'Institut d'Etudes Politiques. Freshman Advisor. Chair, Visiting Prospective
Students Program and Student/Alumni Network.

experience

Summer 1996   UNIVERSAL STUDIOS   LOS ANGELES, CA
**Summer Assistant Marketing Manager, Consumer Products/Interactive
Division:** Worked with Vice President of Sales and Marketing to create business
vision and branding strategy for introduction of new brand in educational interactive products industry.
- Developed brand elements and positioning statements and contributed to
  brand-name generation.
- Created preliminary marketing communications programs for brand launch
  and national product roll-out, targeting both home and academic markets.
- Analyzed economic and consumer trends and conducted competitor analysis,
  resulting in entry strategy recommendation.

1992–1995   THE MAXIMUM MARKETING GROUP   NEW YORK, NY
Associate Supervisor: Directed marketing communications activities for Nikon,
agency's largest account, representing 65% of annual billings at start-up firm specializing in consumer products.
- Created strategic plan to increase brand awareness and loyalty in consumer
  and professional photography markets. Addressed shrinking market share and
  increased competition.
- Managed new product launches from concept development to market for
  existing and new products. Led multifunctional team responsible for product
  positioning, competitor analysis, media coverage, and dealer/sales education.

1990–1992   PUBLIC RELATIONS ASSOCIATES   NEW YORK, NY
Account Coordinator: Developed and implemented national media campaigns
in support of new product launches for Nikon Lite-Touch, Reebok Pump, and
Step Reebok aerobic workout program.

personal   Fluent in French. Active Cornell alumni interviewer and volunteer for youth
hockey program.

To use our old labels, this format is a "multipurpose chronological resume." Note the use of one-word headers and the condensed presentation of educational information. Work experience is first described in general terms, and specific achievements are then highlighted using bullets. The format efficiently uses space and highlighting techniques, including capitalization, bold, and italics. In some ways, this resume is still "they" oriented, presented to meet the (unknown) expectations of the potential employer. We can consider this a solid example of this type of resume, but one that is not quite evolved to the approach we are learning. Samples shown later in this book illustrate techniques for building a stronger resume, including the following:

- Headlines or objective statements that clearly project focus. Well-crafted headlines advertise the nature of your content and reinforce your stated job goal or career focus.
- A comprehensive "summary of qualifications" section, including appropriate terminology and field-focused verbs and nouns, projects a knowledge of self as well as a knowledge of the field.
- Rather than chronologically, information is presented to highlight the most important information first.
- Relevant courses, academic accomplishments, and other pertinent activities are listed briefly.
- Descriptions of work experience appear under headlines in order of significance. They project your capabilities and industry knowledge, as well as your accomplishments.
- Left-justified and text block formats are easy to e-mail and to upload into PDF-based resume banks and posting sites.

The best resumes have common components. They use headlines rather than headers. They include qualification summaries, lists of courses and projects, and highlights of specific accomplishments. The best resumes use field-focused terminology and present information in order of importance.

When you're reviewing these resume samples, examine those that match your field(s) of interest, but don't limit yourself. Review all the samples, and pick out the formats and contents you'd like to model. Be analytical and curious. Your background may be different from the fictional Chris Smith whose qualifications are presented over and over, but you and Chris are not in competition. Avoid focusing your resume on the "they" who will be reading it. Project your knowledge of field and functional goals. Focus on you.

FIGURE 1-1 shows an effective resume for a soon-to-be business school graduate. If it inspired you to think about what your resume should look like, this book has already been effective. Remember that the first two steps in resume-writing involve review and analysis of samples.

The College Graduation Benchmark

The people who most need resume guidance are those who have no, or very little, experience preparing one. Many who find themselves in the market for their first "real" jobs belong in the "college grad" category, which includes the following:

- First- and second-semester college seniors
- Those who have just graduated
- Those whose job search continues at least three to six months beyond commencement
- Juniors, seniors, and others seeking internships

Campus career centers offer counseling and job-search coaching, with seniors being the most likely to take advantage of these services. First-semester seniors spend a lot of time on resumes for on-campus recruiting, career fairs, and other job-placement offerings. On-campus counseling usually produces resumes focused on what the recruiter expects, rather than the candidate's qualifications and focus. In their urgency to create and update their resumes, first-semester seniors often overlook the assessment and research steps that lead to goal-setting. Fear of focus often motivates them to avoid these critical steps to college resume-writing success.

New job candidates usually hope that a large quantity of data will overcome any issues of quality. Anxious about "what recruiters want to see," and hoping that *something* in their arsenal will get them on-campus interviews, they include everything. Myths about recruiters seeking "well-rounded" individuals inspire this kind of "spew." Ironically, candidates are actually screened with narrow, rather than diverse criteria. Reviewers of college resumes are most on the lookout for field-focused majors, high grade-point averages, and pertinent internships.

Second-semester seniors are either inspired by reactions of recruiters gained during the fall, or they become anxious and pessimistic because few responded favorably to their resumes. Those with goals matching the fields and functions that recruiters are looking for often use the same resume and reactive strategies through the spring semester and beyond. Those whose goals do not match recruiters' needs, and those who cannot express their goals, get very anxious around commencement time. This anxiety often inspires unfocused, multipurpose resumes, or leads to procrastination that lingers well past commencement day.

No matter the school, and based on those schools' placement statistics, approximately 30–50 percent of college graduates keep looking for a job after commencement. About 15–25 percent failed to set goals or start their job search before graduation. For these candidates, like anyone else looking for a new job, it's important to work through the seven steps to resume success. The assessment and research steps are particularly effective for gaining and projecting focus. This is critical, as a complete, effective job search mirrors the candidate's knowledge of qualifications and field-specific competencies.

FACT

College graduates are commonly confused by misunderstood job-related data and statistics. Many feel that the top students take all the good jobs, with nothing left by commencement. In reality, recruiting seasons are on-campus anomalies. In the real world, the job search goes on after June. Many, many candidates get their jobs three to six months after they graduate.

Here are a few questions that are common among recent or soon-to-be graduates:

- How do I make my resume stand out?
- What if I don't have related experience or education?
- Should I include education or experiences from high school?
- When and how do I present my most significant work experience?
- If I had one very relevant course and project, how do I highlight both, or either?
- What do I do if I don't have any relevant education or experience?
- If I haven't been successful getting an interview, should I change my resume?

More than any other kind of job candidate, if you are a soon-to-be or recent graduate, you must work hard on identifying and articulating your goals. Identify and analyze what you learned in the classroom and beyond. Pick out your most significant courses, labs, and projects, and present those in terms of their potential for making you valuable and effective on the job. Focus your resume and your search for a job or internship on your academic achievements, but don't forget to analyze what you've learned in terms of your personal exploration and your choice of a career field.

Intern Candidates

About 75 percent of college students use resumes in their search for an internship. Internships are difficult to define. In general, an internship is more sophisticated than a summer job. Some are paying positions. Some internships offer academic credit, while others are more project-focused, offering the opportunity to build skills and explore a field of interest. Some internships are promoted through large, well-publicized and structured programs, and others are identified through networking and self-initiated efforts.

Internships are growing in importance. Students in search of an internship should use their resumes to project their curiosity, competency, and their awareness of the field.

Candidates tend to search for internships out of curiosity, and they tend to use unfocused, multipurpose resumes. Just like any other job candidate, those seeking internships must project focus. Through targeted resumes and articulate letters, they must show how much they have already learned. You're probably looking for an internship to get a deeper knowledge of your field of interest, but—in an ironic twist—you need to project focus and some familiarity with the field before you can get that internship.

First Jobs

This category includes people who have worked two years or less in a volunteer or other nonprofessional position. It also includes people with up to three years of on-the-job experience.

Many college grads do not get their dream jobs right away, nor do they usually start out on a clearly defined career path. Often these young men and women lack the focus to begin their true career development or to implement a goal-directed job search. So, naturally, they find "transition positions."

These positions include a variety of experience. Some people plan to enter graduate school, so they seek "something meaningful to do." The jobs can be "for experience" or "adventures," such as the Peace Corps, Americorps, Teach for America, or maybe a job teaching English in another country. The job might also be something practical, such as a retail sales job, just for a paycheck.

No matter what the position is, the resume must support and inspire a first step onto a true career path. In these cases it is best to avoid the reverse-chronological format, as experience is still limited and the format will make it difficult to project any sense of goal or focus. It's most important to present your potential and identify your goals for the future.

Here are some common questions that new job seekers generally ask:

- If what I am doing now has nothing to do with my goals, how and where do I present my experience?
- What about education, specifically my major?
- Do I highlight what I have been doing for the past few years?

- Where and how do I present my most recent experiences?
- If I wasn't given enough responsibilities to yield achievements, how do I leverage my current job?

Candidates seeking their first jobs must focus their resumes, job-search letters, and interviews on the qualifications they already have and that they will need to succeed in the future. Resumes must target the newly identified goals. Objective must be presented clearly and supported with powerful summaries of your qualifications.

Focus here is critical. You must use the resume-writing process to identify and articulate your goals. (Working through the first five of the seven steps will help.) You must abandon the attitude of "leaving your options open" if you're going to focus on future goals.

Beyond Entry Level

Some people take their first steps (or giant leaps) on their career paths right after they graduate. Two or three years later, they're ready for more responsibility. Career centers' job advice is easy to find for college seniors. But sound guidance is much less accessible later on. Entry-level workers, those with two to five years of experience, can become confused and anxious. As with anyone, fear of change plus fear of focus yields procrastination and anxiety.

Some recent graduates seek change in a subconscious effort to recapture their college experience. In college we get to choose our courses. Our lives change from semester to semester, always offering something new. As a new member of the work force, either seeking promotion or a new position, you must decide what is driving you. Do you miss cyclical changes of academic life, or are you motivated by ambition and the need to develop your career?

Steps four and five of the resume-writing process encourage you to analyze your accomplishments so far and to assess your capabilities.

This proactive approach is positive. It motivates you to present your experience dynamically, in terms of what you've accomplished. As you consider your past achievements, your performance potential for the future becomes clearer.

Resumes for All

Whether you're called an "hourly worker," "nonexempt personnel," or—more traditionally—a "blue-collar laborer," you probably work in an administrative, food-service, customer-service, or manufacturing position. People in these fields often fail to create or update resumes that reflect their potential for continued success. Too often, when it's time to look for a new job, they depend upon applications, references, or word-of-mouth. Everyone needs and deserves a powerful resume. Word-of-mouth can be translated into words on paper, creating an effective resume that mirrors capabilities and projects a clear future focus.

FACT

The word "resume" is not used worldwide. Vita remains the most common term for job-search documentation, used almost everywhere other than the United States and by academicians, physicians, and scientists within our fifty states.

People at the other end of the professional spectrum are also often guilty of overlooking their resumes. In most cases, those we call "senior management" have old, vague resumes or no resume at all. Though they're responsible for large operations and organizations, and though they generally supervise many others, these people are not as ready for the job search as they should be.

Anyone, on any rung of the job-success ladder, should use the resume-writing process to identify and articulate their goals. No matter how diverse your interests or background, creating a powerful resume will enhance your focus and effectively project your qualifications and commitment for your future performance.

The Vitae Alternative

For professors, physicians, and scientists, resumes are not enough to present accomplishments and experiences. Vitae, or "curriculum vitae," are comprehensive documentations of academic and employment performance. Still, it isn't a bad idea for these professionals to prepare a powerful resume that encapsulates their goals and abilities on a single page.

ALERT!

Don't be confused or delay if someone asks for a "vita." Unless you are seeking positions outside the United States or within special fields, respond to requests with your resume. If applying overseas, create a vita by adding information including date of birth, sex, height and weight, and marital status; and all educational experiences, including high school.

Even though vitae are usually lengthy documents, listing publication citations, research projects, presentations, affiliations, and educational and training experiences, they don't have to be passive collections of data. The same qualities that make for a powerful resume—self-knowledge, goal focus, and clear statement of objectives—also apply to a quality vitae. (E)

Chapter 3

Seven Steps to Resume-Writing Success

Just like those popular home-repair shows that teach us to follow well-conceived plans to minimize costs, eliminate errors, and maximize outcomes, this chapter provides you with the blueprint for a great resume. It details do-it-yourself steps, identifies quick fixes, and addresses issues for career builders and job-search architects who might need special tools.

The Process

Resume writing is not as difficult as many believe. Creating your resume is an opportunity to identify the positive things about very important aspects of your life. The process can be simplified to seven easy steps (those we outlined in Chapter 2) that you can use to update or create resumes in just a day. Here are the steps again, in brief:

- Review samples.
- Determine format, content, and order of information.
- Identify objectives and target your audience.
- Inventory your qualifications and achievements.
- Analyze your competencies and capabilities.
- Draft and critique your resume.
- Duplicate it and distribute.

Reviewing Samples

Break out the pens, highlighters, and sticky notes, and start examining the samples that appear throughout this book. Analyze them like a knowledgeable and focused job seeker, excited about the task at hand. Instead of thinking critically, like an editor, identify the qualities you like.

Prospective employers look for certain things as they review resumes. (You can read some of their comments in Chapter 11.) The first thing employers and recruiters do when they want to fill a position is to list the qualifications the job requires. They list these traits in order of priority, according to which are essential, which are optimal, and which are merely desirable (or optional).

Once the employer decides on the qualities he or she is looking for—such as capabilities, areas of expertise, character qualities, employment history, and educational background—candidates are sourced (or encouraged to apply), screened, and, ultimately, interviewed and selected. Sometimes job descriptions and postings include detailed qualification criteria. More often, however, these preferences are expressed vaguely, in broad descriptions.

No matter how inaccurately they express their defined criteria, employers are always aware of them. Employers review resumes and cover letters, conduct interviews, and make their offers with those qualification criteria clearly in mind. In particular, they use written profiles of their desired qualifications for keyword scanning (described in Chapter 5) and behavioral interviews (Chapter 9).

While the job seeker might wish otherwise, employers almost never share detailed qualification criteria. Nor do they thoroughly analyze the resumes they receive. The employer is not responsible for digging through a mass of poorly organized, badly written resumes to find the perfect job candidate. As the job seeker, you are responsible for conveying your goals, objectives, and a clear sense of job purpose. You must create a powerful resume that mirrors your qualifications, and follow that up with an interview that impresses the employers with your capability to perform the job.

FACT

It is helpful to understand the employer's perspective, and it is a good idea to review other resumes. Just remember, this is your resume. You, and not anyone else, are responsible for success.

Format, Content, and Order of Information

Pick out your two or three favorite sample resumes. Examine them from top to bottom. Here are some basic questions to consider:

- What first impression does your resume generate? How is it formatted?
- What appears first on the page?
- How does your resume identify you? Does it include your e-mail address? Do you include both your addresses, and all your phone numbers?
- Will you include a brief yet effective objective and a qualification summary?
- Will you present educational information before or after a qualification summary? Before or after experience? How will you present this information?

- How do you order information about your work history, qualifications, and objectives?
- How can you use as few lines as possible, reserving most of the page for critical content?
- Will you use columns, with dates on the left and descriptions on the right, or a block format?
- Will headlines be centered or left-justified?
- Will they appear under clearly phrased and focused headlines?

We all learned in elementary school that it was bad to write in books. In this book, though, you should write your response to the sample resumes as you review them. Your first response to a resume is often purely visual, and ultimately, it's the human eye that reviews any successful resume. As you read, therefore, note the ways that you can give your resume a greater visual impact.

Formatting Basics

The font you choose is the key to a well-formatted resume. Fonts should be traditional, easy-to-read, and common. You don't want to create a beautiful resume in some obscure font that will be replaced on your reviewer's computer (probably destroying all your careful line spacing and other formatting work as well).

The Best Fonts and Point Sizes for Resumes

Bookman Antiqua 9 Point

Bookman Antiqua 10 Point

Bookman Antiqua 11 Point

Century Schoolbook 9 Point

Century Schoolbook 10 Point

Century Schoolbook 11 Point

Garamond 10 Point

Garamond 11 Point

Palatino 8 Point

Palatino 9 Point

Palatino 10 Point

Times 9 Point

Times 10 Point

Times New Roman 9 Point

Times New Roman 10 Point

Times New Roman 11 Point

For headlines, increase the font size two points at a time until the headline is emphasized but not disproportionate. You can highlight important elements with CAPITALIZATION, **bold face,** and *italics,* as well as with indentations, line spacing, and bullet-points. At one time, e-mailed resumes had to be formatted so they could be easily scanned. Today, PDF is more common. PDF, or "portable document format," is a file format that anyone can read using special viewing software (free from software maker Adobe). Most current word-processing systems let you save documents directly as PDFs. (Your software documentation should explain how you can do this.) The beauty of PDFs is that they allow you to use more creative formatting, such as graphics. Just keep in mind that a cluttered page will confuse your reader; use only those elements that help you present yourself effectively.

Consistency is the key to readability and effectiveness. Resumes are rarely read very thoroughly at all. You want employers to be able to pick up important information just by scanning your page (visually and electronically). Review the samples for illustrations of effective and not-so-effective highlighting techniques.

Identify Yourself

Maybe you don't need an eye-catching logo, but you do need to begin your resume consistently—and your cover letters, and all other correspondence. Letterhead is the best and easiest way to do this. You can design your own very simply, using the features in any word-processing program. Letterhead features your name on the first line. It includes your full mailing address, the telephone number where you can be reached during business hours, and it should include your e-mail address as well. The point of letterhead is to make it as easy as possible for your reader to recognize you and to contact you with minimal effort. Use the same letterhead for all your job-related documents.

Summarize Yourself

Targeted resumes use qualification or achievement summaries to present objectives and goals. Summaries follow or even replace the statement of objectives, depending on what you learn in your self-assessment and goal research (steps four and five). Sometimes these sections come at the end, providing the resume with a solid "bottom line." Chapters 4 and 6 detail issues related to objectives, as well as qualification and achievement summaries.

Putting Your Experience in Order

The best resumes present the job-seeker's most significant experiences first. Entries are grouped under headlines. They include undergraduate and graduate degrees, specialized training, and work history. Education can come at the top, as the first or second category, or you can present it last. Candidates with plenty of valuable on-the-job experience generally list that first, saving the bottom of the page for a summary of their education.

ALERT!

Most recent graduates put their education at the top of their resumes. Your academic achievements may be significant, but you should think about where and how you want them to appear. Don't list education first just because you think you should; you might make important work history, projects, and other achievements look less important by bumping them farther down the page.

Academic achievements and honors can be presented in a bulleted list. To figure out what belongs on this list, think about courses, papers, and projects with special relevance to this field. You might also have pertinent extracurricular or community experience. In general, these activities should follow your education and employment entries. Most good resumes do not have a "personal interests" section. Include yours only if you're sure it emphasizes your goals and qualifications in the field.

Finally, it is important to note that your resume does not need to end with "References available upon request." That's a given.

Identify Your Objectives and Your Audience

This critical step is too often overlooked. You *must* identify your objectives and your target audiences. What do you aim to achieve with your resume? Answer that question, and you will define your goals. You must also define, as best you can, who will be reading your resume. Your reviewers belong to the field. They use particular words, phrases, and other field-focused terminology when they talk about their work. By using the proper language (or "talking the talk"), you project the sense that you can do the job (that is, "walk the walk").

Your resume should clearly state your career objectives. It should project your qualifications as well as your goals. Look through the samples in this book: Almost all are targeted, meaning they are clearly focused on a specific field and, within that field, on a certain job function.

Inventory Your Qualifications and Achievements

Why do so many resume-writing and job-search guides ask you to list your ten most significant achievements? The answer has to do with the power of positive thinking. With your greatest achievements in mind, you are more likely to think about—and represent—yourself as a valuable job candidate, full of potential.

It's not so easy to draft a summary of your qualifications, and don't worry if it takes some time. Start by asking yourself this question: "What skills have I demonstrated in the past that will make me valuable in my chosen field in the future?"

The best way to pick out your important achievements is to think in terms of the job or field you're aiming to enter. Freeform lists of random accomplishment are not as effective. You don't want to rely on your reviewer to figure out or analyze the significance of anything in your resume. It's your job to make your value clear.

Achievement summaries are the heart of any good resume. They should be enough to convince the reviewer of your commitment, your qualifications, and your obvious value. It's important not to skimp on the time or energy you put into summarizing your past accomplishments. To a potential employer, your past has everything to do with the future.

Analyze Your Competencies and Capabilities

It may be physically impossible to look backward and ahead at the same time, but the world of resume writing follows different rules. Great resumes reflect past achievements and, via qualification summaries, project ahead to future roles and responsibilities. You are not limited to talking about what has been achieved. Instead, your resume is the perfect platform to express your confidence and competence to tackle the future.

Drafting and Critiquing Your Resume

Your first draft should be inspired by the sample resumes you've reviewed and analyzed. They will probably influence your choice of content and the order of your information. Let them. Later on, you can go back and determine the best order of presentation and omit unnecessary entries.

As you put your first draft together, don't worry any keeping it to any particular length. If anything, it is better to start long and later edit it down. Write as spontaneously as you can. Don't rewrite as you go, a sure way to inhibit your creativity; there will be plenty of time for that when your draft is complete. Your finished resume should be concise. If after your best editing efforts it is still longer than one page, so be it! Employers do read two-page resumes, as long as they are well organized, with the most important information on the first page.

When drafting, aim to just get the information down. Jot descriptive phrases to help you capture your thoughts quickly. You don't have to use articles ("the," "an," "a"), and you can leave the pronouns out. It's unnecessary to say, "I completed the survey"—in a resume, "completed survey" gets the point across. Without shocking your English teacher, you can feel free to use sentence fragments.

You'll also find plenty of resume-building software to tempt you as you create your draft. Resist the temptation and use a basic word-processing tool. Most, like Microsoft Word, come with resume templates. While attractive, these lock you into a format, and that can limit how you present yourself. Give yourself the greatest control over your resume by starting with a blank page.

You may also be tempted to hire a professional to write or review your resume. Again, resist! Your resume is your responsibility; nobody can present you better than you can, yourself. Besides, you are in the process of learning how to create or update your own resume in as little as one day. Why ask (much less pay) someone else to do something you can do better?

Begin your critique only when you have a complete draft in hand. Some people like to see their resume on paper, and they edit with the old red pen technique. Others revise and edit onscreen. Work the way you're most comfortable, being sure that your method helps you polish your draft to perfection. Critiquing does not mean criticizing. Your revisions are meant to transform your resume into its most powerful form. Be positive. Make immediate changes as you need to, and be prepared to make future changes as your job search progresses.

Duplicating and Distributing

We used to worry about things like typesetting and having a clean ribbon in the typewriter. Then it was a good laser printer, picking the right paper, and finding matching envelopes. Now we have fax machines and e-mail, and those worries are gone.

Most of your resumes will probably go out via e-mail or the Web, though you will need a printed version as well. In either case, it's important to keep making a good first impression in mind. Make your resume effective with strong format, simple graphics (as long as they contribute to your statement), and an attractive design.

Most resumes are created or updated using word-processing software and duplicated on paper using quality printers and photocopiers. Dot-matrix and the older daisy-wheel printers do not produce acceptable quality results. Don't use them. It's best to use standard "portrait" orientation (with the resume reading top to bottom on the page), and while you've probably seen creatively formatted resumes—foldouts or brochures, for instance—you want to stick with the standard. You can't e-mail a brochure.

For paper copies, use a top-quality laser printer or photocopier, and use bond paper. White, ivory, natural, and off-white are your best color options. The content and format of your resume will make your document "stand out," not the color of your paper. If you have your resumes copied, get extra paper and matching envelopes. Use the same paper for your cover letters and other correspondence.

Chapter 4

Goals, Qualifications, and Achievements

Your targeted resume gets its power directly from you. It starts with a clear statement of your goals. Then it follows up with a punchy summary of your qualifications and achievements. In these first few lines, your potential employer meets you for the first time. A strong statement of your professional objectives (that is, your goals) and a convincing summary of your achievements to date convinces your reader that you're worth the time it will take to keep reading.

Scoring with Your Goals

The most effective way to present your goals is to present them clearly as your professional objectives. It's important to know as much as you can about your chosen field and function. The more you know, the better you can focus your objectives. If you name a particular job title, or if a certain job function is your goal, be sure you know the responsibilities that come along with it.

FACT

Career counselors say that lack of research is the reason most job seekers can't articulate their professional goals. Even those professionals who rely on standardized tests to identify their clients' values, interests, personality traits, and skills, agree that research is a key component to knowing goals and what it takes to get there.

Job seekers with a longer employment history have been conducting research naturally. Over the years, as they have progressed from position to position, they have received specialized training, observed successful strategies, and interacted with other professionals in the field. Others, such as recent graduates, get their information from books, periodicals, and the Web.

Qualifications: The "Q" in You

Here's another resume-writing mantra for you to repeat: "You can get any job that you can describe—as long as you can describe it well." This chapter describes the all-important skill of writing good qualification summaries that articulate and support your career goal. Qualifications are critical. As you now know, employers establish and use lists of essential, optional, and desired qualifications to screen, interview, and select employees. You can deduce these qualifications with a knowledge of the field and its functions. The best place to start your investigation is with your personal history. In your work (or education, or volunteer commitments), you have probably performed those very functions.

Plenty of your achievements are relevant to your goals. To decide which are important enough to include on your resume, think like a knowledgeable member of your target field. From this perspective, you can see the criteria that would qualify you for the job. If the field is veterinary science, for instance, your volunteer work in the local 4-H club teaching kids how to care for their livestock would count as a qualification. Review your achievements from a field-oriented perspective. Pick the ten that are most relevant to your current goals. They will be the foundation for your qualification and achievement summaries.

FACT

E-resumes are often analyzed electronically, with database keyword searches. Many major corporations and search firms use these systems, many conforming to the same sets of desired qualities. The more of these keywords you use, the more likely your resume will make the cut. You can make a stab at figuring out the keywords in your chosen field by visiting an online employment site, like *www.monster.com.*

Thinking about past achievements makes you take one step back so you can take two steps forward. Summaries of qualifications talk about the past, but they project your abilities and goals into the future.

Bringing Out the "Q"

Take out three pieces of paper. Title each as follows:

- Employment Achievements
- Service Achievements
- Educational Achievements

Starting from the present and working back in time, list your achievements in each category, like so:

- Note when you accomplished this achievement, including month and year.
- For the employment category, think about full-time and part-time jobs, internships, and other project-by-project roles. The service category should include volunteer work and memberships in service organizations. In the education category, in addition to degrees earned, note important papers, publications, fellowships, or other awards of excellence.

- Think in particular about leadership roles you might have had. The proven ability to lead is an important achievement in any category.
- Name your title, if you had one. Be specific about the context of your achievement (were you an undergraduate when you got that paper published, or a busy grad student?).
- Phrasing should be brief. Edit later for style and to make your descriptions active.

When you finish, your three pages will list past achievements under each heading. But listing all on its own doesn't make for a thorough inventory, and it's an inventory we're after. The next step is to analyze your past.

Making a Self-Inventory

Take out a fourth piece of paper. Title it "Most Significant Outcomes and Accomplishments." Review the achievements you listed on your three earlier pages, and pick the ten that were most significant. Add them to this final page, and include the outcome that resulted from each one.

Finally, transform these accomplishments into bullet-points using an active, outcome-focused style (illustrated in the following samples). Refer to the samples for inspiration, if necessary. You can use these bullet-points on your resume (under headlines like "Experience," "Community Service," and "Education"), or, with a little more work, you can transform them into your qualification summary.

Action Verbs and Action Statements

The following lists include action verbs and sample statements for describing qualifications. Boldface is used in the sample statements for emphasis, not how to format these statements in your own resume.

Most keyword searches scan for achievement-focused nouns in addition to action verbs. Those might include the names of software programs, industry-specific phrases, specialized techniques, conceptual models, or analytical tools.

Action Verbs

Accommodated	Achieved	Activated	Adapted	Adjusted
Administered	Advertised	Advised	Advocated	Affirmed
Altered	Analyzed	Applied	Appraised	Approved
Archived	Assembled	Assessed	Assisted	✶Assumed
Attached	Attained	Audited	Augmented	Authorized

Statements

- **Analyzed** procedures to **assess** overall efficiency and monitor outcomes relative to goals.

- **Assessed** proposals to determine **accuracy** of financial projections and prioritize strategies.

- **Applied** theories to research data, generated hypotheses, **analyzed** data, and then presented trends via written and oral reports.

- **Appraised** value of properties as well as risk **associated** with prospective buyers and mortgage options.

- **Audited** financial and manufacturing performance records to identify cost-sensitive variables.

Action Verbs

Balanced	Built	Braced	Calculated	Calibrated
Chose	Classified	Collected	Combined	Commanded
Communicated	Compromised	Conceived	Condensed	Conferred
Confirmed	Consolidated	Consulted	Controlled	Converted
Coordinated	Counseled	Created	Credited	Curtailed

Statements

- **Built** and **tested** actual and virtual prototype model of bridge and off-ramp.

- **Conceived, implemented,** and **improved** promotional campaign using Web, direct mail, posters, and print media strategies.

- **Conferred** regularly with supervisors, peers, and clients to determine effectiveness of programs.

- **Coordinated** the activities of over 100 volunteers, focusing on serving approximately 5,000 meals.

- **Counseled** students regarding academic performance, class scheduling, test preparation, career options, and college admissions.

Action Verbs

Debugged	Deducted	Decoded	Deemed	Delegated
Deleted	Delivered	Demonstrated	Derived	Described
Designated	Designed	Determined	Developed	Dictated
Digitized	Directed	Disclosed	Discontinued	Discovered
Dispatched	Displayed	Distributed	Documented	Drafted

Statements

- **Designated** specific tasks to individuals, **motivated** maximum performance, and **monitored** outcomes.

- **Described** products and services accurately over the phone, via e-mail, and in written proposals.

- **Designed, implemented,** and **documented** experimental procedures.

- **Demonstrated** effective customer service and relationship sales skills targeting varied markets.

- **Documented** achievements via attendance, sales, and profit figures all in excess of targets.

- **Drafted, edited, finalized, duplicated,** and **distributed** promotional materials and media packets.

Action Verbs

Economized	Educated	Eliminated	Employed	Empowered
Encoded	Encouraged	Engaged	Established	Estimated
Evaluated	Examined	Exchanged	Executed	Expanded
Expedited	Extended	Familiarized	Forged	Formulated
Galvanized	Governed	Grouped	Guaranteed	Guided

Statements

- **Evaluated** program effectiveness using predetermined criteria, then **cited** findings via PowerPoint presentation and written reports.

- **Expressed** views in persuasive yet appropriate ways via verbal and written arguments.

- **Formulated** and **implemented** questionnaire designed to clarify problem areas and assess attitudes.

- **Generated** trust and confidence of clients, parents, peers, and supervisors.

- **Guided** families and prospective students, **answered** questions, and positively **served** as spokesperson for the university.

Action Verbs				
Headed	Heard	Highlighted	Honored	Hypothesized
Illustrated	Implemented	Imposed	Improved	Increased
Informed	Initiated	Installed	Instructed	Interpreted
Introduced	Invented	Inventoried	Investigated	Joined
Judged	Justified	Lectured	Localized	Listened

Statements

- **Headed** committee that **inspired** revision of mission statement, strategies, and methods used to measure adherence to stated goals.

- **Identified** key issues and alternatives, and **detailed** strategies to achieve desired outcomes.

- **Improved** methods used to register clients, retrieve files, and initiate counseling sessions.

- **Investigated** past strategies, resources, and services to establish and implement improvements.

- **Listened** to concerns of customers and **responded** in ways to maximize loyalty and repeat sales.

Action Verbs

Maintained	Managed	Mandated	Matched	Measured
Merged	Minimized	Modernized	Modified	Motivated
Named	Negotiated	Noted	Observed	Obtained
Operated	Organized	Originated	Planned	Prescribed
Procured	Produced	Programmed	Publicized	Published

Statements

- **Managed** time, personnel, and finances efficiently, maximizing impact with minimum resources.

- **Motivated** colleagues to complete program planning, implementation, and evaluation efforts.

- **Marketed** products and services to target groups using specialized strategies and promotional materials.

- **Organized** projects to ensure accurate completion within existing deadlines.

- **Procured** materials donated to renovate homes used for homeless persons and families.

		Action Verbs		
Quoted	Queried	Recommended	Rectified	Reduced
Regulated	Reorganized	Repaired	Replaced	Reported
Represented	Researched	Restored	Revised	Rewrote
Shaped	Simplified	Solved	Sponsored	Stabilized
Strengthened	Studied	Supervised	Supplemented	Surpassed

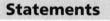

Statements

- **Queried** users regarding customer service, effectiveness of displays, and desired improvements.

- **Reported** findings in PowerPoint illustrated presentation and written report containing charts, graphs, and spreadsheets.

- **Revised** training manual, including role-play interviews, interactive scripts, and inspirational quotes.

- **Suggested** options to improve performance and profitability.

- **Simplified** client greeting and payment procedures to expedite check-in process.

Action Verbs

Taught	Terminated	Took	Tied	Traded
Tracked	Trained	Transcribed	Transferred	Transformed
Transmitted	Tutored	Typed	Uncovered	Underscored
Unified	Updated	Uploaded	Used	Utilized
Verified	Vetoed	Voted	Waged	Wrote

Statements

- **Taught** new paralegals to use LexisNexis and other computerized search systems.

- **Trained** peer career advisors to greet students, conduct quick assessments, and address needs.

- **Verified** effectiveness of promotional strategies via attendance profiling and attitude questionnaires.

- **Used** state-of-the-art CADD techniques to design and test prototypical manufacturing equipment.

- **Wrote** creative promotional materials and **designed** advertising materials in Spanish and English.

Back to the Future

With your inventory of significant accomplishments in front of you, it's time to create a timeline to link those past achievements to the present and on into the future, where your desired job awaits you. Your significant accomplishments don't just belong to the past. They were significant because they made a change in things or in the people involved. Like a stone dropped on a still pond, the effects of your work create a ripple effect of energy that keeps moving, long after the stone has left your hand.

Your goal is to create a resume that, in a glance, gives a potential employer a powerful picture of your job worthiness. You do that in steps:

- A clear statement of **objectives** targets your resume.
- A summary of **past achievements** tells your employer about your abilities and qualifications.
- A description of **outcome** tells your employer about the continuing impact of your achievements.

You can see that it makes sense to talk about outcome. Your next employer is going to hire you as an outcome of your previous achievements; when you make outcome a theme of your resume, you're helping that employer think of a future that has you in it. That's exactly what you want your resume to do.

The following examples are taken from the action-verb statements given in the previous section, with outcomes in boldface. Compare the two versions to see how an outcome description can add impact to your qualifications:

- Counseled students regarding academic performance, class scheduling, test preparation, career options, and college admissions. **Of students counseled, three completed freshman year with honors. One started a successful business straight out of high school.**
- Marketed products and services to target groups using specialized strategies and promotional materials. **Sales increased 20 percent across the board, with polls attributing success to marketing campaign focus.**
- Simplified client greeting and payment procedures to expedite check-in process. **On basis of positive customer feedback, won "Employee of the**

Quarter" award. Received personal recognition at annual meeting from vice president of customer relations.

The difference is dramatic. Reviewing these qualification summaries, it is obvious that the information about outcomes is important. If you were the reviewer, wouldn't it make a difference to know that your candidate was not only qualified but had proved some success?

Not all resumes are "targeted" resumes. We've seen that some resumes are prepared as open-ended introductions, with no specific goal in the job seeker's mind. No matter what advice you get from even your most trusted advocates, remember that employers prefer targeted resumes.

Chapter 5

Your E-Resume

"Recruiting" these days could just as easily be called "e-cruiting." It wasn't long ago that everybody mailed all their resumes. Now we e-mail, fax, and upload them into resume banks. This chapter describes how to create a resume suitable for electronic formats.

Resumes for the E-Superhighway

Almost all resumes today are electronic to some degree. (For instance, we use personal computers and software.) Beyond the means we use to create them, it is important that resumes can be transmitted electronically and that the reviewer can open them easily. After that, our concern as usual is with quality. The aim is to present yourself efficiently, so that no matter who (or what, in the case of a database search engine) opens your resume, it is clear that you are goal-oriented and qualified for the job.

Uploading Your E-Resume

Many potential employers use the Internet to list their job postings. Some use their own corporate Web sites. (The *Everything*® book publisher, Adams Media at ✎*www.adamsmedia.com*, has an Employment link on its home page.) Many also use headhunter sites, where the Web site organizes and displays an employer's advertisement and also makes sure qualified applicants come to the employer's attention.

FACT

The process of uploading a resume from your personal computer is simple. Web sites walk job seekers through the process step by step. The process may vary a little, but in all cases you are using your Internet connection to send the electronic file containing your resume to the online job bank.

File Format for the E-Resume

Uploading is easy, and it is a very effective way of making your resume easily available to many potential employers. However, the electronic file that contains your resume must be in the correct format. Your uploaded resume is useless if the database can't store it.

All online job banks specify the file format you should use. The following are some common formats.

▶ **Microsoft Word.** Almost everyone in almost all professional fields uses Microsoft Word. If you create your resume using another application, you can probably save your file as a Word document.

▶ **PDF.** This format is also very common on the Web. PDF files retain the formatting of the original file and they tend not to be corrupted in their travels across the Internet. You can create a PDF from almost any file format. PDFs cannot be edited or altered, making them a good way of keeping your content exactly as you created it.

▶ **Web page input.** Some job banks ask you to create a resume by filling in the fields of a resume form. In this case, you are not really uploading a file at all. The information you enter into the various fields gets saved directly into the job banks database. Instead of storing resume files, this database contains the information directly.

No matter what format you use, you should do a quality check before uploading your file:

1. Make sure your resume file can be opened, and that it is formatted correctly. Word files can be corrupted, and PDFs can substitute fonts and change things like font size or margins. Do not assume that just because you saved the file or created the PDF that it will meet your requirements.
2. Name your file correctly. Check the requirements of the job bank: They might have a system for naming files. In general, your filename should be short and descriptive.
3. If you are filling in a Web form, take your time entering your information in the fields. Keywords here are essential. You might need to edit your resume, aiming to keep things short while using as many keywords as possible.

Keywords Are Essential

Many job seekers upload their resumes to Web job banks. These are true e-resumes: the potential employer only sees this electronic version.

Often, before any human being lays eyes on these e-resumes, they are subject to review by a search engine. This tool is loaded with certain keywords that the employer has defined as critical to any applicant's qualifications. Regardless of your abilities, if your qualification summaries do not use these keywords, it is likely that you'll never make even the first cut.

Here is where your research pays off. In defining your goals and drafting your qualification summaries, you learned the terms and phrases used in your chosen field. When possible, in your statement of objectives, you should name a particular title that you know is used in your field. The verbs you use to describe your qualifications and experience should mirror those terms as closely as possible.

Here are two statements of objectives that could be used for the same resume. See which one would yield the more fruitful keyword search:

- **Objective:** Position designing logos and graphics for state-of-the-art Web sites.
- **Objective:** Position as Web Designer for software design firm, using skills in XML, DTML, streaming video, Flash animation, Oracle database design, and Web site maintenance.

Chances are that you are uploading your resume into a job bank in answer to a specific job posting. The smartest thing to do, therefore, is to compare the job description to your resume. Does your resume, particularly your qualification summary section, contain the key verbs, terms, and phrases used in the job description? If this job description is short or vague, search the Web for other descriptions of similar jobs. You will notice that they use a common vocabulary to define job functions and desired qualifications.

Keep an Inventory of Keywords

As you continue to search out new job postings, you will learn new industry-specific ways of phrasing your qualifications and summaries. Rather than rewriting your resume every time you find a new, more appropriate term, keep a list. Update your resume when you have a collection of these terms. In this way, your update will not only be more efficient in terms of time, you may come up with better ways of phrasing whole sections, instead of changing a word at a time.

Check the rules of your online job banks. Most allow you to regularly update your resumes. When you do an update, take the time to upload it so all potential employers always see the best and most accurate depiction of your job skills.

E-Mailing Your E-Resume

Some job postings ask you to e-mail your resume directly to a contact person. The process here is very simple: Your e-mail message is your cover letter, and your resume gets included as a file attachment. An e-mail cover letter should be short and direct. The first line should state your purpose ("I am writing in response to your posting for an experienced Web Designer"). Any subsequent text should state your qualifications bluntly ("I have five years of freelance experience designing Web sites for independent movie studios, sometimes using GoLive and Adobe Design software but mostly writing my own code to incorporate movie clips and other complex elements").

QUESTION?

How much info should I include in my e-mail?
It's a good idea to say what made you respond to this posting ("I use links to your site to give visitors access to real-time industry news, and I would love the opportunity to work for you"). E-mails are quick and informal by nature. You know from experience that an overwritten e-mail is hard to read. Be polite, but don't be stuffy.

E-Mail Etiquette

In this case, the question of file formats is particularly important. Pay attention to the stated format requirements, and do not bother submitting a resume that doesn't meet them. You may think PDF is much better than Word, but if Word is what the contact person requests, he or she will not appreciate your superior taste.

The common question with an e-mailed file of any kind is whether the recipient got it in a legible form. If your resume file is huge, with graphics and other special features, it will take a long time to transmit and to open. Nobody appreciates being made to wait, so for e-mailed resumes, it's a good idea to keep things very simple.

Regardless of your care, file attachments do sometimes still get mangled. That gives you an automatic excuse for a follow-up. Ask the recipient to let you know if your file did not come through. Take the opportunity to slip in another quick selling point. There's no harm, as long as you have the contact's address, in sending periodical follow-ups, as long as they are very brief and not demanding in any way.

Addressing the E-Mail

Job postings often ask you to reference a job number in your subject line. Be sure you include this information, as it is unlikely your e-mail (or resume) will reach its destination without it.

Most job postings include a link to the contact person's e-mail. All you have to do to address your e-mail properly is to click on the link. You must also use a personal address, however, in your cover e-mail. Online job postings are notorious for giving little to no information about the contact person. Sometimes all you have is an e-mail address and no name at all. Use whatever information you have. If you don't have a contact name, start the letter immediately after the address, using no salutation at all.

Web-Based Research and Job Search

The Web is full of all the information you could ever need to know about your chosen career. Chances are that your dream job is out there somewhere, too. If only you could find it.

In doing research on the Web, the best place to start is with what you know. It doesn't matter whether you start off in the exact right place. The Web is a job seeker's paradise because it is so easy to follow any trail in whatever direction you choose. Here's an example. We'll let our Web Designer friend Chris Smith take a quick look around the Internet to see what's happening in the working world.

1. Chris is just beginning a job search, so she starts at her favorite all-purpose search engine (we'll say that's *www.google.com*).
2. Chris types in her chosen job title, "Web Designer," in the search field and narrows the search just a little by adding "employment."
3. The Google search engine returns more than a quarter of a million Web sites that are related somehow to the phrase "Web Designer employment." Some of these sites belong to other Web Designers looking for employment. Chris ignores these for now, although later they might be a good way of networking with others in her field. She wants actual job postings. She doesn't have to look very hard to find them. The second listing on the page lists a job posting for a Web Designer.
4. In the next five minutes, Chris finds the following information, just by clicking links that look promising:

   ▶ Dozens of job postings for Web Designers, containing plenty of keywords.

   ▶ Several big job banks, or headhunter sites. These contain not only job postings for Web Designers, they give Chris an idea of what companies are hiring, what industries in her part of the country use Web Designers, and what qualifications employers expect.

   ▶ Salary information. Some job postings include a salary range. But these are not often reliable, so Chris clicks around a little and finds salary statistics on an employment-related government Web site.

   ▶ Sites of individual companies with pages devoted to current openings, all with contact people listed.

   ▶ An online forum of people just like herself, experienced Web Designers of all kinds. Their discussions cover topics like "Freelance Survival" to "Making It Big in the Corporate World."

These are the results of a real Web search, using these keywords, conducted during a quick coffee break. As you can imagine, the real key to getting useful information from the Web is knowing when to stop. Five minutes can easily yield more information than anyone could use in a week. The Web is a huge, chaotic haystack of information; it's true. But as long as you don't worry yourself about hunting for one in particular, you'll find more needles there than you can possibly use.

Vistas for the E-Job Search

Here are a few avenues for beginning your online job search:

- Check with your local librarian to see whether your state sponsors a job bank or whether individual listings can be found online.
- Check the Web sites of companies in your chosen field.
- Use a Web search engine to find the big headhunter sites (like ✍*www.hotjobs.com,* ✍*www.monster.com,* or ✍*www.headhunter.com*).

FACT

Your local newspaper may also list its help wanted ads online. Online listings are usually much easier to search than the printed version. Also, ads often include a link to the company's Web site, where other suitable postings may be found.

Reactive and Proactive E-Strategies

It is easy to think of the Web as a giant fishing pond. You as the job seeker have a certain kind of bait on your pole, and you dangle your line in hope that the right fish is out there, waiting to bite.

This is a reactive job-search strategy, where you the job seeker react to postings and try to model yourself as the best candidate for the job. Sometimes that's all it takes, but a truly effective job-search campaign incorporates proactive techniques as well.

You have already begun using the Web in a proactive manner. When you research your chosen field, for instance, to find the Web sites of the top companies, you are engaging in proactive research. Maybe the company you would most like to work for has several postings that are close to what you're looking for, but nothing that you feel qualified to apply for. You plan to keep checking back, but in the meantime why not write a quick e-mail to the contact person listed for that job. Tell him or her of your interest. Explain briefly how you believe you could be a real asset to the company. Close by saying you will keep in touch, and do it.

Another proactive technique on the employment e-frontier is a twist on our old favorite, networking. Online forums, chat groups, and mail groups cover almost any topic imaginable. They are easy enough to search out (try Yahoo!'s e-group listing, at *www.groups.yahoo.com*) and to join. You probably won't get any job offers, but you can learn a lot about your chosen field and the function you hope to perform in it.

FACT

A recent poll of college career services and corporate recruiters came up with fourteen favorite job-search sites. They include America's Job Bank (*www.ajb.org*), Careerbuilder.com, CareerXRoads.com, Dice.com, Headhunter.net, Hotjobs.com, JobHuntersBible.com, Jobdirect.com, and Job-Hunt.org.

Online Applications

Postings and job bank sites and the actual Web sites of employers increasingly grant you the opportunity to apply for particular positions online. Original copy and paste e-forms are being replaced by PDF systems that allow for uploading of resumes formatted in graphically creative ways. You no longer have to remove bolding or italics, nor worry about tabs, justification, or where dates are presented. But, even with these newer systems you should follow some essential advice.

- Always reflect knowledge of job description within qualification summaries.
- Don't hesitate to use actual phrases appearing in these announcements within summary sections that appear very early (after the objective) in your e-resume.

- Use cover letters created in the same document as the e-resume.
- Update and enhance keyword content of e-resumes.
- Follow up with phone calls and with additional e-mails.

FACT

Estimates regarding how many resumes are stored on or transmitted via Web-based resources vary. Some believe that the numbers of resumes stored in resume banks and connected to postings via mega job-search sites doubled each year over the past five years. While actual totals are difficult to confirm, almost all agree that millions of resumes are stored annually and tens-of-thousands are transmitted by e-mail daily.

Sample E-Resumes

The following sample resumes were all specifically formatted and written for electronic presentation.

Common elements of most successful e-resumes include the following:

- E-friendly fonts.
- Left-justified block text formatting, with minimal tabs or columns.
- Detailed, comprehensive qualification summaries containing key phrases and industry-specific vocabulary.
- Ability to be cut and pasted into e-mails or the fields of Web-based forms.

ALERT!

E-resumes may not be limited to one physical page in length, but you should make sure it is still as concise as you can make it. Keep descriptions brief, use all the keywords you can, and remember: A real person will have to review your document.

While Web-based systems are able to upload resumes in a growing variety of formats, those four characteristics should still be your guidelines in crafting your e-resumes.

Advertising Account Executive E-Resume

CHRIS SMITH

123 Main Street, Hometown, NY 00000, (555) 555-1234, csmith@company.com

ADVERTISING ACCOUNT MANAGEMENT QUALIFICATIONS

Marketing research, strategic planning, promotions, customer service, and sales talents nurtured by in-depth and diverse advertising, promotions, retail internships, and employment. Technical skills gained via courses including: Principles of Marketing, Marketing Projects and Cases, Psychology of Human Motivation and Emotion, Business Administration, Public Relations Writing, Advertising, Mass Media, Persuasion, and Consumer Behavior. Confidence serving on account team and interacting with client colleagues. Special interest in using and enhancing talents associated with market research, segmentation, demographic and media planning, business forecasting, break-even analysis, product strategy development, pricing analysis, financial planning, and publicity concept creation. Capacities to understand 4 Cs: context, company, consumer analysis, competitor analysis, and the 5 Ps: people, product, price, place/distribution, and promotion. French, Dutch, and Farsi fluency, and conversational Spanish capabilities. HTML, Word, WordPerfect, Excel, PageMaker, PhotoShop, and Internet skills.

ADVERTISING AND MARKETING EXPERIENCE
DAYS ADVERTISING, INC., Pittsford, NY
Account Management Intern: Assisted with design of television and radio ads and proposals for varied clients, including Wegmans and Bausch & Lomb. Summer 2001

ADEFFECTS, Rochester, NY
Account Management Intern: Researched and developed promotional materials for retail, manufacturing, and restaurant clients. Suggested changes in advertising materials, consumer outreach strategies, and marketing literature. May 2000–July 2001

PEARLE VISION CENTER, Pittsford, NY
Sales Representative, Summer 2001

IT HAPPENS, Antwerp, Belgium
Marketing Intern: Determined target markets and developed advertising budget for concert, event planning, and entertainment agency. Conducted and analyzed surveys to determine market penetration. Assisted artists with ads, posters, and brochures. Summer 1998

BUSINESS, ECONOMICS, AND LANGUAGE STUDIES
UNIVERSITY OF ROCHESTER, Rochester, NY
Bachelor of Arts, French, with a major GPA of 3.5, May 2002.
Bachelor of Arts, Psychology, with a major GPA of 3.3, May 2002.
Minor: Economics, with a minor GPA of 3.4.
Management Studies Certificate, Marketing and Finance/Accounting Tracks, May 2002.

FINANCE EXPERIENCE
THE FINANCIAL GROUP, INC. DISCOUNT BROKERAGE FIRM, Pittsford, NY
Operations Management Intern, January–May 2001

- Times New Roman font is e-friendly.
- Bullets and special formatting, like bolding, are omitted to make resume easy to upload and/or scan. Boldface, italics, bullets, and other formatting techniques do not interfere with keyword search, retrieval, or printing capabilities.
- Because line spacing and overcrowding are not an issue, spacing was eliminated between headlines and first entries.
- Paragraph-style qualification summary is descriptive and full of keywords.
- This version can easily be cut and pasted into e-mail or a Web-based form and easily reviewed.

Jamie Brown

123 Main Street • Hometown, NY 00000 • (555) 555-1234 • jbrown@company.com

Financial Planning Qualifications and Credentials

- Over a decade of progressively significant roles and achievements within planning, portfolio management, and client services.
- Personal responsibility for more than $210 million client assets.
- Regularly recognized for asset-based performance and customer service.
- Asset collection, asset allocation, asset management, risk management, tax deferment and minimization, portfolio management, generational wealth transition, trust and estate planning, and private placement funding competencies.
- Experience hiring, training, and supervising newly hired FCs and FPs.
- Served as trainer and curriculum developer, using traditional lectures, audiotapes, videotapes, and simulation exercises.
- Licensed Series 6,7,63 and health and life insurance.

Financial Planning Accomplishments

ABC FINANCIAL CONSULTANTS, Princeton, NJ
Financial Consultant/Financial Planner, 1990–present
Serve within comprehensive financial planning roles. Oversee individual and group portfolios. Serve as senior manager, supervisor, and trainer within corporate headquarters of firm responsible for over $800 million in client assets.
- Developed $210 million client asset base via prospecting and targeting.
- Successfully built portfolio that includes stock, bonds, options, and insurance products for more than 450 clients.
- Implemented financial plans through account development and growth.
- Gained estate planning, asset allocation, and wealth succession expertise.

Sales Associate, 1988–1990
- Worked directly with firm's top producer, profiling high net-worth individuals.
- Generated $90,000 for top producer through new account openings.
- Analyzed existing portfolio, assisting in development of accounts.

Account Executive Trainee/Intern, 1987–1988

MAPLEWOOD INVESTMENTS, Maplewood, NJ
Prospecting Intern, Summers 1986 and 1987

Education

IONA COLLEGE, Iona, NY
Bachelor of Arts degree in Economics, 1988
Concentration in Business Management, with courses in: financial accounting, managerial finance, corporate treasury, insurance, statistics, and financial services.

Pharmaceutical Sales E-Resume

DANA JOHNSON
123 Main Street • Hometown, NY 00000 • (555) 555-1234 • djohnson@company.com

PHARMACEUTICAL SALES QUALIFICATIONS

Interest in: AIDS, Antidepressants, Antihistamines, Arthritis, Cancer, Cholesterol, Diabetes, FDA Approval Stages, Heart Disease, Osteoporosis, and Aging. Knowledge gained via research of: Antiulcerants, Antidepressants, Calcium Antagonists, Plain Antirheumatic Non-Steroidals, ACE Inhibitors, Plain Cephalosporins and Combinations, Antipsychotics, Non-Narcotic Analgesics, and Oral Antidiabetics. Record of success within direct marketing and information-driven sales roles. Capacity to understand and share pharmaceutical product and protocol knowledge. Abilities to blend qualitative and communication talents as well as analytical skills to set goals, document impact of sales efforts, and maximize output. Bilingual English-Mandarin abilities and cross-cultural sensitivities.

SALES AND SALES SUPPORT ACHIEVEMENTS

PEARLS AND GEMSTONES CORPORATION, San Francisco, California, 2001–Present
Sales Associate for Loose Diamond Division: Sell and market polished gemstones for an international gemstone and pearl distributor and jewelry manufacturer. Sales methods include appointments onsite, telemarketing, tradeshow exhibiting, and Internet sales. Customers include manufacturers, retail stores, department stores, and catalogues.
Directly involved in sales to house accounts totaling $2.5 million in 2001.
Indirectly involved in sales to salespersons accounts totaling $3 million in 2001.

COMPUTER ASSOCIATES INTERNATIONAL, San Jose, California, 1997
Quality Assurance Analyst: Analyzed business applications and RFPs (Request For Proposal) for marketability. Implemented quality assurance for an inter/intranet-enabled, multiplatform, enterprise management solution used worldwide. *Supported customer service and sales representatives in refining product to match customer needs.*

BUSINESS EXPERIENCE

BANK OF HONG KONG, Hong Kong, Spring 2000
International Securities Dealing Room Trader: Communicated with customers' desires to execute orders in the areas of American and foreign equities, bonds, and options. Received training in and gained working knowledge of Bloomberg and Reuters information systems.

BANK OF HONG KONG, San Francisco, California, 1997–2000
International Lending Department Credit Analyst: Prepared proposals on prospective customers for credit committee. Conducted business and industry research using Bloomberg, Moody's, and S&P analysts and publications.

BUSINESS, ECONOMICS AND LIBERAL ARTS EDUCATION

UNIVERSITY OF CALIFORNIA, BERKELEY, Berkeley, California, 1993–1997
Bachelor of Arts, Political Science, with minor in Economics
Served as Intern for Member British Parliament, London, England, Fall 1995. Served as Intern for Senator Barbara Boxer, U.S. Senate, Washington D.C., Summer 1995.

HAAS SCHOOL OF BUSINESS ADMINISTRATION, Berkeley, California, 1997
Management Certificate for completion of Marketing, Accounting, Economics, Statistics, and Computer Science courses. Developed detailed and fiscally sound marketing plan.

- Times New Roman is an e-friendly font, as is left-justified style.

- Bolding is used as a highlighting technique.

- Qualification summary is placed first, in paragraph form.

- Industry-specific phrasing used. Keywords are included along with rankings of most profitable products.

- This version can be easily cut and pasted into e-mail or Web-based forms. Once retrieved, it can be reviewed with little difficulty.

Chapter 6

Meeting the Employer's Criteria

Let's examine the concepts related to an employer's qualification criteria. When an employer decides to fill a position, they must write up an accurate job description if they hope to attract qualified candidates. That means listing job functions along with requirements such as years of experience, education, training, and any specialized skills or knowledge.

Making the Grade

With a good job description in front of them, an employer's next step is to define what they think is their ideal candidate. Usually, this entails prioritizing criteria into "essential," "optional," and "optimal" categories, reflecting which characteristics their ideal candidate must possess and which would be icing on the cake. Candidates are searched out, screened, interviewed, and selected based upon these predetermined traits. Your potential employer will use your resume and supporting correspondence to determine how well you meet the defined criteria.

With that in mind, it is easy to see that your resume must begin with a clear statement of your job objectives. This makes it clear right from the start that your goals meet the employer's needs.

Objectives Are Not Lifelong Goals

Maybe you have more than one possible career in mind, or maybe you fear deciding on a single option, not knowing whether it is truly the one for you. Don't allow fear of focus to delay your resume-writing or job-search efforts. Nothing says you must limit yourself to a single resume for just one field. If you are interested and qualified for a number of job functions, feel free to apply for them. Objective statements are not difficult to create or update, and it is equally easy to recast your qualification summaries to meet the criteria of different employers.

Your professional objective does not have to state your long-term or lifelong career goals. It is simply a statement of the job title you are seeking. It provides focus for reviewers and influences how they perceive all content appearing afterwards. Your statement of objectives is like a label that names the professional door you seek to enter. When you knock, seeking entry, you introduce yourself via resumes and cover letters. Ideally, after interviewing, you will receive an offer to stay.

Talk the Talk to Walk the Walk

You're probably familiar with those self-help books that use inventive means of self-assessment. They can lead to interesting revelations, but when it comes to an effective job search, the only question you have to answer is "What field do you want to enter, and what job are you looking for?"

As illustrated in samples throughout this book, resume objectives should be simple, stated in as few words as possible. They are best composed of a few nouns, not complex adjective- and verb-filled statements. Top off your powerful page, literally, with the answer to the question: "What is the title of the job you seek?"

"If you can describe a job you can get that job or a similar job" is a simple statement that first appeared in a well-known job-search article called "The Secrets of Job-Search Success." It insightfully underscores the importance of articulating goals. If you can state your goals, that means you have focus. You are shooting for a particular job in some chosen field, which means you understand that job function and how your skills make you qualified to perform it. You have taken the first step toward meeting your future employer's qualification criteria.

Conversation is easy, with almost anyone, as long as the people talking have something in common. In your job-search, including your resume, correspondence, and interviews, you must speak the language that is common to your field of interest. The employer speaks to you in that language in the form of job descriptions and job postings. Your response is in the form of your resume and, later, your interview.

ESSENTIAL

Courses and seminars are another way of learning the criteria for success in your field. If you can devote the time to an internship, or even arrange to spend time shadowing someone who performs your chosen job function (sometimes called an "externship"), you can learn through day-to-day experience.

A good way to focus and state your goals to meet the employer's criteria is to check out a few professional publications. After just a few articles, you should start to notice some common factors. The terminology of the field should become clear, but you should also be able to tell something about individual job functions. Look for interviews or profiles of successful people in the field. What qualifications did they bring to their jobs? Even more general information, such as articles about processes or innovations in the field, should still contain clues. What you're looking for is the collection of characteristics that people share who already work in your chosen field. It is likely that those will be on your employer's list of qualification criteria.

Field Descriptions

Many industry publications compile long lists of criteria to help workers assess their career compatibility and evaluate their potential goals. For you, as a job seeker, simplified field and functional perspectives are enough to help you check whether your qualifications meet an employer's qualification criteria.

The following sections provide brief descriptions for a variety of fields. With this general idea of what comprises a field, you can more easily determine your particular focus and your qualifications for performing a particular function.

Arts and Media

This field includes the performing and fine arts; broadcast, print, and Internet media; and communication-oriented organizations. Settings include, but are not limited to, galleries, museums, radio and television stations, dot-com organizations, publishers, newspapers and magazines, public relations firms, and advertising agencies.

Business

This sector includes almost any profit-driven activities. Most often, the business world is associated with large publicly or privately held companies that provide services or market products. Smaller entrepreneurial ventures, retailers, and hospitality, travel, and tourism sectors are included here as well.

Education

The education field includes private and public preschools, elementary schools, middle and secondary schools, colleges and universities, as well as tutorial and training operations.

Government

Government includes all local, state, federal, and multinational organizations that pass legislation, offer and regulate services, lobby, and promote specific programs and resources.

Health and Human Services

Usually considered a member of the service sector, this field includes both individuals and facilities that offer medical, psychological, social, and related services. Practitioners can be private, government-affiliated, or have nonprofit status. Hospitals, clinics, residential treatment facilities, agencies, and special programs all fit within this field.

Law

The legal field includes services and systems associated with enforcement of laws, such as judicial, regulatory, corrections, investigation, and protection organizations. Employers include government and private agencies, law firms, and nonprofit entities, as well as courts and mediators.

Science and Technology

The tech sector includes organizations and businesses associated with research, development, manufacturing, and marketing of new technologies. Activities can be purely research-and-development-oriented, or they can be product or service-oriented. Government, business, and education entities all fit within this specialized category.

Administration

The administrative field involves general office management as well as oversight of facilities and systems associated with day-to-day organizational activities. No matter their titles, many employees of this field work in administrative, customer service, or labor positions. On the other end of a wide continuum, those serving within these functions are also responsible for large operations and organizations. They generally supervise many individuals, projects, and resources. Job functions include office services, facilities, security, management, and project oversight roles.

Communication

The communication field involves writing, graphics, public relations, publicity, and promotions. It includes all activities associated with creating, distributing, and transmitting text and graphic information via varied print, video, audio, computer, and Web-based media.

Finance

This field involves accounting, budgeting, treasury, auditing, and information systems activities. It includes collection, documentation, and analysis of financial data and the use of this data to make strategic decisions and share pertinent information with investors, regulators, and government entities. It also includes allocation and growth of capital required for annual operations as well as growth.

Human Resources

This field involves recruiting and staffing, compensation and benefits, training and development as well as employee relations efforts. It includes all hiring, career development, compensation, and personnel management activities.

Marketing

Marketing involves new product development, product management, marketing research, product and sales support, advertising, promotions, and public relations, as well as customer services. These functions can take place "in-house," in consumer and industrial product manufacturers, or at specialized consulting firms or agencies.

Sales

The sales field involves direct sales, representative sales, distribution and arbitrage, and retail sales. It includes all activities associated with sales of raw materials used to create products or the sale of products directly to consumers. It can also involve sales of financial or other services.

FACT

Bureau of Labor Statistics data ranks "Sales and Related" jobs as the second largest category of workers, with more than 13 million people performing these functions. For most job seekers it is easy to understand why this is a field worthy of great resumes and even greater job-search activities.

Technology and Operations

This field involves production, materials, traffic, and management of information systems. It includes overseeing or participating in the activities associated with producing tangible products and, with purchasing, receiving, storing raw material, components, or finished products. It is also associated with the allocation of human resources to specific assignments and with the operating, programming, or servicing of computers.

The Field and Function Grid

From the previous list, we can separate these broad descriptions into two categories. Some fields are defined by a professional orientation, or the kind of work they do (government, for instance, or the field of law), while other fields are more function-oriented. Human resources, for instance, is a specific function that takes place in a wide range of industries.

This distinction can be used to draw up and investigate job functions. **FIGURE 6-1** illustrates a seven-by-seven "field and function" grid, in which professions (or fields) go across the top and functions go down the side. This grid is very useful when it comes to defining the sorts of job functions that belong to any given field. As you learn more and more about your chosen fields and job functions, you will be able to create a personalized field and function grid, expanding on the simple job title with information like job duties, education requirements, and qualification criteria.

Figure 6-1: The Field and Function Grid

Field ▶ ▼ Function	Arts and Media	Business	Education	Health and Human Services	Law	Science/ Technology
Administration	Advertising Account Executive	Administrative Assistant, Bank Teller, Branch Manager, Chef, Executive Assistant, Retail Store Manager	Day Care Worker, Nanny, Principal	Case Worker, Dentist, Physician, Physician's Assistant	Paralegal, Police Officer	Chemist, Research Assistant, Telecommunication Manager
Communication	Actor, Musician, Author, Speaker, Publicist		Art Instructor, Sports Information Director			Technical Writer
Finance		Bookkeeper, Budget Analyst, Accountant, Credit Analyst, Financial Planner				
Human Resources		Human Resources Administrator, Recruiter, Training Specialist	Coach, College Professor, Teacher, Tutor	Human Services Counselor, Speech Pathologist		
Marketing	PR Account Executive, Advertising Media Planner	Marketing Brand Manager, Marketing Researcher, Retail Buyer	Admissions Professional			
Sales	Advertising Media Salesperson	Account Executive Sales, Medical Product Sales, Pharmaceutical Sales, Real Estate Sales, Telemarketer, Travel Agent				
Technology and Operations	Architect	Applications Programmer, LAN Administrator, Systems Programmer	Librarian		Legal Researcher	Auto Mechanic, Computer Scientist, Technician, Systems Engineer

As you examine the sample grid in **FIGURE 6-1,** ask yourself a few basic questions:

- Which titles interest you most?
- Do you notice anything missing?
- Where would your specific job-search target appear?

Now is the time to think about the qualification criteria associated with titles that raise your curiosity. Take out a pad or open a new Word document. For each job function that interests you, list the job title, field, and function. Think about the qualification criteria for each. If you were a prospective employer screening resumes, what would you look for? Jot down every qualification you think of. Don't write vague statements like "experience within the field and related education." Be specific and behavioral. **FIGURE 6-2** lists some sample criteria for an entry-level Assistant Account Executive. Notice how each can be worked into a resume or used in follow-up correspondence and in your interview. Together, they form the basis of your common conversation with your potential employer.

Sample Statements of Objectives

As you examine the format, content, and order as well as the objectives of the many sample resumes in this book, think about their simplicity. Think about how they mirror a powerful knowledge of self and of a chosen career field and job function. Though the samples use different approaches, they still have much in common. Some probably have objectives and qualifications that match your goals, and it may be possible for you to adapt some of that content for your own resume. Your abiding goal, here and throughout your resume-writing and job-search progress, is to show your reviewers that you know what it takes to succeed within your chosen field and function. Later, in subsequent chapters and Appendices A, B, and C you will be able to review sample resumes for many of these titles.

Figure 6-2: Sample Criteria

Qualification Criteria	Assets Sought and Interview Questions to Ask
Knowledge of the field	• Previous experience via internships or jobs • Courses in Advertising or Marketing • Vocabulary used in resume and cover letter • "What ads do you like the most and why?" question • "What agency has gained the most significant accounts last year?" question
Curiosity regarding consumer behavior and market research techniques	• Selected courses in Psychology, Anthropology, Marketing, or Sociology • Independent study or research, specifically in social sciences or marketing • Experience with questionnaire or survey development and analysis • "What ads do you like the least, and why?" question
Research and project management skills	• Diverse research or term paper topics, methodology, and outcomes • Multiple extracurricular roles or jobs while in school • Leadership within group projects • Examples of multitasking in internships, jobs, or academic roles • "When were you in charge of a project?" question
Blend of quantitative and qualitative analytical skills	• Diversity of courses, including mathematics, science, social sciences, and humanities • Economics, Business, Psychology, Anthropology, or Liberal Arts Curricula • Independent study or research experience revealed through papers and projects • "What are your strengths and weaknesses?" question
Group communication and task management abilities	• Extracurricular membership and leadership • Independent study, research support, or term-paper research experience • Semester-by-semester analysis of courses taken, motivation, and outcomes • "Describe your most impressive paper or presentation" query
Persuasive oral and written talents	• Majors and courses completed • Research and term paper topics • Cover letter and resume content • "Briefly describe your most impressive paper or presentation" query
Flexibility, curiosity, and ability to accept criticism	• Transcript analysis • Major choice, course selection, research, term paper topics • "Lessons learned from mistakes?" question • "What if I put you on the dog food account?" question • "What have you learned from your mistake?" question

Chapter 7

Resume in a Day

If a picture is worth a thousand words, you would think that a snapshot of your own perplexed face, struggling to update or create your resume, would be worth even more. Smile! This chapter directs you on how to develop new or revised resumes quickly and painlessly.

The Seven Steps Revisited

You should look forward to the opportunity to identify and then describe your most significant achievements. It can be an empowering experience, if you think about it: You get to write a true story of yourself as a qualified, achievement-oriented person. Don't let yourself be intimidated by thoughts of what people expect to see or how they will judge you. Your job is simply to present yourself as effectively as you can.

At this point, you should be grounded in the fundamentals of resume writing for success. You should understand the important of stating your goals, supporting them with a qualification summary, and then spelling out your significant job experience. This chapter is designed to take that confidence and apply it, with the concrete goal of creating or updating a useful resume in the space of just one day.

Maybe the sample resumes in this book have already motivated you to revise your existing resume or draft a new one. In that case, you will be ready to put the fine points on your work. Later discussions on critiquing your first draft and preparing your resume for distribution will come in handy.

Assumptions and negativity aside, great resumes can be created in a day. In truth, they can be drafted and finalized within an hour or two. Your frame of mind is critical to resume writing and all of job search. Remain positive and everything will fall into place painlessly.

As you work through this chapter, think about the seven steps to resume-writing success. Gauge where you are on the continuum and how close you are to completing a powerful resume. Go down your internal "things to do" list. Experience the relief and sense of accomplishment that comes from completing a mental "done that" check. Look forward to the next step. Don't worry or wait. Go for it! Each resume-writing step means that you are closer to achieving your job-search goals. After you finalize your resume, you will be empowered to reactively and proactively complete job-search undertakings.

The Seven Steps as Critical Questions

To inspire action, let's examine the seven steps through a series of questions. Your answers will reveal your readiness to take steps and how close to completion you really are.

- Have you identified two to four sample resumes that you wish to model? Do they match your goals, or do they just appeal to your sense of style?
- Do they have objectives, qualification summaries, and/or achievement summaries? When does specific content appear? What is first and what is presented last? Is education before experience, or vice versa?
- Can you state your objectives concisely? Will they appear first on your draft? If your resume will begin with a qualification summary, will the headline clearly project your goals and can it be easily identified by specific target readers? To whom will you be sending resumes, and why?
- Do you have a collection of your most significant achievements? Do they appear under academic, experience, or other headlines, or do they appear in summary sections? What did you do to achieve these outcomes? What skills, perspectives, or knowledge were involved? Can you list the headlines for all sections that will compose your resume?
- Can you describe the job you are seeking? What qualification criteria would be associated with the position? What fields, functions, and titles best characterize your targets? Have you circled or highlighted relevant summary entries that match your accomplishments and capabilities or criteria for specific jobs? Do you have a collection of keywords associated with field- or job-focused goals? Do you have a listing of accomplishments associated with each?
- Have you typed a draft? Is it longer than a page? Did you do spelling and grammar checks? Did you have someone else proofread and comment on the draft?
- Will you e-mail, fax, mail, or hand-deliver the distribution-ready version? Did you double-check spelling and usage? Do you have a cut-and-paste e-mail-friendly version?

If many of your answers are "no," "don't know," or "huh?" you should think about why. Review the previous chapters to get your bearings again, but don't worry. Most resume writers are overly self-critical and analytical. Begin or keep drafting. You'll have the opportunity to be more critical during the critiquing process detailed a bit later, which doesn't start until you type the final words at the bottom of your page.

If your answers were mostly "Yes!" you are ready to go or, better, almost done! Start on that page you made that has your name and identifying information written across the stop. Start writing! Go for it! Finish your draft right now!

Drafting, Critiquing, Duplication, and Distribution

Don't worry if your first resume is more of a multipurpose than a targeted resume. That might be the best way to get started; that is, by starting from a broad, general base. Later, as you revise, you should aim to create a more targeted version. Remember, writing targeted resumes and taking initial job-search actions are not commitments to specific fields. These are simply important first steps in a particular direction. These steps will, if you choose to proceed, ultimately lead to offers. Once you receive an offer you will have the power to accept or decline; then and only then are you actually making a commitment.

They say the eyes are the windows to the soul. Your resume, with its clearly stated objectives and qualification summary, is your prospective employer's window into your job goals. A resume allows you to display your assets; it also gives others a way of learning about your capabilities and interests. Don't underestimate the two-way powers of targeted resumes.

You should create your resume as a Microsoft Word document. This will make it easy for you to share electronic copies, whether by uploading or by e-mail. Spell check your resume every time you make revisions. The grammar checking tool can be helpful, but remember that in resume style, you are allowed to use sentence fragments. You also commonly leave out personal pronouns (such as "I") and articles (the, a, an).

As you write, stay focused on the aspects of yourself that you want to present. Don't fall into the trap of trying to please some potential employer. In almost all cases, the person who reads and reviews your resume will be a stranger. No matter how hard you try, you have no way of knowing what that person wants or expects to see. All you can do (and it's actually a lot) is put your best foot forward. Show them what you can do.

Additional Inspiration for Action

If you are hesitant or insecure about your ability to create a powerful resume, you are most likely suffering from fear of focus. In your day-to-day life, you may have many interests and possibilities, and you may not be ready to choose one at the cost of any others. That is excellent news. It means you are engaged in a serious investigation of your abilities and of just the right career for you. In the meantime, however, you probably need to get a job of some kind. To do that you need a resume, and to write a resume, you need to define a goal. Don't worry that you're being untrue to all the options in your life; just choose one goal, define it, and use that as your statement of objectives. You can create as many resumes as you like, so if it makes you feel more in control of your future, you can create a resume for each and every one of your professional objectives. The important thing is to use your interests and ambitions to move forward.

When you write your resume, and even when you send it out in application for certain jobs, you are not committing yourself to any field or job function. You might consider this a way of conducting research about the fields you are most qualified for. Any response you get from your resumes will tell you how professionals already working in that field judge your qualifications. If a resume lands you an interview, you can consider yourself a qualified candidate in that field for that position. This is important feedback for anyone just entering the job market who is unsure of how their talents and experience can be valuable. It's also good feedback for the job seeker who cannot decide on any one field. Often, the most attractive field is the one where others consider you an asset.

You are free to submit all the resumes you like and to take any interview offered you. But you should only accept an offer if you are prepared to take the job. Research into that particular position, in other words, ends when and if you are made an offer. If you cannot commit yourself to performing those job duties to the best of your ability, thank the employer for their consideration and graciously decline their offer of employment.

Qualification Summaries

Steps one through five of the resume-writing process all target completion of statement of objectives and achievement summaries. These elements are the cornerstone of powerful and effective resumes and are critical components. Very few (less then 10 percent) of the samples presented in this book do not include some form of qualification or achievement summary.

Start out by reviewing the sample resumes to gain a sense of how these sections are presented. Mark any statements that match your goals or mirror your achievements. You can use them as a foundation for your own achievement summaries. Refer to the list of action verbs in Chapter 4 for inspiration, if needed.

Decide whether you prefer the bullet-point format or paragraph style. Try both to see which one makes your qualifications stand out. You might decide to use your achievement summaries directly after your statement of objectives to begin your resume, or you might choose to put them at the bottom of your page. If you present them first, they will serve as a preview of your work experience. If you choose to put them last, they will summarize your talents, skills, and experience.

Competence and Confidence

The most critical of all your job-search tools is your ability to project your own competence and capability. You must know that you are a qualified, competent worker before you can write a resume that creates that impression in others.

You rely on your resume to convey your abilities to people you most likely have never seen or met. This may seem uncomfortable and embarrassing, but remember that there are two sides to the job-search proposition. You are looking for a job. Your potential employer is looking for someone to do a job. It is unnecessary to think of yourself as inferior in this relationship. The two of you need each other.

When you draft your statement of objectives and your qualification summary, think of them as messages you're sending to potential employers. The message says, "I know what you need. I understand the job and its importance to your company. I am confident that I have the skills and ability to meet your needs and be an asset to your company."

Reflective and Projective Phrases

You must be able to look back over your life in order to write summaries that reveal to readers that you have clear goals in sight. Your qualification summaries must reveal to all that you know a great deal about roles and responsibilities of targeted jobs. This is where you "talk the talk" that will give you the chance, whether in interviews or on the job itself, to "walk the walk." Your aim at first is projected toward the interview. Later, your aim will include job offers and career success. Effective, action-oriented phrasing, in both your statement of objectives and your qualification summaries, will be what shows you are capable of doing more than just talk about the future. You're prepared to make a contribution.

Special Issues for Special Circumstances

Candidates can overcome limited experience by learning as much as they can about their target fields and functions. Research is key. It's difficult to take one logistical step back before taking two forward, but this is in many cases the best approach. Take the time you need to create very detailed qualification summaries and supporting correspondence that shows how much you really do know, whether your knowledge comes from on-the-job experience, school, volunteer work, or other means. Use the correct terminology to show your familiarity with the field.

This advice holds true for recent graduates, those preparing for graduation, people in the middle of a big career change, and for undergraduates looking for part-time job internships. Focus on making your resume show how much you do know, and don't worry about what you don't know. Use your academic achievements to represent the experience you've gained in your field. Take the time to write a clear statement of your job objectives. Follow that up with a carefully crafted qualification summary, and you will have created a powerful resume.

Resumes for recent graduates must clearly project their goal-focused qualifications. If you wish, create and use one multipurpose and several targeted versions of your resume. But don't allow fear of focus to diffuse your goals or strategies. A job search can be frustrating. Don't let yourself lose the focus you need to present yourself as a talented, committed employee. Continue to assess your strategies, and enhance your competencies when needed. It's amazing how one or two goal-specific courses taken at a local community college, in addition to a subscription to a field-focused professional or trade journal, can ignite a somewhat passive, if not dormant, job-search campaign. Keep track of whom you contact in your job search. Follow up, then follow up again.

People in the under-experienced category of job seekers usually have an excellent record of success, yet they can be the most frustrated and easily overcome by self-doubt. A powerful, targeted resume is a sign to yourself and others that you are engaged in a serious job search. It is powerful as a direct contact tool and as a means of networking. Use it with great pride.

If you choose to include your volunteer work with your paid work experiences to save space and make your work history more continuous, make sure to title the section "Experience," rather than "Employment Background" or "Professional Experience."

Drafting, Editing, and Finalizing

Whenever possible, you should create or update your own resumes. While most of the people who provide resume-writing services are highly competent professionals, only you can effectively complete the goal-directed analysis needed to create the very best qualification summaries. Please take the few hours to do so.

Spell Checking and Critiquing

Use, but don't solely depend upon, spell-checking tools within word-processing software. After you have completed your draft, print out a copy. Proofread the old-fashioned way. Read it aloud. When you do, your eyes slow down and your ears also identify potential corrections or changes. Make changes, and then repeat this process one last time. Distribution-ready resumes must be typo-free.

Seek the comments of others, but don't feel obligated to make suggested changes immediately. Many still believe in the old-style tenets. But they might not be best for you. Solicit the feedback of those you respect, particularly of those within your field of interest, and seriously consider their advice. When it comes time to make final editorial decisions, however, you are the one responsible.

Revising Your Resume

In many ways, the first task you complete for a new employer is your resume. This document shows those who review it, at the very least, your project management and communication talents. Resumes and correspondence reveal your ability to collect, analyze, and present information in the most appropriate formats, using the best phrasing and tone. They are like the first business letter you send important clients, colleagues, or customers. Put your best metaphorical foot forward. Show all who review your resume your potential for effective and dynamic communication.

Of course, resumes are not permanent. While seeking "constantly evolving perfection," feel confident to make changes or additions when situations warrant. Job-search circumstances may inspire you to revise strategies and fine-tune specialized tools. The process often requires that you revise resumes for specific jobs, maybe as often as every few weeks.

FACT

There is no better way to review and revitalize job search and facilitate follow-up than by distributing a revised resume. Whenever you desire, revisit the "Resume-in-a-Day Checklist" and "Resume Before-and-After Review" to determine if you are due for a new resume. Three cheers for the inventors of word processing. Thanks to them, you can easily and quickly update your resume whenever you want.

Your Resume-in-a-Day Checklist

Here is an actual step-by-step review of what you must do to create or update your resume today. This list simplifies the actions already outlined and clarified in this one. Have your legal pad or, better, your laptop or desktop computer ready. You should soon be writing or typing, not just thinking. The time for action is here. Without delay, you can now create or update your resume in less than a day.

❏ Identify at least two sample resumes to model. This should now take no more than fifteen minutes.

❏ Reflect upon how and when these samples presented their information. Create a draft listing of headlines you might use, in the order you want them to appear. This step should take about ten minutes.

❏ Concisely state your job-search goal as it will appear in a statement of objectives or as the headline of a qualification summary. This step should also take ten minutes.

❏ With this goal in mind, make a list of significant related accomplishments. This should take about thirty minutes.

❏ Review significant related accomplishments to link past accomplishments with future potential via a qualification summary. It is recommended that you actually draft your entire resume, including the objective, before you take on this task. No matter whether this section is presented first or last, this section should be your last, most important, and, perhaps, lengthiest, task. This could take about an hour, but it can be done quicker.

❏ With model resumes in view, type a draft of your version. Don't think, just type. Later, you will complete self-critiquing and copyediting. This should take at most sixty minutes.

❏ Conduct software-linked spell-checking and grammar reviews. Have someone else review for typos and format questions, then make revisions and complete the final version. Complete the "Resume Before-and-After Review." It should take about fifteen minutes for the self-contained responses to specific questions, but it takes a bit longer to receive the comments of others. While you should respect comments of colleagues and friends, remain confident that you are the best and ultimate judge regarding what should appear in your resume and how it should be presented.

❏ Draft and finalize your cover letter. Distribute your resume. The time it takes to complete this step will depend on whether you e-mail your resume or deliver it by hand.

Resumes Before-and-After Review

Appendix C contains several before-and-after illustrations, and Chapter 10 includes some critiques, illustrating the transformation of a resume from draft to finished version. Once you complete your draft, you must next complete your critique. Your silent or spoken answers to the following questions will reveal whether your resume is ready for distribution.

If answers to the following queries are all "yes, yes, yes," your resume has evolved from "before" to "after" status, and it is ready for distribution. If some answers are "no," keep working. You're on the right path.

✔ Identifying Information
❏ Is your name in larger font and bolded?
❏ Is your address, phone, and e-mail presented using one line?
❏ If more than one address or phone appears, is there a logical reason why, and are they presented using as few lines as possible?

Overall Appearance and First Impression

❏ Is the resume neat, easy to visually scan top to bottom, and in a first-glance logical format?

❏ Is the font type and size easy to read and professional in appearance?

❏ Can you scan down the page and identify a logical pattern of headline placement as well as highlighting techniques?

❏ Are capitalization, boldface, italics, indentation, and page placement used to highlight specific information in easily identifiable patterns?

❏ Can the resume be cut and pasted into an e-mail message and still retain logical formatting?

Objective

❏ Does this statement project knowledge of your desired field and use field-specific phrasing?

❏ Is it presented in as few words as possible?

Qualification or Achievement Summary

❏ Does this paragraph or, better, bullet-point listing support the stated objective?

❏ If no objective appears, does the headline used for this section clearly project your goal?

❏ Does this paragraph or bullet-point listing reveal that you understand the qualification criteria, specialized terminology, and keywords associated with your target job?

❏ Does the headline used inform the reader quickly that you have a sense of focus?

❏ Does this section reveal a thorough projection to the future as well as reflection to the past?

❏ Does the statement reflect upon competence as well as confidence?

❏ Are most significant goal-related qualification statements presented first, and less important last?

❏ If viewed independently from the resume, or within a cover letter, does this section project focus and an impressive knowledge of target-specific field and functional roles?

Education and Professional Development

❑ Do special headlines reinforce objective-related focus?

❑ If a traditional header is used, does it downplay the importance of this section?

❑ Does the order of appearance accurately portray significance, with most important information presented first and least important later, if not last?

❑ Does this section present school(s), degree(s), area(s) of concentration, courses, or honors?

❑ Do courses, papers, and projects listings appear as subheadings or as independent headlines?

❑ For soon-to-be or recent grads, do complimentary (over 3.0) overall or subject-specific GPAs appear?

❑ Is specialized, goal-focused training and development presented under a specific headline?

❑ If specifically related to job-search target, are experiences referred to in a qualification summary?

Experience

❑ Do special headlines reinforce objective-related focus and impact order of presentation?

❑ Do the headlines project knowledge of targeted fields and draw attention to related achievements?

❑ Do headlines catch the eye, revealing through quick review the nature of entries that follow?

❑ If a traditional header is used, does it downplay the importance of this section?

❑ Are entries described using active and accomplishment-oriented phasing, including facts and figures when possible?

❑ Are goal-specific experiences grouped under appropriate headlines, presented in order of significance?

❑ If specifically related to job-search target, is a special headline used and are experiences referred to in a qualification summary?

❑ If entries are simply cited, with no descriptions, are they obviously of less importance than others?

❑ Are organizations, titles, and dates easy to see, revealing an obvious pattern and logic?

❑ Have you, for space as well as goal-directed strategies, presented only the most significant experiences, with most important appearing first, and least important later?

✓ Community Service, Co-curricular Activities, and Special Categories

❑ For soon-to-be or recent college grad, are leadership roles and achievements cited?

❑ If specifically related to job-search target, is a special headline used and are experiences referred to in a qualification summary?

❑ If listed by experienced candidates, do all entries seem relevant to stated goal or do they project a logic for appearing at all?

❑ Are activities presented in easy-to-read and easy-to-follow patterns, avoiding acronyms and an overly lengthy listing of detail?

❑ If specifically related to job-search target, are experiences referred to in a qualification summary?

✓ Overall Presentation, Last Glance, Final Details

❑ Are most important headlines presented first, with most significant information appearing under each?

❑ If your resume is more than one page, is the most important information on the first page and does the second page have your name and a page number header?

❑ If you have more than one targeted resume, are the objectives clear, did you change order of presentation for each, and are summaries of qualifications target-specific?

❑ Does the resume present a professional image, with easy to recognize highlighting patterns, and with a top-to-bottom and in a last-glance logical format?

❑ If a qualification summary appears last, does it summarize goal-directed competencies and capabilities accurately and dynamically?

❑ Can you elaborate upon the resume in a cover letter?

❑ Would a prospective employer sense goal-oriented competence and confidence even without an accompanying letter?

❑ Can you elaborate upon the resume and use it as a clear guide during an interview?

❑ Are you ready to duplicate and distribute your resume?

Your answers must all be affirmative to all these questions, or you are not ready for the final steps. Don't be overanalytical or self-critical. Finish and use your resume. If needed you can always update and it will only take another day!

Duplicating and Distributing

Resumes can be printed each time one is needed, or they can be copied using a quality photocopier. Good laser and ink jet printers create copies on quality bond paper in conservative and easy-to-fax colors (white, off-white, and ivory). Traditional laid or linen bond (not parchment) paper is best for mailing, faxing, and hand delivery. Use blank pages and envelopes that match for job-search correspondence. If you create a master copy on plain paper, then photocopy on better paper; duplicates must be clean and toner residue-free.

FACT

Today, most resumes are in some way electronically transmitted (fax or e-mail), so issues related to duplication have changed. Anxieties and old causes for frustration and procrastination have been diminished if not eliminated. You have no excuse to delay creating, updating, duplicating, and distributing your resume today.

Circumstances will dictate whether you fax, e-mail, or mail your resumes. While you can combine two approaches to the same employer, it's not a good idea to do all three unless you are specifically requested to do so. Usually it's fax then e-mail, or fax then snail mail, that are the appropriate first steps. Eventually, you will use the telephone and other letters as you follow up on your resume distribution. As you can see in the closing comments of almost all our cover letter samples, it is always appropriate to follow up a resume with a phone call confirming its receipt and, if possible, requesting an interview or clarifying strategically sound next steps.

Remember, sending resumes is only one of the eight steps to job-search success. These powerful pages must be used as part of a comprehensive strategy. You will use your resume to get interviews, and you will use it during your interviews. You will get offers and make good decisions. In behavioral and motivational terms it's the person, not the page, that succeeds. Ⓔ

Chapter 8

Resumes, Cover Letters, and You

Y ou've heard all your life that "You can't tell a book by its cover." While this may be metaphorically true for some publications and people, it's not the case for resumes. A cover letter is the basis for your employer's first impression. It inspires your reader to examine your resume thoroughly. This chapter examines the relationships between your resume and the letter that covers it.

Always Send a Cover

It's easy to focus too much job-search attention on resumes. But the cover letter is just as important. Regardless of the means you use to submit your resume, and regardless of who the person is, never send your resume without a cover letter. While a complete letter may not be necessary in all circumstances, at the very least a quick note should accompany your resume.

Your cover letter represents you. It tells your readers what you most want them to know about you and your goals. Just like your resume, your cover letter mirrors your knowledge of self and your knowledge of qualification criteria associated with specific positions or functional areas.

In the old days, a standard cover letter asked readers to "assess my candidacy and determine the most appropriate fit." Today, you must quickly and clearly state your goals, briefly present your qualifications, and then refer your reader to the resume. While cover letters are most definitely written for others to read, they are in many ways personal tests of your abilities to state and support job-search targets. They are written quizzes that you must pass before you make it to the job interview.

ESSENTIAL

Always cover your resume with a letter or a note. If you are told to "just send a resume," what you should hear is, "Send a resume and a supplemental document focusing the reader's attention on your desired goals." While you may not actually hear that lengthy phrase, you should always send some form of letter. Resumes should, in good taste, never be naked.

Ideally, every cover letter you send will be addressed to a particular person. "To whom it may concern" or "Sir or Madam" are never appropriate salutations. If you don't know the recipient's name, start the letter immediately following address information, or use a memo format. Correspondence-style or memo-formatted documents can be faxed, e-mailed, or actually mailed. Know your target readers and write accordingly.

The best cover letters and resumes can stand alone, soliciting and supporting consideration. Readers can look at either independently and have enough information to judge the candidate's worthiness for an interview. But when they're combined, the impact of the two is much greater. Cover letters have a number of potential target readers (some at first electronic, yet all ultimately human), and they can be entitled and defined by a few common terms.

Other Types of Job-Search Correspondence

There are many other kinds of letters you will be called upon to write as you progress through your job-search campaign. The following sections describe a few of them.

Letters of Introduction

A letter of introduction does just what it says; it introduces you and your circumstances to readers. You also clearly identify what you would like the reader to do next and what you will do next. You can seek assistance, specific information, or referrals. Readers are, most often, prospective network members and advocates, or persons who can offer answers to specific questions. They are, less often, potential employers from whom you solicit consideration.

Letters of introduction are most effectively used as research and information-gathering tools. They ask readers to conduct information conversations or for referrals to persons, organizations, or Web sites that might be of assistance. Always phrase your requests in ways that require more than "yes" or "no" responses. They should inspire readers to forward names, e-mail addresses, phone numbers, Web sites, or other desired information. In closing, you note whether you will "patiently wait for an e-mail response" or "follow by phone to discuss your reactions to this request."

Don't ever ignore the power of a brief cover note, most often an e-mail. Effective communication does not always have to be formal nor lengthy. You can first briefly ask for some very specific information, and then follow up with more detailed documentation. In fact, people today may respond better at first to a number of quick e-bites, rather then one lengthy multiparagraph document. While it is always a good idea to attach resumes to any job-search letter, you do not have to do so with these briefer messages. Eventually, through follow-up efforts, you will send resumes to everyone you contact.

Letters of Application

A letter of application is a reactive tool used specifically to apply for a posted position. Within this letter you first state the job title (and number when given), where you saw the posting, and your desire to interview for the position. Later, you support requests for consideration by offering an accurate assessment of your qualifications. These two or at most three subsequent paragraphs show readers that you know the field, function, and title in question and that you have thought about what it will take to succeed.

These middle sections are where you very thoroughly share with readers what you learned through qualifications and achievements inventories and goal-focused competencies and capabilities analyses. This could be done simply via rephrasing your resume's qualification summary. You are the one required to look back, then look forward, and, most important, share your future-focused and confident views. After review of these paragraphs, readers must sense that you are worthy of an interview.

Be prepared to reflect knowledge of the job, and use words contained in the announcement. Show readers that you have more than the minimum qualifications. Refer to "the attached resume," and expand upon the qualification summary. Again and again, the more you talk the talk, the more likely you will walk the walk, down the path toward job-search and career success.

FACT

More and more resumes are transmitted by methods other than the U.S. mail. At one time all resumes were delivered by the postal service. Then FedEx and other express carriers came along. Now electronic transmission is possible and, more important, popular and convenient. As paper folded into envelopes has been replaced by e-mail messages and attachments, the world of resume writing and job searches has changed.

You most definitely should use phrases from your resume that reflect upon past achievements, with a preference for those that project knowledge of the future. Maintain and share your always-improving target vocabulary in letters of application. Use words from the actual description and from Web sites and articles written about the firm. Through this targeted letter of application, you are applying for a particular job with a specific organization. Give them a clear sense of your focus.

For creative fields, including public relations, advertising, and publishing, you can take more creative approaches, but for others, goal-direct yet formal phrasing will do. Some jobs allow you to take a more humorous approach, while others may require you to illustrate your abilities to create and send formal business communication skills. Know your audience, and keep in mind that you can share creativity in follow-up letters, rather than in first contacts.

Whenever possible, close letters of application with a statement like "I will call to confirm receipt of this letter and to discuss next steps." You must remember to follow up initial correspondence with phone calls and, if needed, with e-mails, then phone calls again. Do leave voice mail messages if you don't get through when you call. Don't call too often. Be persistent, yet not obnoxious.

Later in this chapter, samples illustrate a very user-friendly and quick approach to creating effective letters of application.

Letters of Inquiry

A letter of inquiry is a proactive tool, used to inquire regarding current opportunities and, most often, to inspire individualized consideration for future ones. In order to gain consideration, you must reinforce the sense of focus represented in your resume. In fact, the more effective you are at revealing your knowledge of the field, the more likely it is you will get an interview. Show reviewers that you have done your homework about the field, function, and firm. Ironically, the last is very much the least important. If readers are impressed with your knowledge of the field and with your abilities to serve within specific functions, you don't need to impress them with your knowledge of their firm. You'll have the opportunity in the interview to show how much you know about the particular organization.

A letter of inquiry is your opportunity to state in very clear terms what field and within what functions you are focusing your search. Ideally, you can cite some commonly used job titles, but they don't have to be specific to any particular organization. Like letters of application, the middle two or at most three paragraphs show readers that you have analyzed what it will take to succeed. You support your request for consideration by offering your summary of qualifications.

Address queries like the following:

- Why have you chosen the particular field?
- What does your background have to do with the field and the function you wish to serve within?
- What are the key qualities required to serve within the desired day-to-day roles?

Answer these questions proactively, and you will have the opportunity to answer others reactively, via the phone or in person via an interview. Use phrases and vocabulary that are field specific, and you will truly have the chance to talk the talk more and more as you continue to walk the walk on the path to offers and career success.

ESSENTIAL

Samples appearing later illustrate user-friendly and effective letters of inquiry. Some "inquiry and referral notes" can be brief, and followed by a more detailed letter, but you should always be clear regarding the focus you possess. A very brief, three or four-sentence expression can close with "a more detailed letter will soon follow" statement, but always include what functions you are interested in.

Some letters of inquiry begin with a "I'm contacting you at the suggestion of" a specific person who is serving as an advocate or network member. A name recognizable to the reader at the very beginning of your correspondence should ensure that it will be thoroughly read and, you hope, that an interview will follow. Close all letters of inquiry with "I will call to confirm receipt." You might also wish to copy your contact person to generate some behind-the-scenes supportive communication. Don't hesitate to identify the option of "meeting to discuss current opportunities or informally discussing future options."

Networking Requests

Requests for networking assistance should be clear and concise. Not everyone shares a common definition of this term. With a letter, you can seek "information about your career biography," "advice regarding how to gain consideration within your organization," or "referrals to others who can provide information or consideration." At the pre-research (research before job search) stage, you might focus on the first and third requests. When in job-search mode, you might focus on the second and third.

When communicating with alumni, family, or friends, do not be vague in your requests. If you want the names and e-mail addresses of specific people, ask for them. If you want to know "How do I break into your field?" or whether they will forward the attached resume to the right person, ask. Regardless of your request, be appreciative in tone and in words. Be sure you say thank you. Then say it again, for good measure.

To simplify, "networking" involves clearly stating your goals, then asking for specific help of others to attain these goals. These requests can be of persons you know or of those you would like to know. They can follow or be included in letters of introduction to individuals who are at first just names gained via articles, professional association directories, or search engine referrals. As with all communications, the impact will come from follow-up efforts.

Follow-up Letters

Ideally, everyone you contacted would respond promptly and positively. But, as you know, job-search undertakings are most often far from ideal. Effective campaigns involve follow-up communication. While patience is a virtue in some circumstances, it is not a characteristic of a strategic job search. Your challenge is to figure out what to say next and when to say it.

Your cover letters will broadcast your intent to call and confirm receipt of your resume. Don't expect much out of this exchange. Very few of them will result in any kind of positive response. Most likely, you will leave a message with a receptionist or via voice mail. Do leave voice mail messages. State your name, identify that you sent a cover letter and resume and that you wish to "confirm receipt and, ideally, set up a phone or in-person interview."

You should alternate your communication approaches—phone calls, e-mails, and faxes—and be sensitive to how often you are contacting potential employers. Because most resumes today are e-mailed or faxed, your initial confirmation call can take place within twenty-four hours. The old "I will call within a week" standard closing phrase is most definitely passé. If next-day calls get through, that's great. If they lead to interviews, wonderful. Most likely, they will yield a polite "please be patient." If you talk to an actual person, ask when you should call back. Then follow the suggested timeframe. If you were told next week, don't call before. In general, one contact a week for the first three weeks, then one contact a month after is a good rule of thumb.

FACT

Whenever you make a revision in your resume, you have a good reason to send a brief follow-up letter. Whether it's because you've changed your address, added a new course or seminar, or seen another posting on a Web site, after you've updated your resume, send it accompanied by a cover note. Refer quickly to past contacts, yet focus on what is new and directly related on the resume.

You can follow calls with brief telegram-style e-mails. A message like the following is appropriate:

"Tried to call today, but could not get through. Understand how busy you are. Just wanted to confirm receipt of resume and cover letter. Can we talk by phone or in person? Thanks."

For the first follow-up contact, you can include another copy of the cover letter and resume. For the following two (maximum) follow-up contacts, you can include just a copy of your resume.

Thank-You Letters

Expressing appreciation is a very effective form of job-search communication. While it may sound trite, you can say thank you at every step along the way. Everyone knows to send a thank-you note after interviews, but too few communicate their gratitude before then. A thanks for confirming receipt of your resume, including an expression of continued interest and a clearly expressed wish for a telephone or a face-to-face interview, is usually the first of these efforts.

A thanks for clarifying status, including an expression of continued interest, with a statement regarding when you might follow up again, is most likely the second. Too often ignored, a thank you for a rejection letter or e-mail is also appropriate. Respond to a "your background does not match" letter or e-mail with an "I remain very interested in your firm, and ideally we can discuss where my qualifications best fit" statement. Be careful of tone, but do seek continued consideration as well as some additional focus.

Appreciation should always be expressed to network members and advocates who have referred you to postings or persons. By keeping these individuals informed of your efforts you are subtly, or directly, inspiring their own follow-up efforts. Follow-up calls or e-mails by network members to their contacts, requesting "special consideration," often lead to interviews and speed up an otherwise slow process. In many ways your follow-up networking letters are as important as those to organizations you wish to work for.

Confirmation, Acceptance, and Declining Letters

While it's usually not legally or logistically required, it is a good idea to confirm most activities and decisions in written form. Whether these expressions are transmitted via electronic means, faxed, or mailed is not important. But it is important that you communicate continually and effectively. The growing use of e-mails has made this process quicker, easier, and less awkward for most.

You must call or e-mail a few days before each interview to confirm the time and date and to assist with your preparation for this important series of conversations. When making decisions regarding offers, you must continue to communicate enthusiastically. After you have made a decision, you will accept or decline via a brief note, either faxed or e-mailed.

These continued communications are good habits to get into and they set the scene for future positive interactions. Pre-interview contacts facilitate critical next steps, and post-offer communications impact salary and other discussions. In many cases, they can lead to consideration and offers years from now.

Communication Not Simply Application

If you have ever cracked open a fortune cookie and read, "He who hesitates is lost," you probably understand the overly simplistic yet profound importance of continued communication. So-called "application processes" are, by nature, reactive. They inspire you to be passive. When applying to college, to graduate school, for a mortgage, or for an association membership, waiting is appropriate. When applying for employment, communication is more than desired. It is required to succeed!

ALERT!

Never send only a resume. Always complement this document with a brief or detailed cover page. Clearly identify your desired outcomes. In most cases this would be an interview, but sometimes it is an information conversation or a referral. No matter which, politely make your request and support it with particular entries on your resume.

Resumes are the most common symbols of job-search communication. While they may lead most to assume that you are in job-search mode, you use supporting and continued documentation and follow-up communication to confirm your status and provide you and those you contact much-needed focus. Ironically, the most common mistake made by job seekers is over-dependence on resumes. No matter how powerful the words on this page, they must be continually supported by your assertive and appropriate actions, reactions, and continued interactions.

E-Mail versus Snail Mail

Those who remember walking uphill both ways in the snow to get to school and to go home without shoes, also remember that job search was different in the "olden days." Today, e-mail is the most common and acceptable way to send resumes and all follow-up letters. But do not forget that alternating media can diminish the potential for oversaturation and negative consequences. Fax, phone, express mail, and, yes, even "snail mail" can be used.

"Snail mail" is the cute Y2K phrase used for the slow but sure (we think) U.S. Postal Service. At one time the only persons who delivered resumes, cover letters, and all other correspondence were the men and women in red, white, and blue. Today we have wearers of the brown (UPS), blue and orange (FedEx), and others who can guarantee delivery in one or two days. Don't ignore the impact of express delivery on specific individuals, particularly those with whom you have spoken over the phone, but remember that e-communication is now the most cost-effective, immediate, and (in this "sad, but true" security-sensitive world) safe forms of delivery.

ALERT!

If you think recipients may be concerned about virus-carrying e-mails, copy and paste your resume straight into the text box. Do not identify it as an attachment. Remember to note the title of job desired and the words "enclosed resume" in the e-mail subject heading.

You can follow some electronically transmitted letters with hard copies, just to be safe and traditional, but do not depend solely on paper, envelopes, and stamps as your job-search tools. When you do send items by mail, make sure you have the correct postage. Match your resume and cover-letter paper, and use large mailing envelopes so you don't have to fold your contents.

Phone and Fax

These communication and transmission techniques are underused. With the increased popularity of e-mail, fewer people use phone and fax as follow-up tools. You are encouraged to use the phone whenever possible and, in order to place an actual document within someone's hands, the fax as well. While at first awkward for most, phone skills and confidence enhance with each call. Do call to confirm receipt of documents, to identify next steps, and to make a clear "can I schedule an interview" request. Leave brief, slow, and clear voice mail messages whenever you call. Don't appear to be a pest, but do be persistent and professional.

After you have left a message or two, fax or e-mail a note. Alternating communication techniques can be effective. Always briefly and clearly state who you are, when and how your earlier contact was made, and what you would like to happen next. Don't be afraid to state, "I would like to meet with you," or more assertively, "I would appreciate an interview." Also, ask if they would like another copy of your resume to refresh their memory regarding your background. It is okay to provide one with the first two follow-up letters, particularly those that are faxed.

Sample Cover Letters and Follow-up Letters

The following samples are offered to share insights into the job-search efforts of our fictional friends. Through a longitudinal glimpse at these initial contact and follow-up letters you should be inspired to create or update effective documentation.

Additional samples also appear. To maximize the effectiveness of your resume and correspondence, make them personal. Whether you are a soon-to-be or recent college grad, an experienced candidate or someone seeking a promotion, the content and style of your communication will impact success. Be inspired by the samples that follow, but make sure the documents you use are perceived as yours and that they clearly connect to your goals. Your written and spoken voice during your job search must sound like you.

Advertising AE Letter of Application

CHRIS SMITH

123 Main Street • Hometown, NY 00000 • (555) 555-1234 • csmith@company.com

August 23, 20–

Jamie Stenson
Account Supervisor
Saatchi and Saatchi
8765 Broadway
New York, NY 14623-0450
FAX (555) 555-5555

Ms. Stenson:

I would like to interview for an Assistant Account Executive position. Relevant courses in Marketing, Finance, and Accounting, as well as independent marketing projects have enabled me to develop practical skills and perspectives. Knowledge of strategic planning, marketing research, budgeting, advertising techniques, and related report-writing and presentation skills have been fine-tuned in varied settings. In general, I offer:

- Marketing research, strategic planning, promotions, customer service, and sales talents nurtured by in-depth and diverse advertising, promotions, and retail internships and employment.
- Technical skills gained via courses including: Principles of Marketing, Marketing Projects and Cases, Psychology of Human Motivation and Emotion, Business Administration, Public Relations Writing, Advertising, Mass Media, Persuasion, and Consumer Behavior.
- Confidence serving on account team and interacting with client colleagues.
- Blend of research, analysis, writing and presentation talents.
- UNIX, HTML, Word, WordPerfect, Excel, PageMaker, PhotoShop, Netscape, and Internet skills.

Specific qualifications that match those cited on your Web site as required include:

- Marketing research, strategic planning, promotions, customer service, and sales talents nurtured in advertising and promotions internships.
- Blend of quantitative, analytical, and creative problem-solving talents.
- Capacities to conduct and analyze research, and then translate data into persuasive proposals, reports, and graphics.
- Intense curiosity regarding consumer behavior, varied products, and industries, and the nature of market segmentation.

I graduated from University of Rochester with dual majors, a minor in Economics, and, most significantly, a Certificate in Management Studies in Marketing. As my resume indicates, I have had a number of related internships with local as well as international firms. I would welcome the chance to discuss my qualifications. I will call to confirm receipt of this fax (originals to follow by mail) and, at your convenience, to arrange a brief meeting.

Sincerely,

Chris Smith

- This letter of application is used when applying for a posted job.
- Addressed to actual contact person. Name gained via company Web site, then confirmed by phone.
- Document first uses abbreviated qualification summary from resume to present overall candidacy.
- Second set of bullets paraphrases qualifications in actual ad. These must be changed for each letter of application, depending upon the job and requirements.
- This "copy-and-paste, then change" technique can be used when applying for almost any posted job. Make sure the specific qualifications highlighted match the position sought and contain keywords used in the posting and within the field. This is crucial for keyword searches associated with Web-based resume collections.
- In some cases, the specific qualifications may appear before the general ones.

Advertising AE Follow-Up E-Mail

- E-mail used as initial contact via referral from original communiqué.

- Font as per e-mail setting.

- This follow-up supplements a "letter of inquiry" for general opportunities within a particular field or a "letter of application," in specific application for a posted job.

- The candidate is making first contact with a person whose name has been referred by another.

- E-mail is a quick way to transmit follow-up communiqués.

- Document covers original letter as well as resume. It is copied and pasted into the actual e-mail text box, with other documents sent as attachments.

JAMIE BROWN

123 Main Street • Hometown, NY 00000 • (555) 555-1234 • jbrown@company.com

August 23, 20–

Jane Green
Recruiter
jgrecruiter@company.com

As shared with Jamie Stenson via the attached letter, my post-graduation objective is to begin a career in advertising. It is with focus and enthusiasm that I seek to interview for an account management focused position at Saatchi & Saatchi. After speaking with Ms. Stenson's assistant, Kim, I understand that you coordinate all requests for consideration, and that recent graduates can be considered for internships as well as post-baccalaureate opportunities.

Relevant courses in Marketing, Finance, and Economics, as well as many independent marketing projects, have enabled me to develop practical skills and perspectives. Knowledge of strategic planning, marketing research, budgeting, advertising techniques, and related research, report-writing, and presentation skills have been fine-tuned in varied roles and settings.

As my resume indicates, I have had a number of internships in the past five years. Each has taught me much and nurtured advertising related skills. I would welcome the chance to discuss my qualifications with you and your Saatchi & Saatchi colleagues as soon as appropriate. I will call to confirm receipt of this e-mail (originals to follow via mail) and, at your convenience, to arrange a telephone or in-person interview.

Trips to New York are easy to arrange. Perhaps we could meet when I am next in the city? I am committed to this field and I will persevere to succeed through job search and beyond. Thank you for your consideration.

Sincerely,

Jamie Brown

Letter of Introduction and Networking E-Mail

DANA JOHNSON
123 Main Street • Hometown, NY 00000 • (555) 555-1234 • djohnson@company.com

August 23, 20–

Marty Jones
Account Manager
DDB Needham
mjones@company.com

Mr. Jones:

The advice and support of a University of Rochester alumnus would be much appreciated. My post-graduation objective is to begin a career in advertising. It is with focus, enthusiasm, and curiosity that I seek to learn about your career biography and, respectfully, request referrals to persons within your firm and other agencies who might grant me an interview.

Through telephone or, if convenient, in-person discussions I can learn about your background and gain insights regarding how I can enter the field of advertising. Ideally, I would do so as an assistant account executive. Specific suggestions regarding how to network and successfully solicit interviews would be well received.

The attached resume is offered to quickly familiarize you with my background. A more detailed cover letter can follow if you judge my candidacy worthy of consideration by you and your DDB Needham colleagues. As the resume indicates, I have had a number of related internships over the past five years, and my academics have given me strong conceptual foundations upon which I have built field specific skills. I will call to confirm receipt of this e-mail and, at your convenience, to arrange a phone conversation or a meeting. In advance, thank you for your assistance.

Sincerely,

Dana Johnson

- E-mail introduction sent to initiate networking activities with alumnus.

- Expectations clearly cited.

- Candidate's background only briefly noted.

- Illustrates a "letter of introduction" and a "networking letter," used to gain information and referrals within a particular functional area.

- The candidate is making first contact with a person who might serve as a network member or advocate. Initially, contact was gained through online alumni directory.

- This document seeks specific consideration for a position with the alumnus' firm as well as general referrals.

Advertising AE Letter of Inquiry

FRANCIS WILLIAMS
123 Main Street • Hometown, NY 00000 • (555) 555-1234 • fwilliams@company.com

August 23, 20–

Marty Jones
Human Resource Manager
Ogilvy and Mather
123 West 49th Street
New York, NY 14624
FAX (555) 555-5555

Ms. Jones:

I would like to interview for an entry-level account management position! Independent marketing projects, related internships, and relevant courses in Marketing, Finance, and Accounting have enabled me to develop practical skills and perspectives. Knowledge of strategic planning, marketing research, budgeting, advertising techniques, and related report-writing and presentation skills have been fine-tuned in varied settings.

Diverse account management qualifications and capabilities include:

- Marketing research, strategic planning, promotions, customer service, and sales talents nurtured by in-depth and diverse advertising, promotions, and retail internships and employment.
- Technical skills gained via courses including: Principles of Marketing, Marketing Projects and Cases, Psychology of Human Motivation and Emotion, Business Administration, Public Relations Writing, Advertising, Mass Media, Persuasion, and Consumer Behavior.
- Confidence serving on account team and interacting with client colleagues.
- Blend of research, analysis, writing, and presentation talents.
- Knowledge of International Business approaches gained living and working in varied North American, European, and Middle Eastern settings.
- German, French, Dutch, and Farsi fluency, and conversational Spanish capabilities.
- UNIX, HTML, Word, WordPerfect, Excel, PageMaker, PhotoShop, Netscape, and Internet skills.

I graduated from University of Rochester with dual majors, a minor in Economics, and a Certificate in Management Studies in Marketing. As my resume indicates, I have had a number of significant advertising-focused internships. During an interview I can expand upon internships as well as the above bullets, learn more about the nature of opportunities at Ogilvy & Mather, and support my candidacy for account management-related positions. I will call to confirm receipt of this fax (originals to follow by mail) and, at your convenience, to arrange a brief meeting. Thank you.

Sincerely,

Francis Williams

Advertising AE Thank-You Note

COREY DAVIS

123 Main Street • Hometown, NY 00000 • (555) 555-1234 • cdavis@company.com

September 17, 20–

Jane Green
Recruiter
Saatchi and Saatchi
jg@company.com

Ms. Green:

I appreciate the opportunity I had to share qualifications for an account assistant position. The more people I meet, and the more I learn from enthusiastic professionals like you, Jamie Stenson, and Bill Burton, the more eager I become to join you and your colleagues on the Saatchi & Saatchi team. I do look forward to hearing soon regarding the outcome of the interview. The writing sample we discussed will soon be forwarded by e-mail or fax.

Thank you again for your time and consideration. I do sincerely hope to soon begin an achievement-filled career with Saatchi & Saatchi. As a dedicated account assistant I will contribute to the multifaceted research, analysis, campaign development, and client relations roles associated with this critical area. It was exciting to see how enthusiastic your colleagues were about their particular accounts, particularly those who have Hershey as a client.

As discussed during the interview, I will strive to personify the blend of creative, quantitative, analytical and communication talents required to add value to the account team, the client, and the firm.

Sincerely,

Corey Davis

- This is a simple thank-you note. It was e-mailed immediately following interviews to the recruiter who coordinated a series of meetings. All others involved were named. Additional notes will be sent. It's not important that they all be different. But it is important that they all receive quick positive and appreciative reactions.

- The middle and last paragraphs refer briefly to particular points addressed during their particular meeting. While some use thank-you notes to reinforce qualifications, they can also just be simple expressions of appreciation.

- Also, this note reminds the reader that supplemental materials will soon be forwarded.

Advertising AE Acceptance E-mail

CHRIS SMITH

123 Main Street • Hometown, NY 00000 • (555) 555-5555 • csmith@company.com

September 27, 20–

Jane Green
Recruiter
Saatchi and Saatchi
jg@company.com

Ms. Green:

It is with great pride that I confirm through this e-mail that I accept the account assistant position. I understand that my immediate supervisor will be Bill Burton and that my starting salary will be $28,000 annually. The start date of October 1st seems ideal, and I will visit your office within the next few days to complete all required forms. I am eager to join the Saatchi & Saatchi team and begin an achievement-filled tenure as an account assistant. Ideally, this will mark the beginning of a long and productive career with the firm.

As we discussed after the offer was extended, I do appreciate your agreeing to a performance and salary review after six months, and another one year after my start date. This will allow me to prove my value and earn a raise that will ease the financial burden of my relocation to the New York City area. Of course, the relocation allowance of $500 is most generous and will be used appropriately.

My personal thanks go out to you for your efforts throughout all stages of the consideration and interview process. I will see you soon, when I visit to complete paperwork. If you wish to contact me for any reason, please do so via the phone or email above.

Sincerely,

Chris Smith

Public Relations Letter of Inquiry

JAMIE BROWN
123 Main Street • Hometown, NY 00000 • (555) 555-1234 • jbrown@company.com

April 8, 20–

Marty Jones
ABC PR
234 East 45th Street
New York, NY 00000
FAX (555) 555-5555

Mr. Jones:

How about an honest cover letter as a refreshing alternative? When first asked, "What do you want to do after graduation?" my answer was "I don't know." After introspection and active research, I can now confidently, enthusiastically, and ambitiously answer "Why PR?" and state that this field would require the use of existing talents and require that I develop new ones. Assets I offer today include:

- *Abilities to conduct research on various topics, identify key trends, then present findings in verbal and written reports, promotional materials, feature articles, or press communiqués.*
- *Interest in transforming understanding of behavior and motivation to strategic campaigns, promotional efforts, fundraising events, persuasive publications, and educational activities.*
- *Capacities to use statistical techniques to analyze and present data.*
- *Confidence planning and implementing events independently or in groups, with particular focus on creatively identifying goals, logistics, and details required to succeed.*
- *Experience using Word, Excel, PowerPoint, and Internet applications for academic, creative, and other projects.*

Serving within entry-level or internship capacities, I will achieve my professional and personal goals. I will become an effective event planner and creative writer, a strategist working with clients to develop and implement targeted campaigns, and a peer who will brainstorm with, support, and inspire those around me. Yes, occasionally I will be a colleague who laments about "clients who just don't understand," or that "so-and-so who doesn't like my writing," but I will always be a responsible professional who will continue to improve her skills and complete tasks accurately and on time.

I will call to confirm receipt of this letter and accompanying resume and, ideally, arrange telephone or in-person conversations regarding opportunities at ABC. While I am seeking a full-time position, I would welcome consideration for internship or part-time options. Most important, I want to speak with you, a successful professional, about your career, my talents, and about your firm's needs. An honest and creative person must always share dreams and be confident that they will someday become realities. If initial communiqués don't do the trick, follow-up communication will. I look forward to continued communication and interactions.

Sincerely,

Jamie Brown

- Identifying information notes addresses from which letter is sent.

- Left-justified block text format is e-friendly; can be uploaded to Web sites and copy-and-pasted into e-mail.

- Illustrates "letter of inquiry" for opportunities within a particular field.

- Candidate is making first contact with a person on her hit list. Contacts are identified via printed directories or Web sites, then confirmed through telephone conversations. This was gained through a professional association membership directory.

- Requests consideration for entry-level or internship options, and introduces the concept of an informational interview.

- It raises a variety of options that must be addressed during follow-up communication.

Pharmaceutical Sales Letter of Application and Follow-Up

- Detailed introductory paragraph reveals field-focused research.

- Second paragraph highlights most significant experience.

- Closing presentation of qualification summary as it appeared in resume serves to tie all concepts together.

- This cover letter illustrates a "letter of inquiry."

- The candidate is making first formal contact after a telephone conversation, facilitated by a referral from a physician.

- The letter is detailed because the contact encouraged him to "include everything you know, but keep it to a page." Many pharmaceutical firms ask for supplemental goal sheets. This candidate incorporated some of these concepts in the letter.

- Candidate identifies geographic target, yet raises relocation option.

- Faxing provides a hard copy to be forwarded to others.

Dana Johnson

123 Main Street • Hometown, New York 00000 • (555) 555-1234 • djohnson@company.com

April 7, 20–

Ms. Marty Jones
District Manager
Pharmaceutical Giant, Inc.
100 San Paso Way
San Francisco, CA 12121
FAX: (555) 555-5555

Ms. Jones:

Thank you for speaking with me the other day. As I have discussed with you and Dr. Smith, my goal is to begin and succeed within a pharmaceutical sales career. Ideally, that career will be with Pharmaceutical Giant. Most critical, I am confident that I can enhance market share of Pharmaceutical Giant products and personify the profile of a physician, patient, and profit-inspired professional. Regular reading of *Pharmaceutical Representative Online* and other related sites and publications reinforce my goals. It was exciting to see that Pharmaceutical Giant has brands within many of the top profitable categories for the past fiscal year. These include antiulcerants, cholesterol & triglyceride reducers, antidepressants, calcium antagonists, plain antirheumatic non-steroidals, ACE inhibitors, plain cephalosporins and combinations, antipsychotics, non-narcotic analgesics, and oral antidiabetics.

Detailed on the attached resume, contributions to my current employer helped turn 2001 into a successful year despite the effect of the recession on sales of luxury items. Unlike traditional sales positions where the relationship between salesman and customer ends with the close of a deal, my position requires the establishment of an ongoing relationship, similar to those built between pharmaceutical representatives and physician customers. I am required to convince my customers to turn to me for all their needs, just as a Pharmaceutical Giant representative inspires physicians to prescribe represented medications on a regular basis. In summary, I offer:

- Record of success within direct marketing and information-driven sales roles.
- Confidence nurturing existing relationships and developing new clientele via direct calls using information dissemination strategies.
- Capacity to share knowledge pertaining to pharmaceutical products and protocols.
- Abilities to blend qualitative and communication talents as well as analytical skills to set goals, document impact of sales efforts, and maximize output.

I will call to confirm receipt of this letter and, I sincerely hope, to continue our discussions. Ideally, I will soon have the opportunity to support my qualifications via a formal interview. Until then, informal conversations would be most welcomed. Also, while eager to apply my talents to opportunities in the Bay area, I would definitely consider relocating for the chance to join Pharmaceutical Giant.

Sincerely,
Dana Johnson

Investment Banking Template Letter of Inquiry

FRANCIS WILLIAMS

123 Main Street, Apartment 13 • Hometown, NY 00000
(555) 555-1234 • fwilliams@company.com

TO: Contact Name
             Company Name

DATE: February 27, 20–

FAX: (555) 555-5678

SUBJECT: **Analyst Position**

As an Economics major at Harvard I completed several key economics and statistics courses. In addition, I took undergraduate courses in finance at Boston University. As noted on my resume, I have also served in diverse finance-focused internships. While I have proven that I can excel academically and within internship capacities, I now seek the challenges associated with succeeding as an Analyst at [COMPANY NAME].

Basic qualifications I offer include:

- Knowledge of the industry and economics gained through upper-level and honors courses, as well as substantial internship experience.
- Analytical ability honed by Honors Microeconomics and fundamental finance courses.
- Ability to work long hours and succeed, demonstrated by academic performance, extensive internship experience in finance industry, and broad cocurricular leadership.

Specifically associated with the responsibilities of an Analyst, I offer:

- Experience completing research projects within demanding, pressure-filled, deadline-driven financial institutions.
- Capacities to quickly understand, examine issues, and identify trends associated with capital formation products and services, including: derivatives, IPOs, Mergers and Acquisitions, Bond Markets, and [FIRM SPECIALTIES HERE].
- Technical skills gained as an intern included: using spreadsheets for sophisticated as well as simple modeling; investigating investment worthiness and profit and loss leverages; and presenting findings to critical and analytical colleagues.

Extensive computer skills and exceptional analytical capacities will also help me succeed at [COMPANY NAME]. I will call to confirm receipt of this fax and, I do sincerely hope, to arrange an interview. At present I have some interview trips to New York City planned. Perhaps I could meet with you during my next visit?

Sincerely,

Francis Williams

- Template developed for targeted field; changed slightly for each firm.
- Memo format easy to read and transforms well into template format.
- Set up via database to facilitate mass mailing.
- Summaries of general and specific qualifications are focal points.
- Specific summary allows insertion of firm specialties.
- This database-driven format allows for mass mailings with small variances in each letter. Contacts are identified via printed directories, Web sites, and alumni directories, and then confirmed through telephone conversations.

- Illustrates a "letter of application" as well as a "follow-up letter," because it is written in response to a referral from a third-party teacher placement agency.

- It can serve as a "personal statement," a document often required of candidates for teaching positions.

- Faxing is a quick way to make contact (with originals sent later by mail).

- This document uses qualification summary adaptation as an easy and effective way to present overall qualifications.

- It also contains sample lesson-plan descriptions and expresses great enthusiasm for teaching.

Chris Smith

123 Main Street • Hometown, NY 00000 • (555) 555-1234 • csmith@company.com

March 22, 20–

Marty Jones
Headmaster of the ABC School
2345 School Street
Princeton, NJ 12321
FAX (555) 555-5555

Headmaster Jones:

Commencement signifies "a beginning," when I will start new experiences, yet never stop learning. Being a teacher requires self-motivation for ongoing learning and the inspiration of others to do the same. As a teacher at ABC, I will empower students as they progress towards their commencement. Too many students have aversions towards studying languages, towards exploring theories associated with making and spending money, and towards examining timeless themes in books not mentioned on talk show television.

Teaching would allow me to use lessons similar to those of my favorite instructors. I can imagine teaching vocabulary in an interactive and engaging manner. I would group students and teach vocabulary for foods by having them make and use picture flash cards. Students would show cards, then ask and respond to questions such as, "Which food do you like best?" I would relate economics to the world of high school students. For example, I could use pizza and wings to explain diminishing returns to scale. The first piece of pizza could be described as the most delicious while the twelfth may perhaps be nauseating. English literature would involve powerful relations and comparisons between different works of literature and society.

A position at ABC will allow me to begin my teaching career, provide intrinsic rewards associated with inspiring students, and provide me the continued learning that I crave. In return, I offer:

- Confidence in tutorial roles, assisting peers with college and secondary courses.
- Sensitivities to ability levels and communication styles of varied learners.
- Desire to teach French language and literature as well as science or economics courses.

My desires to become an effective teacher, mentor, and motivator will drive me as I continue to learn at ABC. I am pleased that Professor Sanders informed you of my candidacy, and I am most eager to discuss my qualifications by phone or in person. Thank you for your consideration.

Sincerely,

Chris Smith

Chapter 9

Resumes as Interview Preparation and Motivation Tools

Somewhere you've read this advice: "Use resumes to get interviews, and interviews to get offers." An even more accurate statement would read: "Use your resume to get interviews and resumes during interviews; then you'll definitely get offers." This chapter identifies how to use resumes as both interview preparation and motivation tools.

The Resume, Interview, and You

Never interview without a copy of your resume in your hand, in your heart, and in your head. The interviewer will refer to this document to inspire questions. You can use it to inspire answers as well as attitudes. While it may seem simple and somewhat silly, read the following statement aloud: "as you can see on my resume." Yes, aloud! Listen to yourself saying these seven words. Do so with enthusiasm and confidence. This phrase is the verbal and strategic foundation for planning and maintaining interview communications.

Interview preparation begins with a thorough, job-specific review of your resume. With a job title and job description clearly in mind, develop a list of qualification criteria. Highlight the most relevant experiences on your resume. Identify at least three things on your resume that you must discuss in the interview. Select the bullet-points from your qualification summary, accomplishments from your experiences, or educational achievements that you must cover. This is your general review. Later in this chapter, a step-by-step pre-interview regimen takes you through the process in detail.

Your resume should be a psychological security blanket, nurturing confidence and diminishing anxiety, as well as a guide to the key points to cover. Your resume is not just for the interviewer. It is a preparation and implementation tool for you. To maximize your interview performance, use your resume before to identify and link qualities and accomplishments to the job you are interviewing for. Use the resume during your interview to guide the conversation and ensure that key points were covered.

Easy Job-Search Conversations

Preparation is how you avoid perspiration. By being prepared, you will skillfully facilitate conversation. Conducting pre-interview preparation builds your confidence, provides focus for communication, and enhances outcomes. Too many candidates spend hour after hour researching historical facts and obscure figures associated with an organization, increasing anxiety via off-target, yet well-intended efforts. These individuals research companies too much, and their own backgrounds and job descriptions too little. They don't review resumes, and they limit qualification criteria analysis to a quick perusal of brief, oversimplified job announcements.

Verification is for many a missing link to interview preparation. Call a few days before any interview to confirm your meeting and, whenever possible, to arrange an informal conversation with someone who knows about the job you will be interviewing for. Clarify logistics of the day, particularly for callback interviews, arranged after initial telephone or in-person screening discussions. Know how many people you will be seeing and what to expect of your visit. Don't fear "stupid questions," including asking for directions, for the more information you have, the smarter you will appear on the day of the interview.

Pre-interview research does not have to be completed covertly, so specifically ask, "Is there information I should be reading, or can you provide me with a very detailed job description prior to my interview?" You might also ask: "Are there particular questions I should be thinking about prior to my interview?" Verify and be curious before, so you can be effective during any interview.

Last-Minute Tips and Strategies

You've spent hours hunting books that might help with resume writing, interviewing, and job search. Yet bookstore employees often hear from frantic customers, "I've got an interview tomorrow. What is the best book for last-minute preparation?" Here are some easy-to-follow guidelines for last-minute prepping.

Call Ahead

Two or three days before your interview, e-mail or call the employer to confirm your meeting and to request a copy of the job description and a company profile. Offer to stop by to pick up the information or ask if it can be e-mailed, faxed, or express mailed. Specifically ask this question: "Are there questions or issues I should focus on to prepare for our meeting?"

Imagine how well you can prepare if you receive a list of potential questions or critical issues to examine. You would be surprised how often interviewers will provide this information when asked. Queries can be made by phone. If you can't get through to the appropriate person(s), leave a voice mail message, followed quickly by an e-mail or faxed note, and then, later in the day, by another call. If you start a few days prior to the interview, you have a greater chance to receive a response.

Specific Research

Conduct an Internet search or visit a reference librarian, seeking information on the firm and, most important, on general current events articles on the field involved. If possible, enter a few keywords into a general search engine or into search options within the company's Web site. Don't dwell too long on researching the prospective employer. Basic and topical information on the field involved is often much more valuable. You should be able to discuss industry trends, major players, and "what's hot and what's not" within the field. While somewhat "retro," reference librarians are still competent problem solvers. They thrive on the challenge of locating hard-to-find information under the pressure of a pending deadline. Also, just as a sports fan regularly reads the sports section of the newspaper, don't forget to read the business or related sections of local papers and professional publications.

Complete a Pre-Interview Resume Review Inventory

It is critical that you be prepared to share anecdotes of your achievements. On the back of your resume, list at least three times when you used specific skills to complete a project or achieve success. For each, be able to describe actions that yielded specific outcomes. Review your resume to enhance your job-search memory, but don't memorize it. You may also use the back of your resume to identify key points to make in the interview and to remember questions to ask during the two-way exchange.

Timing Is Everything

Arrive exactly one-half hour early, check in, and, if you haven't already done so, ask if you can review a copy of the job description as well as literature describing the nature of the organization and significant events of the past year. Sit down in a comfortable area and review your resume and cover letter. It's amazing that most job seekers forget this very simple preparation activity. Think about it. What do interviewers review when determining whom to meet? What do they review immediately before and during the interview? Most definitely, the answer is "your resume and cover letter." Don't forget to review these documents before your interview. Mark critical points or make notes on the back. This one-page "personal note sheet" can be very effective. Have extra copies of your resume available in case you meet with someone who doesn't have one.

Answers and Questions

Ask two questions within the first ten minutes of the interview, and bring copies of your work to show. Questions should be variations on "What are the qualities you are seeking for this position?" and "What specific expectations in terms of output and outcomes do you have for the person who holds this job?" This will allow you to gain a greater understanding of the position and reflect qualifications later in the interview. The more you learn early in the conversation, the better. Remember, an interview is simply a conversation with a purpose. It is not an adversarial "right-or-wrong" or "the interviewer is out to get me" process. Be enthusiastic, optimistic, and inquisitive.

Inject some humor to relieve any stress. Write a funny "relaxation association phrase," a silly childhood nickname, or a doodle at the bottom of the resume page. Or place a cartoon sticker somewhere on the resume. It's hard to stay tense when looking at the words "Mickey Mouse," "Pooh," "Breathe," or "Smile." You cannot help but smile if you quickly glance at a picture of Snoopy or Tigger. Relax, enjoy, and go for it!

Putting It All Together

While for some, interviews can yield the appropriate excitement and anticipatory "edge," for others it can manifest in negative ways. Sweaty palms, knotted guts, and beads of sweat are too frequent physical and psychological symptoms on interview day. If you prepare and have the proper attitude, interviews can be fun. When else is it okay to brag and speak about yourself in positive ways for an hour or two? After creating and reviewing your resume, you should be very appropriately egocentric, focusing on you. You're a great candidate, or you would not have been invited to interview. Enjoy the chance to share your pride in your achievements as well as your personal visions of your future.

Your Resume as a Guide for Interview Day

As qualification criteria were used to review resumes and identify whom to interview, these same qualities are the yardsticks from which all interviewers will measure you. To determine your potential to walk the walk to success within a particular job, your interview talk will be heard and then analyzed. Those you interview with will be listening for verbal cues that reveal how strongly you match predetermined criteria. As they listen, they will process what they hear and create an overall impression of your potential to succeed within the specifics of the job.

Focus your thoughts first and then your statements on roles and responsibilities of the job. Prospective employers have already identified connections between your resume and their desired and required competencies. All you now need to do is reinforce these resume-linked connections while sharing communication as well as personality style.

Interviews can flow as conversations, but you should figure out ahead of time what key points you want to address. You don't go into academic exams without focusing on specific topics. You don't conduct presentations without some notes or AV tools. Pre-interview resume review activities focus on topics and provide needed visual cues.

It is easy to use this process-oriented knowledge. Before each interview, create a list of qualification criteria for the position. What specific criteria would be associated with an ideal candidate for the position you will be interviewing for? Identify the basic qualities sought and how one would determine who possesses these traits. Most important, use your resume to create a carefully conceived strategy and list of discussion points.

Pre-Interview Resume Review Inventory

Before each interview, complete the following exercise on the back of a resume. This will organize your thoughts, identify what last-minute information needs to be collected, and clarify what to highlight during the discussion. Using these notes, you will be focusing the interview into a target-specific conversation. Review your notes beforehand, and use them during the interview.

What, When, and Where

Answer the basic questions first. Briefly note the organization and describe the position you will be interviewing for. If you can do it in, let's say, 100 words, you are ready to move on from this exercise. If you cannot, you have some fact-gathering or thinking to do.

If you have not yet reviewed a detailed job description, request a copy and do so. Then summarize what you have read in your own terms. Describe it as if you were speaking to the fifteen-year-old son or daughter of a close friend. In this way you will force yourself to simplify and describe actions and outcomes associated with the job in basic behavioral and functional terms.

Define Qualifications

Second, cite three key points that make you qualified for the position in question. Review your resume's qualification summary section, then identify three of those cited or define "broader connections" that clearly match qualifications for the position you are interviewing for. In general, you are completing the statements "Thinking about this job, specifically, my three key assets are . . ." or "Thinking about the job, the three key points I want to raise in the interview include . . ." Ideally, these will match some of the phrasing used on the qualification criteria list you have already created for the job. Each of the three bulleted points should be no more than fifty words.

Illustrate Your Abilities

Third, note three anecdotes that illustrate your capabilities to succeed on the job. Stories should support the three key points cited, linking skills used when taking goal-directed actions and, ultimately to achieve results or finish a project. Start out by very briefly noting the story. Then, identify actions, results, and tasks that were associated with your accomplishments. Last, cite the key skills used and enhanced as a result of each particular experience.

List three questions you would like to ask the interviewer. Ask one question in the first five minutes of the interview and another in the second five minutes so that you can use your interviewer's response in the discussion as it progresses. These initial inquiries should focus on day-to-day job responsibilities and on how performance will be judged. Clarifying and confirming shared expectations early in the conversation will ensure that you raise appropriate issues. Often, the answers you receive inspire immediate re-establishing of key points you wish to discuss later. If three won't do, prepare a list of additional questions to ask during and at the end of the interview session.

ALERT!

While you should definitely prepare for interviews, identifying key points and reviewing typical questions in advance, do not memorize. Have some anecdotes to share. But don't attempt to deliver previously written soliloquies or word-for-word responses. The oxymoronic phrase "planned spontaneity" describes the best results.

By writing all of the above on the back of your resume, you will have used existing printed text to create new supporting documentation. You will have a handwritten focal point containing well-conceived key points, anecdotes, and employer queries.

Two Key Phrases You Must Think or Say

Interviewers constantly use your resume as a point of reference for forming particular questions. You can and must do the same, by stating things like "as you can see on my resume," or "as my resume illustrates." Refer interviewers to key experiences or education, and use the phrase specifically in advance of anecdotal discussions. Let the interviewer's eyes focus on specific sections, and don't be surprised if they highlight text or take notes while you speak. This key phrase perks interest and invites magnified attention. Use adaptations or precede with a simple "again," but do refer to your resume regularly.

In response to questions, do state aloud or allow your internal voice to focus thoughts on the phrase "thinking about the job." These four words verbally or internally preceding your response will inspire you to "connect" past achievements and related qualities to "job-specific requirements." Find creative ways to restate this phrase. Creatively, you might change it to "thinking about your answers to my questions about the job," or "thinking about the job description as posted on the net." Or, you might refer to your past answers by stating: "thinking about job-specific issues I addressed earlier." This is a very effective technique.

ESSENTIAL

Don't practice too much, and don't overanalyze and dissect each role-play or actual interview. You don't want to become stiff or appear too rehearsed. Preparation is meant to relax you and provide stimuli for normal interactions.

You will be amazed at how powerful these two simple phrases can be and how using them in various forms can improve your interview skills. At first, do so via role-play interviews. Have someone ask you typical interview questions, and then respond aloud, as you would in an actual interview. This is perhaps the best way to complete final preparation efforts. While the person asking the questions will be playing the role of interviewer, you will remain yourself and answer as you would in a real interview. Be yourself! Don't be the person you think the interviewer wants you to be. Sincerity during the interview will yield honesty-based relationships as well as the personality and capability required for on-the-job success.

Common Questions and Universal Themes

Almost every job-search resource contains a list of common interview questions. What makes this book unusual is the emphasis it places on using the resume as your foundation for identifying themes to address when answering these and all questions.

Basically, interviewers determine through very special questions and answers whether you have the potential to succeed. Because potential can be a mercurial concept and very difficult to measure, much of the interview process is subjective. No matter how difficult to predict, it is a process that is easy to prepare for. You just have to translate past actions into words and, using appropriate tone, project confidence as well as your knowledge of self and your knowledge of job-specific qualifications.

Past behaviors are cited on your resume. Your ability to connect your past to the future and to your desired goal will be the basis upon which your interviewing skills will be judged. In fact, a popular interviewing trend these days is called "behavioral interviews." This technique allows interviewers to quantify and objectify a traditionally subjective process. It is based upon the principle stating that past behavior is the best predictor of future performance. Moreover, more recent behavior is a better predictor of future performance than older behavior, and trends in behavior are better predictors than isolated incidents.

Interviewers present "what did you do when" scenarios or ask you to identify past incidents when you used certain behaviors to reach a goal. Before the interview, a behavioral interviewer determines the behaviors that are desired. Basically, the interviewer arrives with a pre-established "checklist" for determining if you have the qualities associated with success in a particular job. Be prepared for this, and don't get rattled by any open-ended questions. Note-taking by the interviewer is not unusual, so don't interpret it as negative or positive. Interviewers may seek clarification or contrary evidence of your statements by continually probing, so don't become rattled or express frustration.

No matter the style, whether it's conversational, traditional, or behavioral, a review of common questions is extremely helpful. Attempting to memorize answers can do more harm than good, so, please use the list to stimulate thoughts and inspire you to share ideas effectively during interviews. You might ask a friend, family member, or peer to select five and ask them aloud, initiating a role-play interview. Hearing the questions as well as your answers, rather than just thinking about responses, is valuable.

Traditional Interview Questions

To maximize your use of this list, after you review the general as well as behavioral queries, identify a "top five" list of questions that related to a specific job matching your goals. Then conduct a practice session, having a friend or family member ask you these questions. Remember, there are no right answers to particular questions. Responses during an interview must seem well conceived, yet spontaneous. Think of this interaction as a conversation, not an inquisition. It is best to complete this exercise aloud, even if you are doing so alone.

- Why are you interested in this particular field of employment?
- What academic or career achievements are you most proud of?
- Why did you choose your major, and how does it relate to your goals?
- What classes did you find most stimulating, and did they nurture job-connected skills?
- What would you like to be doing in five years?
- What are your greatest strengths and weaknesses?
- How would you describe yourself and how would others describe you?
- How would you characterize career-related success?
- What are your three most significant employment or school-related achievements?
- When did you use persuasive skills or sales talents?
- Why should we hire you?
- What are your long-term career goals?
- How have your academic experiences to date prepared you for a career, and what are your future academic goals?

- What would you do differently with regards to academic or career experiences?
- What was your most difficult decision to date, and how did you go about making it?
- Why did you attend your alma mater?
- What do you think it takes to succeed in the job you are being interviewed for?
- What lessons have you learned from your "failures" or "mistakes"?
- What are your geographic preferences, and are you willing to relocate?
- What concerns do you have with regard to this job/academic program and our organization/school?
- How would you describe this opportunity to friends and family members?
- What additional information do you need to determine if this is the "right" opportunity for you?
- What motivated you to first contact us?

Behavioral Interview Questions

Behavioral questions, and those that might be used during what some might call a traditional interview, include the following:

- Describe when you faced problems at work that tested your coping skills. What did you do?
- Give an example of a time when you could not participate in a discussion or could not finish a task because you did not have enough information.
- Give an example of a time when you had to be relatively quick in coming to a decision.
- Tell me about when you used communication skills in order to get an important point across.
- Tell me about a job experience when you had to speak up and tell others what you thought or felt.
- Give me an example of when you felt you were able to motivate coworkers or subordinates.

- Tell me about an occasion when you conformed to a policy even though you did not agree with it.
- Describe a situation in which it was necessary to be very attentive and vigilant to your environment.
- Give me an example of a time when you used your fact-finding skills to gain information needed to solve a problem; then tell me how you analyzed the information and came to a decision.
- Tell me about an important goal you've set and tell me about your progress toward reaching this goal.
- Describe the most significant written document, report, or presentation you've completed.
- Give me an example of a time when you had to go "above and beyond" to get a job done.
- Give me an example of a time when you were able to communicate successfully with another person, even when the individual may not have personally liked you.
- Describe a situation in which you were able to read another person effectively and guide your actions by your understanding of his/her individual needs or values.
- Specifically, what did you do in your last job in order to plan effectively and stay organized?
- Describe the most creative work-related project you have completed.
- Give me an example of a time when you had to analyze another person or a situation in order to be effective in guiding your action or decision.
- What did you do in your last job to contribute toward a teamwork environment? Be specific.
- Give an example of a problem you faced on the job and how you solved it.
- Describe a situation when you positively influenced the actions of others in a desired direction.
- Tell me about a situation in the past year when you dealt with a very upset customer or coworker.
- Describe a situation in which others within your organization depended on you.

- Describe your most recent group effort.
- Describe the most challenging person you've interacted with and how you dealt with him or her.

Questions You Can Ask Potential Employers

Questions you might ask potential employers during an employment interview or during a pre-interview information conversation include the following:

- How would you describe the job in terms of day-to-day roles and responsibilities?
- What qualities are you seeking in a candidate?
- What type of person would most likely succeed in these roles?
- What advice would you give someone who would seek to achieve as quickly as possible?
- What should I expect of myself over the first few months on the job?
- How will my performance be judged, and by whom?
- Whom should I use as a role-model for this position and would it be appropriate to contact this person?
- What characteristics does it take to succeed within this organization and within this position?
- What are the best things about the job and the most challenging requirements of the position?
- Who would have highest expectations of me, or be the one(s) who would be most difficult to impress?
- What is the typical career path and time frame associated with career development?
- How will I be trained, and how can I appropriately seek skills enhancement?
- Who last served in this position, and what is he/she doing now?
- What goals do you have for the person who will serve in this job?
- What project would you expect to be completed first, and what would be involved?

Conversations, Not Cross-Examinations

Each interviewer has a personal style, but most interviews can be identified using a few common labels. Many interviews will be "conversational" or "traditional," in which interviewers chat with candidates and ask fairly typical interview questions. Some are "behavioral," in which interviewers ask about past achievements, seek details regarding behaviors (and skills) that contributed to these undertakings, and ask candidates "what would you do in this situation" questions. Occasionally, particularly for consulting firms, interviews are "case studies," in which interviewers ask candidates to analyze specific situational cases and problems; revealing how candidates "think on their seats" in response to specific analysis-driven cases.

ESSENTIAL

Interviews should not be thought of simply as a series of questions and answers. They are conversations with a common purpose for you and the interviewer. Both use qualification criteria to assess the other's potential to succeed within a specific set of roles. During the exchange, the more verbally inspired images of success that are sent and received, the more likely an offer will be made.

No matter the label used, resumes are tools for you to use during any interview. Interviewers review these documents during your conversation with a particular purpose, so you should do so too. Bring the resume with you to the interview. To prepare, review typical questions. Identify three key points and three anecdotes associated with academic and experiential achievements. Don't memorize the answers to any questions, but be prepared to expand upon the key points and anecdotes you identified as illustrating qualifications. Bring a resume with you to every interview.

Don't be shy! Talk about your achievements with pride. Interviewers have limited time to get to know the real you. Don't think there are right answers. When asked a technical question, if you don't know the exact answer, talk the interviewer through how you would find the correct information. Don't wait to do so, but always ask questions when invited.

Don't overanalyze or dissect your performance after each interview. Decision-making is very subjective. The process changes from initial screening through call-back stages and, ultimately, through selection interviews. If your style and strategies remain sincere, no matter the interviewer's style, technique, or temperament, you will find a good fit. If you don't receive an offer, never stop to ask why. Instead you should, via follow-up contacts, seek "consideration for the next available similar opportunity." Remain confident and enthusiastic. More often than you think, you can transform someone who rejected you into a strong advocate and network member who might interview you again very soon.

Bring extra resumes with you in case you unexpectedly meet additional interviewers. You might also wish to bring "supporting materials" to serve as illustrations of your work. Some fields, specifically publishing, public relations, and journalism, require writing samples or "portfolios." Be ready to detail what samples you have included and why they demonstrate specific talents.

Ultimately, you will communicate motivations and, most important, qualifications successfully via phone and in-person interviews. Have confidence in your abilities to project qualifications and capabilities. Always check in advance regarding how many people you will be interviewing with and how long the entire process might take. Specifically ask, "Are there any materials you recommend I read prior to my interview?" Also, look your best and dress appropriately.

What You Wear and What You Say

Also inquire regarding appropriate mode of dress. Some situations and organizations are "casual khaki," when neatly pressed slacks, an ironed shirt, and a tie (with sport coat optional) would be appropriate for men, and slacks or skirt, ironed shirt, or sweater would be appropriate for women. Others are "business formal," when suits, ironed shirts, polished shoes, and ties are a must for men, and suits are required for women.

What was once known as "casual Friday," has become "confusing Monday-through-Friday" for contemporary candidates. Old-fashioned rules regarding power suits, colors, and ties may not seem to apply today. But because what you wear may impact what you say, and how others perceive your professionalism, in truth, they still do. Your interview image, revealed by your attire, is a projection of "common sense" rather than "fashion sense." While there are varied fonts you can choose for your resume, it's always recommended that you remain conservative and traditional with the font you choose and with the clothing you select for interview days.

Ties can be loosened, jackets removed, and sleeves can be rolled up. It's easy to transform business formal into something more casual, but the opposite is not possible. Unless specifically told otherwise, and the circumstances of the interview confirm that casual is the only appropriate attire, dress more formally. Suits are always appropriate and required for banking, financial services, consulting, and conservative fields. For other settings, blue blazers, gray or khaki slacks or skirts, crisply ironed shirts, and appropriate neckwear may seem like prep school uniforms, but these basics are always good bets for interviews.

After reading this chapter, you are ready to use your resume as an interview preparation and implementation tool. You have learned how to use this document to focus preparation prior to and during these crucial conversations. On interview days, simply looking at your resume should instill confidence and generate effective communication. Resumes contribute well beyond the initial contact stages. Used effectively, they impact all actions and outcomes.

FACT

A recent salary survey for college graduates revealed interesting averages and more intriguing totals. Average salaries include the following: $35,719 for sales, $48,208 for consulting, $34,058 for management trainee, and $38,532 for private accounting.

Chapter 10

E Resume Review and Critique

You will examine before-and-after reviews that contain insights regarding critical changes. This chapter reveals details that will inspire you to maximize your efforts to create or update great resumes. As you read, and as you see one resume transformed into three, it will be as if you have your own resume coach at your side. This word-for-word review will inspire you to immediate actions.

The Heart and Head of the Resume Coach

Some fans believe a coach can cost a team the game or even the championship ring. Instead of firing the team, owners fire those paid far less than players and those who have no playing time. We've all waited with anticipation the naming of MVPs, but what about coach-of-the-year ballots? Does anyone care?

Amateur and professional sports coaches can and do contribute to wins as well as losses. Decisions they make do impact the outcome of games. As almost all agree, coaches can impact the efforts of teams and individual players, maximizing performance potential and desired outcomes. Resume-writing coaches can do the same. These professionals, mentors, or advocates do not write documents, but they do inspire you to improve your resume-writing skills.

The job seeker uses both his heart and head while writing a resume. These two different approaches yield different resume-writing and job-search strategies. You've learned how emotional perspectives and hopes must blend with intellectual and strategic thoughts to yield success. Step-by-step strategies inspired you to unite attitudes and actions in order to conduct comprehensive job-search campaigns. Resume-writing and job-search coaches possess and share contradictory yet complementary views as well.

The Heart of the Resume Coach

The heart of the resume coach would like to return to the old-style-resume days, encouraging you to seek the holy grail of "what they want" in order to create resumes their way. While appearing optimistic to some, heart-driven advice can be unrealistic for most. It is characterized by statements, queries, and often unrealistic hopes that include the following:

- Keep your options open. Do not limit yourself by placing goals on resumes.
- Send out as many multipurpose resumes as possible; respond to almost every posting.
- Even if you don't have any experience, just send out multipurpose resumes and let employers judge your potential to succeed.

- Don't worry about distance. Apply for any job, anywhere; even overseas.
- The broader the entries on your resume, the better. You want to appear well rounded.

The Head of the Resume Coach

The head of the resume coach projects the philosophies unique to targeted resumes. These views guide you to take active and proactive steps in logical sequence. The related advice and strategies are realistic and logistically sound, yet they are also inspirational. This view is characterized by statements, queries, and realistic hopes that include the following:

- Focus proactive efforts on three fields and two functional areas within each, but respond reactively and creatively to as many postings as you wish, using targeted resumes.
- Complete goal identification, qualification inventorying, and analyses needed to create targeted qualification summaries for all of your resumes and many letters.
- Be prepared to clearly articulate realistic goals, maintain awareness of qualification criteria associated with related jobs, and always use field-focused phrasing in documentation, conversations, and interviews.
- Take responsibility for projecting goals as well as qualifications through effective resumes and job-search communication.
- Complete the assessment and research needed to set and share realistic goals and to mirror qualifications via targeted resumes and very focused supplemental documentation.

Both the heads and hearts of resume coaches agree that you should create your own resume. While some professional resume writers do create effective documents, especially for very experienced candidates, it is always best to personally go through the resume-writing steps. But the perspectives of experienced coaches can be extremely valuable. The following represents a detailed word-for-word, step-by-step critique as it was conducted. Project from past to present and imagine what your interactions would be like if you had access to a qualified resume coach.

First you will be privy to the thoughts and actual changes associated with transformation of one last "before" version into an effective multipurpose "after" model. Then you will learn how this one broad resume can become three much more effective targeted versions.

FACT

Most believe that only 20–25 percent of all jobs are posted. Maximum estimates for the "posted versus hidden job ratio" are one-third hidden to two-thirds posted. No matter the numbers, all agree that you should never limit efforts to postings. Proactive actions are the only way to uncover hidden opportunities.

A Few Detailed Reviews for You

The sample that follows was that of an actual soon-to-be graduate, but the lessons learned from the detailed critiquing are applicable to all resume writers. Recently laid-off workers, soon-to-be and recent college grads, inexperienced workers, experienced executives and mid-managers, and those seeking basic employment will become educated and motivated by these detailed resume reviews. All job seekers can gain much from the words of the resume coach who will critique these documents. Someday soon, your internal voices will echo the knowledge of these concepts and phrases. You will become your own strongest resume coach and, perhaps, support the efforts of others.

Multipurpose Resume Before Critiquing

Chris Smith

123 Main Street	987 Centre Avenue
Apartment 13	Philadelphia, PA 11111
Hometown, NY 00000	(555) 555-5678
(555) 555-1234	csmith@company.com

EDUCATION

Bachelor of Arts, Political Science, University Of Rochester, Rochester, NY, anticipated May 2001
Dean's List. Completed cluster of three thematically linked courses exploring the natural sciences in physics and astronomy. Completed cluster of three thematically linked courses in Spanish. As member of Student Senate, organized campus activities and worked to ensure a maximal educational experience.

EXPERIENCE

Server, Burgundy Basin Banquet Hall, Pittsford, NY
Greeted customers. Took orders. Maintained accurate records of receipts and gratuities. 2000-present

Research Assistant for Professor Harry Smart, University Of Rochester, Rochester, NY
Scheduled subjects, conducted interviews, input and analyzed data, and completed library research. Completed comprehensive interview assessing husband-and-wife relationships. Scored, coded, then input data, ensuring easy retrieval and data analysis by graduate students and faculty. Conducted extensive library and Internet research, identifying studies related to husband-and-wife relationships. Spring 2000-present

Intern/Assistant to the President, The Ardmore GROUP, Ardmore, PA
Reported directly to the president of a multidivisional enterprise that included political consulting, special-interest lobbying, bidding on and awarding state government contracts in health care, social work, and welfare administration. Organized luncheons and various meetings for political operatives and office holders. Conducted research as to what contracts were available for bid and what resources would be necessary to produce that bid. All research with recommendations submitted in written report to the president. Work involved independent trips to the State Capitol and attendance at networking sessions to procure clients. Summer 2000

Assistant to the CFO, Philadelphia Physicians Associates, Philadelphia, PA
Reported directly to Medical Records Supervisor and CFO of regional medical practice. Audited medical records for accuracy. Distributed those records to doctors, attorneys, and insurers. Organized records for depositions. Distributed work to clerical staff. Part-time and summers 1998-1999

Coach's Comments, Queries, and Quick Corrections

Here's what the resume coach has to say:

▶ **First, visually this resume is organized and easy to read, yet it lacks something.** The Monaco font is basic, often used as a default setting for e-mails, and it does not really project a professional image.

▶ **Are you looking for jobs in the Philadelphia area?** If yes, then leave both addresses, but do not use as many lines to present this information.

▶ **Do you have a job-search goal?** A general field of interest? Particular functions in mind? It's okay to start with a multipurpose document, but you should use targeted ones for each of those areas you stated. The format, content, and style of this one are not presented effectively for some of those goals. Let's create one general and then a few targeted versions.

▶ **You use two very clear and appropriate headers, but don't you want to tell readers a bit more about some of your educational and practical achievements?** Think about themes you want readers to be aware of as we create a better multipurpose resume and the targeted versions. How would you characterize your education? If you used a multiword headline for education, what would it be? What words best describe the type of education you received? Would the header be different for different targeted resumes?

▶ **You highlighted your degree using bolding and position on the page, but what about the school?** Isn't University of Rochester one of the top schools in the country? Doesn't this school have a unique cluster-oriented curriculum? Shouldn't you proudly highlight the school's name?

▶ **The information under education and experience headers is well written, but it isn't highlighted.** Have you thought of other ways to present both degree and school as well as employer and position?

▶ **The header for experience is also very traditional, but it doesn't allow you to break away from the reverse chronological order rule.** You've blended some very interesting and sophisticated experiences with other less significant experiences. In fact, your first job is a waitress position. What experience themes do you want readers to quickly recognize as you create the better multipurpose resume and targeted versions? How would you characterize your experience? If you used multiword headlines for groupings of experience, what would they be? What are the two most significant and sophisticated experiences? Is there any way to present them more prominently? Would the headers be different for different targeted resumes?

▶**You highlighted your experience titles using bolding and position on the page, but what about the employer?** Some of the organizational titles might focus the reader's review of descriptions cited.

▶**Look at all of your academic as well as practical experience.** What are your most significant achievements? What skills and abilities yielded related accomplishments? Can you make a profile containing your greatest assets?

▶**Okay, let's review a bit.** We're first going to create a better multipurpose resume. Later, we will create targeted resumes for each of your stated goals. These fields include consulting, advertising, and law. Let's not worry about it now, but you will very soon have to review the newly updated multipurpose resume and think about specific qualifications for these fields and what entries to highlight. We'll use order of presentation as well as headlines to highlight the selected skills.

▶**Now, we will proceed from top to bottom.** Use one line for each address, rather than five. We most likely will need those extra three lines somewhere else. Place bullets in between entries, graphically creating separation for what was on individual lines before.

▶**Next, we will create a general summary of qualifications.** This will contain four or five bulleted phrases that reveal to readers some of your basic qualities and characteristics. Again, look at all of your academic and employment experiences. Which are most important? Yes, I agree. Your courses were all research-oriented and your research assistant position, political consulting, and medical practice management experience all required strong research, data analysis, writing, and presentation skills. One of your summary statements will reflect this. Oh, you think of yourself as a good writer. What kind of documents have you written for academic or other purposes? Can you detail how you did so? Do you have samples?

Yes, computer competencies are important. What software can you confidently use? Can you teach others to use these systems? Course titles are often left off resumes, but they can reinforce some of the qualification statements. For the multipurpose resume, you can list a few general ones, but later, think about including only those related to particular goals.

▶ **Changing your headers to headlines should be relatively easy.** The education headline can now reveal that you've had some liberal arts, science, and political science studies. Better, the headline can reveal that your academics seemed research focused. The experience section can reinforce the same themes. It can show you have had research-driven achievements. Let's think about distinct categories for your research experience, project management, and general business experience.

▶ **For education, using all caps to highlight the name of your school, and presenting it first, followed by city and state, would be effective.** On the next line you can still use bold for the degree. If you have enough room, use bullet-points to highlight extracurricular achievements. Let's see if everything fits. So far, so good. How many semesters did you make the dean's list? What were your overall and major GPAs? Let's not include those, nor enter dean's list if it was for your first semester freshman year.

▶ **Now, let's focus on headlines for experience.** Yes, I agree that the most important experience should go first. The way information now appears you highlight titles and not organizations. We'll use the same format for experience used for education. Make the organizations all caps, followed by city and state. Then, bold the title. Ideally, well describe overall responsibilities under the title and follow with bulleted accomplishments. And the dates can go on the same line as the title, justified to the right margin. In fact, let's justify dates as well as cities and states on the right margin. There, what do you think?

▶ **Yes, I know, we still haven't created headlines nor divided up the experiences by importance and nature of roles.** Okay, the two most important experiences are the research assistant position and the one with the governmental firm. Let's definitely group these two. Yes, add the medical practice management position to this section. The three will appear under a headline that clearly notes the research, writing, and time management skills you possess. Let's leave off the waitress entry. Yes, it does show that you work hard and contributed to educational expenses. But did you gain significant skills? I know it's hard to take this off and someone advised you to put it on. If we have room, let's list it at the end of the page. If space permits, it'll stay. If not, it'll go. Okay?

▶ **Let's focus a bit on the actual job descriptions, particularly on the accomplishment bullets.** After we do, we'll revisit the qualification summary to ensure that it reflects the skills used to achieve these outcomes. Now, are the most significant achievements noted for each position? Is anything missing? Would someone who worked with you in these settings approve? Action phrasing does not require embellishment or deception.

▶ **Okay, the first draft is complete.** Let's play with the font and spacing a bit to fit on one page. Times, Times New Roman, and Bookman Old Style are fine, but Garamond might allow the most to fit. Yes, it does. Oh, we'll play with some of the blank spacing between headlines and entries and between entries. Shrinking it from ten-point to four-point does add a line or two.

▶ **Now that we're close to being finished, let's try something dramatic.** Put education last. Your experience is so strong that it deserves to be more prominent. The fact that courses are in the qualification summary serves the purpose of introducing specific topics. The degree and school don't carry as much weight as your significant work experience. What do you think? I know every one of your friends lists education first. Do they have strong GPAs and academic honors? Are their majors directly related to targeted goals? Remember, this is your multipurpose document. The targeted ones might have a different order of presentation.

▶ **Will you be uploading this resume into resume banks or other Web-based systems?** After we're done, you should conduct some Web and library research to focus on the vocabulary and keywords used within your three fields of interest. Consulting, advertising, and law do have their own lexicons, and when your resume is reviewed, they must be identified. No matter whether the keyword scanning is done electronically or visually, by a person or machine, these words and phrase will be—well, as silly as it sounds, "key!" After your research, we'll transform your multipurpose document into three targeted ones.

▶ **Finally, let's think about all visual and content issues.** I know, it's not that easy. Let's use a collection of questions from a wonderful book. It's weird, but it's best to read and respond aloud. What are your answers to each?

"Before-and-After" Checklist for Determining Distribution Readiness

The queries on the "before-and-after" checklist following formalize those that would informally or intuitively be asked by a resume coach before drafts are considered final versions. Visually scanning the resume from top to bottom inspires the following questions of both coach and resume writer. What would your answers be for the sample that immediately follows? Is it ready for duplication and distribution? Do you like the before-and-after transformation of this multipurpose document? What about the experience phrasing and bulleted accomplishments? How would you change it into targeted versions?

- Is the identifying information accurate, including your e-mail?
- Is just one address and phone enough?
- Is it visually appealing, with information presented in a logical format, and easy to read?
- Can you identify a logical pattern for headline, content, and highlighting techniques?
- Can it be copied and pasted into an e-mail?
- Is the objective brief, and does it use field-specific phrasing?
- Does the summary of qualification section support the stated objective?
- Does this paragraph or bullet-point listing reveal that you possess the qualification criteria for target jobs?
- Does this section project to the future as well as reflect upon the past?

- Are most significant goal-related qualification statements presented first?
- Do special headlines for experience and education project objective-related focus?
- Does the order of appearance effectively portray significance?
- Does the education section present school(s), degree(s), area(s) of concentration, courses, and honors?
- Do courses, papers, and projects appear somewhere?
- Is specialized training presented under a special headline?
- Do headlines project knowledge of targeted fields and draw attention to related achievements?
- Do headlines, quickly reviewed, identify the nature of entries that follow?
- Are all entries described using active and accomplishment-oriented phasing, including facts and figures?
- Are goal-specific experiences grouped under appropriate headlines, presented in order of significance?
- If entries are simply cited, with no descriptions, are they obviously of less importance than others?
- Are organizations, titles, and dates easy to see, revealing an obvious pattern?
- For space as well as goal-directed purposes, are only the most significant experiences thoroughly described, with most important appearing first?
- If listed by soon-to-be or recent college grad, are leadership roles and achievements cited?
- Are most important headlines presented first, with most significant information appearing under each?
- If your resume is more than one page, is the most important information on the first and does the second page have your name and a page number header?
- If you have more than one targeted resume, are objectives for each very clear?
- Did you change order of presentation for each resume and are summary of qualifications target-specific?
- Can you elaborate upon the resume in a well-crafted cover letter or brief cover note?

- Would readers sense goal-oriented competence and confidence without an accompanying letter?
- Can you use the resume as a clear guide during an interview?
- Are you definitely ready to duplicate and distribute your resume?

Coach's Final Words on the Multipurpose Resume

▶ **While your responses to the before-and-after checklist were not 100-percent positive, because we're working on a multipurpose document, I think it's ready to go.** What do you think? Yes, you can upload it into your school's resume collection and on-campus recruiting system. You can now begin responding to postings and networking with alumni. But, we have to finish those targeted versions if you are to maximize your efforts. Of course, we need to work on cover letters as well.

▶ **Targeted resumes with objectives and qualification summaries are best.** While you should be proud of yourself and your newly created general resume, it's not quite the best document. You must support your targeted reactive and proactive efforts with clearly focused resumes. No, focus is not bad. It does not limit you. You will be using appropriate resumes and supplemental documents for each field. You can use this wonderful multipurpose version to get the process started and whenever something "unique" might arise. Remember, it's your responsibility to share and support goals, not the employer's responsibility to interpret resume content and magically identify goals for you.

Multipurpose Resume After Critiquing

Chris Smith

123 Main Street, Apartment 13 • Hometown, NY 00000 • (555) 555-1234 • csmith@company.com
987 Centre Avenue • Philadelphia, PA 11111 • (555) 555-5678

Qualification Summary

- Confidence conducting detailed research using library and Internet resources.
- Data collection, trend analysis, and writing talents nurtured via practical experiences, as well as academic papers and research projects.
- Confidence in research, writing, editing, proposal development, presentation, event planning, and project management roles.
- Windows, UNIX, HTML, Word, Excel, PageMaker, PhotoShop, and Internet utilities.
- Skills, interests, and perspectives gained from courses including: Applied Data Analysis, Economics, Debate, Psychology of Business, Arguments in Politics, Political Theory: Politics in the Mass Media, Political Systems, Social Psychology, and Adolescent Psychology.

Research, Writing, and Project Management Accomplishments

UNIVERSITY OF ROCHESTER   Rochester, NY
Research Assistant for Psychology Professor Harry Smart   Spring 2000–present
- Conducted extensive library and Internet research, identifying studies related to husband-and-wife relationships. Summarized findings and developed detailed listings of citations. Presented findings to weekly faculty-led research team meetings.

THE ARDMORE GROUP   Ardmore, PA
Intern/Assistant to the President   Summer 2000
- Reported directly to the president of a multidivisional enterprise that included political consulting, special-interest lobbying, bidding on and awarding state government contracts in health care, social work, and welfare administration.
- Conducted research regarding contracts available for bidding and what resources would be necessary to produce that bid. All research efforts were transformed into written recommendations submitted in reports to the president. Yielded about one hit per month.
- Work involved independent trips to the State Capitol, attendance at networking sessions and sharing of information with colleagues and supervisor to determine appropriate next steps.

PHILADELPHIA PHYSICIANS ASSOCIATES   Philadelphia, PA
Assistant to the CFO   Part-time and Summers 1998–1999
- Reported directly to Medical Records Supervisor and CFO of regional medical practice.
- Audited medical records for doctors, attorneys, and insurers.
- Organized records for depositions in specialized formats facilitating access by attorneys, arbitrators, and judges addressing specific points of law.

Research-Oriented Studies

UNIVERSITY OF ROCHESTER   Rochester, NY
Bachelor of Arts, Political Science   anticipated May 2001
- As member of Student Senate, effectively interacted with peers, administrators, and others, transforming goals into decisions to implement freshmen housing model.

Coach's Internalized and Verbalized Before-and-After Review

This chapter has already revealed a detailed critique, illustrating the transformation from a before draft to a finished after version. Step six of the seven required to create or update resumes involves drafting and critiquing. Questions on the before-and-after checklist reveal for you, with great confidence and closure, whether a resume is ready for distribution.

Resume coaches think about and ask these questions aloud of those creating or updating documents. Silent or spoken answers inspire attitudes needed to stop drafting and start distributing. What would your answers be for the new multipurpose version and, more important, for the targeted versions that follow? For each sample on the pages that follow, see if you can you identify obvious and subtle changes made from one resume to the others.

ALERT!

If after you have sent a cover letter or resume you have updated the resume or wish to add additional information, do not hesitate to send follow-up documentation. Refer to earlier communications, yet highlight in your follow-up communiqué all critical new issues and assets on your revised resume.

As you recall, when all responses to the before-and-after checklist are "yes," a resume is ready for distribution. If some answers are "no," the document can be revised or used until changes are made. While questions asked by coaches, advocates, and others do help, you now have a written script that they might use. In many creative and confidence-building ways, you now have what can be viewed as the very best coach's queries printed on just a few pages. To inspire continued re-evaluation, you might wish to photocopy the before-and-after checklist and post it in a clearly visible location whenever you are creating or updating resumes.

One Multipurpose Resume Equals Three Targeted Resumes

As the resume coach's reactions revealed, targeted resumes will be created to match stated goals. Many job seekers should do the same. One resume cannot do all things for all candidates. The first step to updating and creating resumes involves reviewing samples. This section offers annotated reviews of three resumes created from one. Comments offered by the coach should inspire you when you create one, two, or three targeted resumes.

Coach's Comments for an Advertising Resume

▶ **So, the multipurpose resume is finished.** Oh, you have a new research position. Yes, it's too early to cite many accomplishments, but let's describe it now and you can add more as you progress. Let's add it. No, don't worry about room until we've drafted again. We'll think of some space-saving approaches later.

▶ **Now let's get to the targeted versions.** Have you done your homework? Did you research the fields? Oh, that's okay. We'll start with advertising and then go to the others. Continued research will reveal information and, most significant, key phrases that will be added to updated resumes and supplemental letters. Let's not delay. You need some targeted documents to maximize posting responses as well as self-initiated contacts with prospective employers.

▶ **Now, let's focus on advertising.** Is there a particular job title or functional area of interest? Can you describe it in terms that anyone can understand? Can you describe it using specialized terms? That's good! So, account management is your objective. We'll first create a distinct objective statement, but we might have to blend the objective with a qualification summary to save space.

▶ **Yes, the qualification summary is now the most critical component of your resume.** Targeted versions must reveal that you know your goals and that you know what is required to succeed within these roles. In many ways, the rest of the resume will stay the same. But, we will think about order of presentation, headlines, and specific descriptions.

▶ **Thinking about your newly found knowledge of the field, what are your most significant academic or employment accomplishments?** Have you had directly related experiences that should be highlighted via the qualification summary? The summary must show that you know about this field and that you know about particular skills you possess that are related. In the cover letter you will show more, but the qualification summary must quickly reveal your goals and basic qualifications.

▶ **We do have some space issues, so we must get very creative.** Will you be applying for advertising positions in Philadelphia, or just New York? Well, no matter. Let's just use one line for identifying information. You can add the second line to cover letters targeting Philly firms. Also, let's make sure that your course listing is as concise as possible and presents most important classes first.

Coach's Final Words on the Advertising Resume

▶ **Your responses to the short and long list of questions were close to 100-percent positive.** That's great. You should research the field more and constantly improve the qualification summary, but I think it's ready to go. Of course, you must convey much of the knowledge already gained through research in your cover letters as well. With advertising, you can be a bit more creative and add humor to these covering pages. Also, for each firm you can refer to some particular clients and recent awards or sales gains. For this field the cover letter may be as important as the resume.

▶ **Definitely start sending resume and cover letters to the many, many firms on your hit list.** Also, network with alums. Learn about their career biographies. Increase knowledge of field appropriate phrases and terminology. Ask if they can consider you for positions on their client teams, or if they can forward your resumes to someone who can.

▶ **Yes, targeted resumes with objectives and qualification summaries are best, but starting with a headline like the one you used takes the place of an objective statement.** Remember, we had some space issues and this allowed us to save a line or two.

Chris Smith

123 Main Street, Apartment 13 • Hometown, NY 00000 • (555) 555-1234 • csmith@company.com

Advertising Account Management Qualifications

- Curiosity regarding consumer attitudes and behaviors and confidence using data collection, trend analysis, and writing talents to develop client-focused campaign strategies as well as proposals, and to assess campaign effectiveness.
- Experience in roles requiring attitude assessment, brainstorming, persuasive communication, and creation of reports and proposals.
- Confidence independently or as team member developing proposals and presentations, planning events, and completing special projects.
- Interests and perspectives gained from diverse courses including: Psychology of Business and Industry, Applied Data Analysis, Economics, Debate, Arguments in Politics, Politics in the Mass Media, Social Psychology, and Adolescent Psychology.
- Abilities to use Word, Excel, and PageMaker for quantitative analyses, reports, proposals, and related campaign support documents.

Political Consulting

THE ARDMORE GROUP   Ardmore, PA
Intern/Assistant to the President   Summer 2000
Reported directly to the president of a multidivisional enterprise that included political consulting, special-interest lobbying, bidding on and warding state government contracts in health care, social work, and welfare administration.

- Conducted research regarding contracts available for bidding and what resources would be necessary to produce that bid. All research efforts were transformed into written recommendations submitted in reports to the president. Yielded about one hit per month.
- Attended networking sessions to procure clients, and sharing of information with colleagues and supervisor to determine appropriate next steps.

Research, Proposal Writing, and Project Management Accomplishments

UNIVERSITY OF ROCHESTER   Rochester, NY
Research Assistant for Psychology Professor Harry Smart   Spring 2000–present

- Conducted extensive library and Internet research, identifying studies related to husband-and-wife relationships. Summarized findings and developed detailed listings of citations. Presented findings to weekly faculty-led research team meetings.
- Scheduled subjects, conducted interviews, input and analyzed data, and completed library research.

Speech and Hearing Center Research Assistant   Fall 2000–present

- Identified methodology to be used to measure effectiveness and target criteria impacting therapeutic outcomes.

Liberal Arts Studies

UNIVERSITY OF ROCHESTER   Rochester, NY
Bachelor of Arts, Political Science   anticipated May 2001

▶ **Again, I think this one is ready to go.** No, focus does not limit you. You will be using different resumes and cover letters for each field. I realize that you don't truly know what you want to do, yet advertising is one of your top choices. This resume clearly reveals your goals. Additional documents and, eventually, interviews will show how much you have learned about advertising and how easy it is for you to speak using field-focused vocabulary.

▶ **Hey, if you can, why don't you sign up for a marketing or advertising course or seminar.** Local chapters of professional associations might offer brief seminars. You don't have to take courses for credit, and they can be offered at a local community college. The more you demonstrate true interest in the field, the more your actions will speak as loudly (or more) than your words on this great resume.

FACT

The terms *cum laude, magna cum laude,* and *summa cum laude* are all lowercase and should be put in italics.

Coach's Comments for a Consulting Resume

▶ **So, now the advertising version is finished. See, it didn't take long to adapt the multipurpose resume to a specific purpose.** In fact, each adaptation should take much less time than the original process, not much longer than thirty to forty-five minutes. The next two probably won't take much more than twenty minutes each.

▶ **Okay, consulting is the next field.** Again, have you done your homework? Did you research this particular field? I understand it's not an easy one to enter for undergrads. Yes, it's that selective, but you don't know if you have what it takes to get an interview if you don't try. Continued research will reveal more information and additional key phrases that will be added to updated resumes and supplemental letters. But let's get the first ones out soon. This field screens candidates and completes initial interviews early in the on-campus and off-campus recruiting cycles.

▶ **Now, let's focus on consulting.** Is there a particular job title or functional area of interest? Yes, each firm does have a variation on the titles used for entry-level opportunities. Some call them Associate Consultants, some use Analysts, and others use Research Analysts. So, instead of an objective statement, we'll use the headline and summary of qualification strategy again. Can you describe what these first post-baccalaureate jobs are all about? What do recent grads do who work for consulting firms? In fact, can you describe what a consulting firm does? That's good enough, but you cannot stop your research now. It must continue even after you've sent your first group of resumes and cover letters. Follow-up letters can reveal when you've gained additional insights.

▶ **The qualification summary remains the most critical component of this targeted resume.** This section must reveal that you know your goals and what is required to succeed within these research and analytical support roles. Like before, the rest of the resume may stay the same, but you might change order of presentation, headlines, and specific descriptions.

▶ **Now, for the qualification summary, you must project knowledge of self, knowledge of the field, and knowledge of particular job functions.** What are your most significant consulting-related academic or employment accomplishments? Yes, you did work for a consulting firm already. It wasn't exactly a management consulting firm, but it was a consulting firm. Let's include that in the qualification summary and bring that entry as high on the document as we can. Oh, and we'll use a good headline as well.

Order of presentation will be crucial. The first two entries must be impressive. Yes, I agree. You do want to de-emphasize education. In this case it's not your greatest strength. Leave it last on the page, but make sure we highlight specific courses and concepts in the summary.

▶ **The summary must show that you know something about consulting and that you know about the particular skills you possess that are related.** In the cover letter you will show more, but the qualification summary must effectively reveal your goals and basic qualifications. With a selective field, it may be the most important section of the resume. Because it is read first, if it doesn't grab the attention of the reader, the rest might not be read.

Consulting Targeted Resume After Critiquing

Chris Smith

123 Main Street, Apartment 13 • Hometown, NY 00000 • (555) 555-1234 • csmith@company.com

Management Consulting Qualifications

- Confidence developing proposals and presentations and completing special analytical projects within a consulting firm's deadline-driven and detail-oriented environment.
- Knowledge gained via Economics, Applied Data Analysis, and Psychology of Business courses.
- Experience using economic models, Excel, statistical analyses, and other approaches to quantify data, identify trends, and present findings to colleagues, supervisors, and clients.
- Curiosity regarding strategic planning, profit profiling, industry trending, and competitor analysis.
- Experience in hypothesis testing, brainstorming, and creating reports.
- Abilities to use Word and Excel for financial and marketing analyses, reports, and case documentation.

Consulting Accomplishments

THE ARDMORE GROUP   Ardmore, PA
Intern/Assistant to the President   Summer 2000
Reported directly to president of multidivisional $10-million annual billing enterprise that included political consulting, special-interest lobbying, bidding on and awarding state contracts in health care, social work, and welfare administration.

- Conducted research regarding contracts available for bidding and what resources would be necessary to produce that bid. All research was transformed into written recommendations submitted to the president.
- Involved independent trips to the State Capitol, attendance at networking sessions to procure clients, and sharing of information with colleagues and supervisor to determine appropriate next steps.

Research, Analysis, and Project Management Accomplishments

UNIVERSITY OF ROCHESTER   Rochester, NY
Research Assistant for Psychology Professor Harry Smart   Spring 2000–present
- Conducted extensive library and Internet research, identifying husband-and-wife relationship studies. Summarized findings and developed listings of citations. Presented findings to weekly faculty-led research team meetings.
- Scheduled subjects, conducted interviews, input and analyzed data, and completed library research.
- Completed comprehensive interview assessing husband-and-wife relationships.

Speech and Hearing Center Research Assistant   Fall 2000–present
- Identified methodology to be used to measure effectiveness and target criteria impacting therapeutic outcomes.

PHILADELPHIA PHYSICIANS ASSOCIATES   Philadelphia, PA
Assistant to the CFO   Part-time and Summers 1998-1999
- Audited medical records for accuracy prior to distributing records to doctors, attorneys, and insurers.
- Organized records in formats facilitating ease of access by attorneys, arbitrators, and judges.

Education

UNIVERSITY OF ROCHESTER   Rochester, NY
Bachelor of Arts, Political Science   anticipated May 2001

Coach's Final Words on the Consulting Resume

▶ **Your responses to the questions did reveal some anxiety associated with the selectivity of the field, but they also showed that you think the resume is ready.** You can now begin responding to postings, sending self-initiated contacts to firms, and networking with alumni.

▶ **I believe for this field that networking will be most crucial.** When selectivity is involved, it's often the name of someone stated at the beginning of the cover letter or, better, the fact that this person forwards your documents to the resume screener that impacts success. Use your past consulting employer as a source for referrals. Don't be shy about leveraging his name and his network of colleagues and associates. He can help you identify some other smaller, entrepreneurial and privately held firms.

▶ **You now need to work on cover letters.** In this case you must first show that you have the research, analysis, and presentation skills required to effectively fill the roles desired. Read and think about some Harvard Business School case studies and refer to this activity within your correspondence. Pick up and read one of those books on introductory business management. Review some Harvard Business School cases. A liberal arts student like you can very quickly pick up appropriate phrases and concepts applicable to consulting. When you do, quickly update both resume and cover letters. Oh, you can follow up with firms who may have already rejected you. You have nothing to lose.

▶ **While this resume is ready for distribution accompanied by a great letter, you can and should enhance both as your job search progresses.** Continue to read about consulting and network with individuals in the field. Enhance your business-related knowledge and lexicon as you read. Update both documents whenever you wish. Send them anew or again when strategically appropriate.

Coach's Comments for a Paralegal Resume

▶ **This should be the easiest version to complete:** You've done two already, you have some significant experience, and you are sincerely interested in the field.

▶ **Of course, you've thought a great deal about the field already.** Yes, it's a very attainable goal. Many large and a few small firms regularly hire legal researchers and paralegals with academic backgrounds similar to yours. They appreciate the breadth and depth of research skills gained as a liberal arts student, specifically a political science major with a career interest in law. In your case you have also had directly related experience and a strong skill set.

▶ **The qualification summary remains the most critical component of your resume.** This targeted version will reveal that you are seeking a paralegal or legal research position and that you have all of the competence and confidence required to succeed within these roles.

▶ **The qualification summary must effectively reveal your goals and basic qualifications.** To save space, let's use the headline approach again. The words selected for this first headline will clearly state your goals. The bulleted statements that appear next, with the most important first, will summarize what you have to offer. They will serve to preview as well as review all of the qualities and capabilities you possess. No, you cannot use the same as you used for consulting, although some might remain. Think specifically about those experiences and skills that relate to paralegal and legal research.

▶ **A revised order of presentation will make this resume most impressive.** Yes, I agree. You do want to emphasize the law-related experience immediately following the qualification summary. Can you add to the description or accomplishment list? Make sure readers understand how much of this job was law related. The rest of the resume will look very much like the consulting one, except for a new header for education. You are interested in someday applying to law school, right? Many of your courses were taken as an exploration of law, government, and political science topics, correct? So, let's use "Pre-Law" in the headline. Okay?

▶ **It may seem too quick, but we're done.** It's time again to ask aloud the questions that determine if the resume is distribution ready.

Paralegal Targeted Resume After Critiquing

Chris Smith

123 Main Street, Apartment 13 • Hometown, NY 00000 • (555) 555-1234 • csmith@company.com

Paralegal and Legal Research Qualifications

- Confidence conducting research using library and Internet resources as well as interview techniques.
- Experience in roles requiring detailed collection and review of documents and creation of reports and indexes.
- Confidence developing proposals and presentation, planning events and completing special projects.
- Knowledge gained from courses including: Applied Data Analysis, Economics, Debate, Arguments in Politics, Political Theory, Politics in the Mass Media, Political Systems, and Social Psychology.

Legal Research and Litigation Support Accomplishments

PHILADELPHIA PHYSICIANS ASSOCIATES — Philadelphia, PA
Assistant to the CFO — Part-time and Summers 1998–1999

Reported directly to Medical Records Supervisor and CFO of regional medical practice, supporting day-to-day business, law, and insurance-related functions.

- Audited medical records for accuracy prior to distributing records to doctors, attorneys, and insurers.
- Organized indexes and record packets for depositions in specialized formats facilitating ease of access by attorneys, arbitrators, and judges and focusing on specific points of law in question.

Research and Project Management Accomplishments

UNIVERSITY OF ROCHESTER — Rochester, NY
Research Assistant for Psychology Professor Harry Smart — Spring 2000–present

Assisted with study assessing perceptions impacting husband-and-wife relationships.

- Conducted extensive library and Internet research for husband-and-wife relationship studies. Summarized findings and detailed listings of citations. Presented findings to weekly faculty-led research team meetings.
- Scheduled subjects, conducted interviews, input and analyzed data, and completed library research.

Speech and Hearing Center Research Assistant — Fall 2000–present

Assisted with planning and implementing study assessing effectiveness of speech and language therapy services.

- Scheduled home visits, explained services, helped clients complete assessment questionnaires.

THE ARDMORE GROUP — Ardmore, PA
Intern/Assistant to the President — Summer 2000

Reported directly to president of multidivisional enterprise that included political consulting, special-interest lobbying, bidding on and the awarding of state government contracts in health care, social work, and welfare administration.

- Conducted research regarding contracts available for bidding and resources necessary to produce bids. All research was transformed into written recommendations submitted to the president. Yielded one hit per month.
- Developed and distributed detailed pre-event and post-event documentation and correspondence.

Political Science and Pre-law Studies

UNIVERSITY OF ROCHESTER — Rochester, NY
Bachelor of Arts, Political Science — anticipated May 2001

Coach's Final Words on the Paralegal Resume

- You should be very proud of this targeted resume. It will easily and effectively support reactive and proactive efforts. You can respond to postings and send this out immediately to firms of interest in New York, Philadelphia, and Washington, D.C.
- But just because the resume is so strong, don't undervalue the potential impact of your cover letter. Within this supporting document share qualifications as well as motivations. Reveal that you know the ideal profile of paralegal candidates and those who serve within these roles. State that you wish to apply to law school only after the appropriate tenure with the firm. If confidentiality allows, within these letters note the firms involved and a summary of some of the cases that were related to your experience with the medical practice.
- Make sure you add the Philadelphia address to the letterhead used for letters targeting firms in your "home city." This will enhance your chances to be invited to interview.

An Actual Resume Success Story

Many of the sample resumes in this book are adaptations of those used by actual job seekers. Ideally, these real-life documents reveal the most effective use of concepts and themes presented within the preceding pages. Most significantly, the final versions presented in this chapter were, in somewhat different forms, used by a successful recent graduate.

This clearly strong, yet typical candidate used all of the varied formats that we examined here. They won her several interviews. She used the resumes in preparation for and during these discussions. She got several offers. Ultimately, this talented individual accepted an offer to work as a paralegal.

FACT

This chapter revealed how a draft can become a more powerful finished resume and how one multipurpose resume can, with coaching support, be transformed into targeted versions. You have learned to become your own resume coach.

Chapter 11

What They Say about Your Resume

We solicited the comments of recruiting and human resources professionals to get an idea of their thoughts on the resumes they review. Many responded to a brief open-ended query. Their comments were edited for length, not content. The fields represented are diverse, and views varied (sometimes contradictory), yet some common themes emerge.

Jill Furick

▶ Jill Furick is a recruiting coordinator for the law firm of Wiley Rein & Fielding LLP.

You know me, I am not a "sweet talker," I just say it as I see it. My views may be specialized for law, but generalized for other fields and candidates. They include:

- A resume only needs to go back ten years. I truly don't care what you were doing in 1970; it's probably outdated by now anyway!
- Don't put your salary on your resume. Inevitably you will be ruled out because you are too high or your salary is so low we don't think you could have the experience needed.
- I would rather see your computer skills than your personal interests. It doesn't matter to me that you like riding horses or playing basketball: Can you use MS Office?
- Provide references when asked and make sure you have the right information. Nothing is more annoying than trying to track down a person for a reference! After the interview, call each reference and tell them they may get a call from a potential employer.
- Make the HR person's life as easy as possible!
- You can't network sitting on your couch or in front of a computer! Job seekers who think hunting for jobs solely on the Internet frees them from having to network and conduct disciplined, diverse searches are fooling themselves.
- Last but not least, put your resume on the Internet and then get off your rear end and hit the streets! Contact every company you are interested in and hand-deliver, e-mail, or fax a resume. Don't expect an interview, but you never know whom you will run into!

William C. Belknap

▶ William Belknap is a partner in the firm Performance Leadership Incorporated. Here are a few of his thoughts (from a guy who has been working with resumes for thirty years).

- The first time around, the reader gives the resume about a ten-second scan. It is critical that your resume is structured to attract their eye to your accomplishments.
- Hiring managers are interested primarily in what you can do for them. "How many home runs will you hit, and how many bases will you steal?" It is all about performance.
- The resume becomes doubly critical in a tight market because the buyers can afford to be choosey.
- Well-written accomplishments, good appearance, user-friendly (lots of white space), no typos can mean the difference of making it into the "A" pile versus the "C" pile or worse, the "round file."
- Attention has to be paid to what makes you different; an accomplishment bullet does just that.
- Every accomplishment bullet must answer the simple question, "So what?" Said another way, what was the business impact of this effort?

Joshua D. Shapiro

▶ Joshua Shapiro is Chief of Staff for U.S. Congressman Joseph M. Hoeffel.

In my capacity as Chief of Staff to a United States Congressman, it is typical for me to receive upwards of 350 resumes for a single vacancy on the staff. It is impossible to read each one thoroughly. A resume must stand out—it must grab my attention at first glance. To do this, the successful applicant should:

- Use catchy headings that stand out and tell the reader what you've done. A resume from a typical college grad should have about five to seven headings, including schooling, internships, work experience, etc.
- Think brevity, brevity, and brevity. It is not necessary to tell your whole life story on your resume—leave something for the cover letter and the interview.
- Keep it to one page.
- In this digital age, make sure you have your resume in the proper format to be mailed, faxed, and e-mailed. The economy and the times demand a quick response.

- Put one thing on your resume that is unique. I once interviewed someone (who was just as qualified on paper as lots of other applicants) because he listed on his resume that he "has a proclivity for tea." Seems strange, but it was enough to get my attention and grant him an interview to give him the opportunity to prove himself. It worked. He got the job.
- Remember, the resume is just to get you a seat at the table; your interview and references are also important in my business.
- Remain positive. Keep an open mind. Relax. Be yourself. Be unique.

Stephanie Chiesi Reh

▶ Stephanie Reh is a Senior HR Generalist at Hand Held Products (a Welch Allyn Affiliate).

- Tailor your resume to the position description as much as possible. Many candidates apply for several positions at several different companies and submit the same resume for each. When preparing to apply for a position, you should first verify that you have the experience and qualifications necessary to perform the job. If you do not meet the advertised criteria, your chances of being selected are slim, because you are competing against the most qualified candidates. Recruiters are looking for the best resume that most closely resembles the job specification.
- I often receive cover letters or phone calls from candidates who attempt to amplify their resume by providing me with extra information because, "you can't put everything on your resume." I disagree. Unless a recruiter is convinced by your resume that you may be a good fit, he or she will not read your cover letter. Cover letters are best kept brief, including only pertinent information such as salary and relocation requirements, and where you saw the position advertised (particularly important if it is an employee or colleague referral). All other information should somehow appear in the resume itself.
- Paper resumes are, for the most part, a thing of the past. Therefore, format and length are much less important than relevant, thorough,

well-written content. It takes time and considerable attention to detail, but it will be worth your effort.

- Customizing your resume shows the potential employer that you want a particular job, not just any job.

Jonathan Bujno

▶ Jonathan Bujno is a Recruiting Specialist for the research and development arm of GE Corporate.

- The resume, like the diary or journal, is an introspective look at a person's past and present life. One major difference is that the resume's intent is often to lead you to employment, to money, and to success. Perhaps this is why it is such a difficult process. One thinks, "If this is no good, I won't be interviewed and I won't earn this job." This is generally true in my opinion. Initially, resumes are relied upon to screen candidates in or screen them out. It is often impossible to screen every candidate by phone, and managers will rely on the resume to represent skills and accomplishments. You may be the most qualified for the position; however, if your resume is a poor representation of your background, you may not be considered for the position. Therefore, one must take a careful approach to resume writing to ensure that they accurately portray potential.
- Writing a resume can be a lot easier than most people make it. The problem is, people tend to update it at the last minute—it's hard to remember what you did on the job for the last four years. Here are a few tips: If your Human Resources Department gives you a job description when you're hired, keep it and file it somewhere. Also, buy a notebook and take it to work with you. Each time you do something new or accomplish something on the job, write it down. Updating your resume will now be much easier. Instead of trying to remember what it is you did, you can "calmly" refer to these resources and piece together your resume. Also, include examples of work-related initiative, diligence, and character on your resume. If you filled in for someone at the last minute and saved the company $30,000—include that.

- Your resume will be used as an interviewing tool. A good recruiter will probe everything you put on there. Know it well and be careful of inconsistent information.
- Regarding format, keep it simple. Simple fonts, simple paper, simple color, and simple bulleted facts that are relevant to the position you are applying for. Design your own resume rather than using the standard MS Office template. This will help your resume stand out. Include a summary of professional objectives, education, experience, and technical skills. From there, you may add (to name a few): certifications, publications, accreditations, community organizations, and additional education.
- Proofread and when you think it's perfect, give it to someone else and let them look it over. Finally, we all know "references will be available upon request," so you don't need to include that.

Preparing your resume doesn't have to be a frustrating experience. But if you do feel yourself becoming a bit heated, then pound the table, take a walk, scream and yell, do what you do; just don't rush to get done! Remember, your resume can screen you out or screen you in. The latter is the goal.

Danilo Minnick

▶ Danilo Minnick is the Senior Recruiter for the Peace Corps Regional Office and a retired Peace Corps volunteer who worked in The Gambia.

I view tons of resumes—not only volunteer applicants but also for staff positions. Believe me, I have gotten good at recognizing poor versus well-constructed documents. It really is the most important element of one's job search, and along with a professional cover letter, the first step to "selling" yourself with the hope of being called for an interview. The essential "basics" and extra "frills" that do get my attention include:

- One page, especially for "newbies" (students or inexperienced workers). Of course, midcareer professionals or execs can go beyond that, but when a twenty-something submits three pages, I wonder if they're full of themselves.

- Bold and bullets recommended (no underlines or abbreviations except for the U.S. states).
- No salary or personal information.
- Identification includes name, address, phone, and even e-mail, centered on the page.
- Education and training are musts, even if just listing high school or certificates.
- When describing job responsibilities, use action words and accomplishments.
- Use bullets or concise three- to four-line paragraphs; a big block of type takes too long to browse quickly.
- Use a "Professional History" or related subheading to summarize many jobs. Through this section, expand upon qualifications that don't quite belong as detailed descriptions under each listing.
- Concise, consistent, dynamic phrasing that stresses result and accomplishments.
- Include a targeted or generalized skills summary.
- Avoid pronouns, use proper verb tenses, and check many times for spelling and mistakes. We do ask for revised ones if an applicant isn't represented professionally, because documents are shared with the host before they decide whom they want to work in their countries.
- Don't ever lie.

Mark A. Indovina

▶ Mark Indovina is Vice President of Engineering at Improv Systems, Inc.

- To me, your resume is your personal sales brochure or data sheet published to highlight work history and qualifications.
- Once submitted for consideration, your resume is used as the road map that guides discussions during a phone screen or face-to-face interview.
- I am against the prevailing attitude that resumes should be as short as possible. How can a single page of text adequately describe the

accomplishments of a career individual? I expect an individual with over five years of experience to have a two- to three-page resume (particularly true for technical fields).

- My fundamental resume "law" is very simple: be detailed, but factual (honest!!!) with items documented on your resume. As I noted earlier, the resume is the data sheet used during any discussions with the candidate. Expect to be asked detailed questions about the statements you make on your resume. On too many occasions when interviewing a student, questions about classes taken were answered with "I don't remember." These meetings are cut short and, obviously, the candidate didn't get the offer.

- These days I would expect face-to-face interviews for technical positions to be held in a group setting with the candidate as the center of attention. This can be very intimidating, but I find the process to be an excellent barometer of how well the candidate blends into the group.

- Infrequently, but regularly, throughout the meeting you might be asked to stand up and solve simple problems at a white board. If so, don't hesitate to ask questions if you're confused. I would also be prepared to be "chatty" (those doing the interview are nervous too!); the astute candidate will also know when to shut up.

Jerry Jung

▶ Jerry Jung has been Technology, Product Development, and Manufacturing Recruiter since 1980 at Jerry L. Jung Company, Inc.

I do not write resumes for a fee, but I help many people redo resumes so they can get a positive response from my employer clients when I introduce them. Almost in every case when I help a person with a resume they get an interview. Here is my take from twenty-two-plus years of recruiting:

- Anybody with more than five years of experience should have two to four different resumes.

- The biggest difference for each should be the objective and slant of experience to support that objective.
- Today's job market is not one for a generic "one resume fits all" approach.
- The idea of a one-page resume is crazy for anyone beyond fresh grads.
- Hiring managers, headhunters, and others don't have the time to invest in calling up people to find out the whole story. It should be told via the resume.
- The best format is still the old-fashioned one, with most recent job first, then back to first job.
- Spell out duties and experience. Describe using action verbs and accomplishments.
- Functional resumes are poorly received in technical markets.
- Resumes using special headings, such as Management Engineering, Projects, Sales Experience, then using the most recent job first format are okay.
- Make sure basic buzzwords associated with specific skills, talents, and methods, are specifically used in the resume.

Nancy D. Miller

▶ Nancy Miller is Executive Director of CEO VISIONS: Services for the Blind and Visually Impaired.

I am most impressed with resumes that are:

- Neat, twelve- to fourteen-point type (ten-point is too small).
- Clearly organized, simple to read, not in color so that copying is easier.
- Chronological with dates of employment starting from most recent.
- No more than two pages (preferably one); includes talents, hobbies, specialties.
- Neat and typo-free and without whiteout.

I am most impressed with resumes that include:

- Computer or software expertise.

- Languages spoken and/or written other than English.
- For recent grads, part-time and/or volunteer work statements that specify which jobs were paid.
- Education, with university, date and degree received.

Because a cover letter is as important as a resume:

- Write to me and refer specifically to the job I am advertising or that you are conducting a general search.
- It should be personalized.
- Let your personality show through without being cutesy.

Barry Goldman

▶ Barry Goldman is Critical Skills Internship Manager at Lawrence Livermore National Laboratory.

While the first half of my career was as a recruiter, the latter part has been administering internships—including placing students in projects at an R&D facility. I have over thirty years of experience in Human Resources, ranging from recruitment, staff relations, compensation, and education. Past employers include McGraw-Hill, Stauffer Chemical, Exxon, and Westinghouse. The following are my thoughts on the topic of resumes:

- A resume is not intended to get you a job. It is intended to get you in the door to be interviewed. As a result, resumes should be targeted to the specific opening for which you are applying. The initial reviewers of a resume may very well be just screeners without any technical expertise. The resume will be reviewed against established criteria for the posting. Therefore, use the same wording as the ad—otherwise, a nontechnical person might not recognize your match and screen you out instead of in!
- There are many kinds of resumes or formats for resumes. Determine the format that is appropriate for the application. Keep in mind there are also differences in resumes that will be hand submitted or

included with a cover letter versus one that may be sent electronically.

- Every word on a resume should have meaning. If it doesn't, omit it.
- While not about resumes, it's okay if you're able to interview with others based on family and contacts of friends. Remember, if you are offered the job, it is not usually because of whom you know but your skills and what you are bringing to the job.
- If you are applying in response to an ad, as mentioned previously, use the language from the ad. If applying as a cold call, it is even more important to research the company. Check out their home page. Maybe there is a search engine that will allow you to research your interests in line with company programs. Check out their organizational chart and job postings. Postings will give you a flavor for their needs and types of openings. Possibly they have Web links to publications that are available externally?
- The more you can identify project or employee names that can be referenced on your application, the more you will increase your chances of being successful by getting it to the attention of the right people.
- As a past recruiter, a thank-you letter after an interview is advised. Anything to keep visibility on your name, availability, and makes you different than other applicants. Managers also like this form of follow-through as they would like to see this characteristic also in their employees.

Jerri Striegler

▶ Jerri Striegler is a Human Resources Specialist with the National Park Service.

I've been in HR for close to twenty-nine years with the Department of the Interior. We look for employees who are dedicated to the preservation and protection of our natural and cultural resources. From among the thousands of applications and resume documents I have reviewed, there have been handfuls that have really grabbed me and said—"Find a way to hire me." There is a very fine crevice into which the best ones fit. It squeezes between the professionally prepared "buzzword of the month" resume and the offhand, "I don't really care about this" submission. My views include:

- The good resumes say "I am a real person and what I do as a vocation must be something to which I can dedicate my energies, something I really care about. I sincerely want this particular job, and I have been preparing myself so that when it becomes vacant, I will be the best candidate. I would really enjoy this work, and I would be a nice person with whom to work." They don't actually say those words but they bring a sense of those qualities.

- The not-so-good resumes say, "I need a good job. I have worked hard to get to where I am and I deserve to be selected. This particular job will be a punch on my ticket to success—it will look good on my next resume. My professional knowledge and abilities obviate skill in communication and interpersonal relationships." Or, they say, "I need a job, I need money to live, any job will do as long as the money is right. Even though I don't have the appropriate background, I'm sure I can learn what you want me to do." Once again, they don't say those exact words, but that is the sense they bring readers.

- A good applicant for one job may not be a good applicant for another job. The same resume doesn't work for every job for which you apply. You may want to have several different versions of your resume—one general resume that you can throw in for any job, just in case—plus several others that are fine-tuned to each of the several career fields you would consider. Don't spend a lot of time applying for positions for which you are not well suited.

- Do spend your time fine-tuning the application for the job you really want. Always check the resume over and make changes so that it appears to have been prepared for the specific job for which you are applying.

- Also, remember that anyone can list skills on a resume, and that evaluation of skill level is very subjective. Back up the skills you list with some of your accomplishments. Researchers provide vitae that show scholarly publications, presentations, memberships, and offices held in professional societies, awards, university and professional affiliations, etc.

- No matter what your field, it would be good to provide any similar information that strengthens your image. Also, be sure to add information about your other interests—to show your human side.
- Remember that the hiring process in any bureaucracy (public or private) may be full of land mines. You should do your best to familiarize yourself with the organization and their policies and practices. Thoroughly read all information provided in the job announcement or on the Web site, and be sure to follow the instructions provided. If you know someone who understands the particular system in which you are applying, it can make a huge difference for you as a candidate.

Alan Soane

▶ Alan Soane is a Recruiting Specialist for Xerox.

As a recruiting professional who has reviewed thousands of resumes, I am continually asked what I look for in a resume or what are considered "best practices" as far as format, content, and length. To the usual chagrin of the asker, my response is there is no best or magic template for all resumes. Each individual resume should clearly answer the questions that intended audiences carry as a filter and lens.

A good resume will prompt the intended reviewer to fully read the document by being attractive, informative, and concise. A common perception of a resume is that it gets "your foot in the door," the means of gaining an interview where you will actually have the opportunity to sell yourself.

Although this is still true to an extent, with the advent of the Internet, e-mail, and commercial job boards, a resume has never had to stand on its own more than the present day. The information age has enabled job openings to be communicated to larger and larger pools of job seekers, which is a positive, but it has also buried recruiting, HR, and management professionals in an avalanche of resumes.

Thoughtful presentation of your relevant experience, skills, and personal attributes against the position for which you are applying is the best course to take.

Jennifer Gage

▶ Jennifer Gage is Manager of Employee Relations at Transmation, Inc.

- Your resume is your introduction to a potential employer—your marketing tool. It should be an accurate representation of who you are and what you have accomplished.
- If there are clerical errors, overuse of clichés, lots of style, and no substance—the reader will most likely make some unflattering assumptions.
- There are no hard, fast rules for resume length, but if you have more than a one-page resume, make sure it is full of valuable information.
- Most recruiters see hundreds of resumes per day—you may only have thirty to sixty seconds for your resume to make an impression before it is filed away somewhere, never to be seen again.
- It is important to highlight your unique contributions in your resume. The resume should not simply be a laundry list of your job duties.
- Include action-result statements, or statements that detail an action that you took and the resulting benefit to your organization. If possible, quantify these results (percentage of time saved, cost reduction, etc.) These statements show that you did more than come to work and do your job—you contributed to the bottom line profitability of the organization.
- It is important to remember that, in most cases, the resume is simply your ticket in the metaphorical door. However, if you don't make it through, you'll never have a chance at the job. A resume will get you the interview—an interview will get you the job.

Joyce A. Ponserella

▶ Joyce Ponserella is the Medical Officer Recruiter for Navy Officer Programs.

- A resume that includes a college or university address, as well as their home address is wonderful. Phone numbers are a must for both locations, and anyone who doesn't have or use e-mail is nuts. It's the quickest and easiest, not to mention cheapest, way to reach someone.

- Since the programs I recruit for are highly competitive, it is important to know the applicant's GPAs, particularity in their major, but also overall.
- Experience is a very important area as well. However, if your experience doesn't relate to the area you want to work in, why bother with it. For example: Major: Biology; GPA: none listed; Course Highlights: Ecology, Genetics, Endocrinology, Microbiology; Experience: Customer Service Assistant, Enterprise Rent-A-Car. This is fine if you are looking for a job in the car rental business, but useless if you are applying for most everything else. Also, if I have to draw my own conclusions about GPA, I will assume you weren't proud of it, and therefore I am not interested in you for my organization.
- In another example: Major: Neuroscience major, Psychology major; GPA: 3.67 overall, Psychology: 3.82, Neuroscience: 3.49; Experience: Summer 2001, Harvard Medical School Summer Undergraduate Research Program doing full-time research in Alzheimer's disease research unit; Summer of 2000, Burke Rehabilitation Hospital, Intern in Traumatic Brain Injury unit, assisting staff with patient care and day-to-day evaluation of patients. This individual has really given me some useful information. I know exactly what this person can do for my organization.

Frank Bell

▶Frank Bell is President of Bell Associates International.

I hate resumes, but they are a necessary evil. As a professional recruiter, a resume has one purpose—to get my attention—so I start asking questions and get curious enough to telephone the person. As an international recruiter my priorities are:

- English plus a language of the country where the job is or will be oriented.
- Relevant experience in the United States and preferably overseas (if in the country of a search, even better).

- Adaptability, survivability and willingness to travel or live overseas (I specialize in searches for U.S. companies in emerging markets).
- A pithy one-page resume is ideal.
- If I am interested in the candidate for a client (the client pays the fees), I will use the back of the resume to write notes on, occasionally referring to the front of the resume for details.
- I once felt guilty when I spent less than a minute initially reading a resume, but I felt better when I read that the VP of Human Resources for a major company spends less that ten seconds per resume.
- The best resumes are like "carpenter's checklists." They require knowing what the client (employer) is looking for. Like a carpenter building something, if he needs eight-penny nails, you list that you are a strong, eight-penny nail, nothing different. Most recruiters and companies are too lazy to really thoroughly search. If your resume says you are exactly what they are looking for, they will "check" on you.
- I hated creating resumes so much, I became a recruiter so I didn't have to write them. Instead, I can read them and pontificate about them.

Dave Bassi

▶ Dave Bassi is the Recruiting Manager for the State of Wyoming Department of Corrections.

Are there three sides of a fence? If so, I've been on all of them! Initially, I was a college student, trying desperately to compose the perfect resume that would land me a job that paid far more than I was worth! Later, I was employed as a Career Counselor for six years. This involved instructing job seekers on the art of marketing themselves to prospective employers through the use of the various resume formats. Currently, I am a Recruiting Manager who reviews anywhere from thirty to fifty resumes each month. Consciously, or maybe subconsciously, I look at each resume and critique them from all locations on the "fence." What is the applicant trying to tell me (or sell me)? What parts of the resume were good? And, what parts were not so good? And finally, how can this applicant help me? Much of resume writing is common sense (with a little showmanship thrown in for good measure). I feel a little ambivalent sharing because I don't want to come off sounding like a know-it-all. All I can do is try to relate some of my experiences from each side of the fence:

- A good resume won't guarantee you a job. However, a bad resume will guarantee you won't get the job you want! The goal of the resume is to get you an interview. A poorly written resume decreases your chances of being invited to interview and increases chances of receiving dreaded rejection letters!

- When writing your resume, be truthful. Sometimes, you may feel the need to embellish qualifications to make you appear more competitive in a tight job market. Don't do it!

- Put your most marketable assets toward the top of your resume.

- Always have a current resume handy.

- Read the job announcement carefully. Read the job specs, compare against your assets, decide to apply, and reflect your analysis of assets versus requirements.

- Edit your resume for form and content. Ensure the layout is eye-catching yet uncluttered.

- Think like the employer. Put yourself in the place of the person doing the hiring. Would you rather read about someone's exciting work accomplishments and scholastic achievements, or would you rather read about his/her interest in bug collecting? Target your resume contents to the needs of the employer—don't list inconsequential niceties that you're happy to see in print.

- Tell me what you want in a cover letter, and show me in your resume why I should give you what you want: an interview and a job.

- If you send me a resume by e-mail, that does not excuse you from your obligation to write a cover letter.

- Find out my name! If you want to apply to my agency, call to find out who gets the application.

- Your resume is only one tool in your job-search arsenal, albeit a very important tool. Rarely, if ever, has an applicant been hired solely on the basis of a resume. But until someone comes along with a better way for applicants to get noticed, you better have a good product at your disposal.

Jennifer R. Jenkins

▶ Jennifer Jenkins is the College Recruiter at The May Institute.

I am a college recruiter for a very special place; therefore, my main focus is on soon-to-be and recent college grads seeking to work with special needs clients and patients. With this target group in mind, my views on resumes include:

- One of the recommendations I often make (to this population of job seekers) is to live their resume rather than just writing it. I encourage students to create their resumes by exposing themselves to a variety of experiences such as volunteer work, internships, and/or co-ops. If they are able to gain experience throughout college, they are literally building a resume.
- When I am working with a soon-to-be graduate who has not had these types of experiences, they tend to have a very basic resume. In many cases, this tells me very little about who they are, their post-college focus, or their areas of strength.
- I realize that many college students have cumbersome schedules and don't want to jeopardize their school grades by getting in over their heads. However, I worked in college admissions for many years, prior to Human Resources, and I was impressed with the number of students who combined their work-study job with their area of study. For example, Psychology students often sought out Admissions jobs, which allowed them the opportunity to build on their counseling and people skills.
- Another option is to do an internship/co-op during the summer months. These may even be paid positions. The May Institute, a nonprofit human service agency, hires a number of college students during the summer months, as well as throughout the school year. These opportunities offer them great hands-on experience, exposure to the field, flexible schedules, and an income!

Lindsay R. Greene

▶ Lindsay Greene is the Fund Development Specialist for United Way of the Texas Gulf Coast.

Here are my thoughts on resumes and job searching:

- There are several styles of resumes. Some are more formal than others. Choose the style that best fits you. Your resume is the first impression an interviewer has of you.
- The two most important factors on a resume are accuracy/attention to detail (no typos!) and conciseness. Keep it to the point, complete sentences are not necessary, bullets are much easier to read.
- Keep your resume limited to one page unless you have a Ph.D.
- Have someone else review your resume for typos and ask them if your resume is easy to read. After looking at your document for several hours, it is often hard to see your own errors.
- Your resume should quickly tell the interviewer if you are a good candidate for the open position through your skills and job experience.
- Include any volunteer and civic activities you are involved in locally. These additional experiences show that you are a well-rounded individual and may display additional skills you possess that are not necessarily evident from your past work experience.
- Your cover letter, and please do write a cover letter, should expand on these skills and experiences. Your resume will not get you hired for a job, and so therefore, the main goal of your resume and cover letter should be to get an interview. Once you get your foot in the door, you can then impress the interviewer with your charming personality and knowledge and your goal will then change to being hired for the open position.
- During the interview, you can refer to your resume and will often be asked to explain or expand on something on your resume. Be prepared for this.
- If possible, relate the skills learned from that position to the current job opening. Do some research on the company that is interviewing you and as necessary, refer to this research.

- I am always impressed when the person I am interviewing has done their "homework." The Internet is very helpful today for this sort of information. Use it!
- Write a thank-you note to everyone who interviewed you.

This chapter provided insights into the thoughts of recruiters and others who review resumes, determine whom to interview, and actually conduct interviews. The diverse views of professionals from varied industries and employment fields were presented, yet some common themes arose. The common threads woven through the colorful tapestry that is resume writing and job search became visible. These metaphorical threads include the following:

- Tailor your resumes to job descriptions, and customize your resume and cover letters to match specific jobs. Use "buzz phrases" specific to fields and functions and wording that appeared in the announcement. Omit information not relevant to your stated goal, or to the position you are applying for. When possible, include specific skills, including computer competencies.
- Note accomplishments that are target-specific, addressing "so what" issues that are raised during screening as well as interviews. Inform readers what past accomplishments have to do with the specific job. Allow focused achievement presentations to enhance the potential that your resume is placed in the "yes pile."
- The resume is as important as the cover letter and vice versa. Customize both and show that you understand and that you can appropriately use field-specific concepts and words. Be detailed and factual.
- Be prepared to use your resume as an interview tool and be ready, when asked, to expand upon entries. The resume should be used by both employers and candidates during interviews.
- Use a format that allows for mail, fax, and e-mail distribution. Specifically, be prepared to use e-mail today.
- The idea that one resume can fit all needs is crazy. Create target-specific versions as needed.
- Use bold and bullets, as well as special headings and order of importance to highlight.
- Gain focus and share focus. Remember, focus, focus, focus are the keys!

Sample Designs

This first appendix contains fifteen common resume formats and designs. Look each one over carefully and experiment with combining different formats to get the results you feel best match the image you wish to convey.

Chris Smith

123 Main Street • Hometown, NY 00000 • (555) 555-1234 • csmith@company.com

Consulting Qualifications

- Specialized knowledge of e-business models and techniques related to market segmentation.
- Skills gained conducting real and academic focused case analyses related to Wal-Mart and Dell Computers and projects investigating marketing and distribution strategies.
- Capacities to research, analyze data, identify trends, and create proposals, plans, and documents.
- Word, Excel, Power Point, PageMaker, Netscape, Explorer, and Internet talents.
- German and English fluency and conversational French and Swedish talents.

Economics, Business, and Mathematics Studies and Honors

1999-2003   UNIVERSITY OF ROCHESTER, Rochester, NY
Bachelor of Arts, Economics, with Mathematics Minor, anticipated May 2003
Economics GPA of 4.0 and **Overall** GPA of 3.92 and **Mathematics** GPA of 3.91
- John Dows Mairs Economics Prize for a Junior achieving the best in the field
- Golden Key Honour Society and Omicron Delta Epsilon Economics Honor Society
- Courses at Uppsala University, Uppsala, Sweden, Fall 2001

1999-2003   WILLIAM E. SIMON SCHOOL OF BUSINESS ADMINISTRATION, Rochester, NY
Management Studies Certificate, with Marketing Track, May 2003
- Simon Scholar tuition scholarship applied to future enrollment at Simon School

Selected Business, Economics, and Mathematics Courses

Financial Accounting, Statistics, Principles of Economics, Intermediate Micro- and Macroeconomics, Economic Growth in America, Economic Thinking, Teaching Assistant for Microeconomics, Probability and Statistical Inference, Advanced Microeconomics, Econometrics, Marketing, Economics of the Organization, International Organizations.

Research and Policy Analysis Experience

2002   EUROPEAN PARLIAMENT, Brussels, Belgium
Intern: Supported efforts of German SPD delegation and 35 MEPs. Performed competitive analysis of German parties impacting federal elections of 2002. Also, researched and wrote paper on topic of emissions trading from an environmental, economic, and industrial standpoint.

Business, Strategic Planning, and Quantitative Experience

SAATCHI & SAATCHI ROWLAND, Rochester, NY
Summer 2002   **Freelance Media Assistant:** Assisted media team with DuPont 2002 and 2003 media planning.
Winter 2001   **Account Management and Media Intern:** Assisted with customer profiling and competitive ad spending runs for DuPont Teflon.
Summer 2001   **Account Management and Media Intern:** Performed product research and customer profiling, interviews with sales representatives to construct marketing plans for various Bausch & Lomb products, such as ReNu, Purevision, and Ocuvite.

Chris Smith

123 Main Street • Hometown, NY 00000 • (555) 555-1234 • csmith@company.com

CONSULTING QUALIFICATIONS
- Specialized knowledge of e-business models and techniques related to market segmentation.
- Skills gained conducting real and academic focused case analyses related to Wal-Mart and Dell Computers and projects investigating marketing and distribution strategies.
- Capacities to research, analyze data, identify trends, and create proposals, plans, and documents.
- Word, Excel, PowerPoint, PageMaker, Netscape, Explorer, and Internet talents.
- German and English fluency and conversational French and Swedish talents.

ECONOMICS, BUSINESS, AND MATH STUDIES AND HONORS

UNIVERSITY OF ROCHESTER   ROCHESTER, NY
Bachelor of Arts, Economics with a Mathematics Minor   anticipated May 2003
- Economics GPA of 4.0 and Overall GPA of 3.92, and Mathematics GPA of 3.91
- Recipient of John Dows Mairs Economics Prize for a Junior achieving the best in the field
- Golden Key International Honour Society and Omicron Delta Epsilon Economics Honor Society

WILLIAM E. SIMON SCHOOL OF BUSINESS ADMINISTRATION   ROCHESTER, NY
Management Studies Certificate, with Marketing Track   anticipated May 2003
- Courses include: Financial Accounting, Statistics, Principles of Economics, Intermediate Micro- and Macroeconomics, Economic Growth in America, Economic Thinking, Probability and Statistical Inference, Econometrics, Marketing, and International Organizations
- Recipient of Simon Scholar tuition scholarship applied to future enrollment at Simon School

BUSINESS, STRATEGIC PLANNING, AND POLICY ANALYSIS EXPERIENCE

EUROPEAN PARLIAMENT   BRUSSELS, BELGIUM
Intern   2002
Supported efforts of German SPD delegation and 35 MEPs. Performed competitive analysis of German parties impacting federal elections of 2002. Also, researched and wrote paper on topic of emissions trading from an environmental, economic, and industrial standpoint.

SAATCHI & SAATCHI ROWLAND   ROCHESTER, NY
Freelance Media Assistant   Summer 2002
Assisted media team with DuPont 2002 and 2003 media planning.
Account Management and Media Intern   Winter 2001
Assisted with customer profiling and competitive ad spending runs for DuPont Teflon.
Account Management and Media Intern   Summer 2001
Performed product research and customer profiling, as well as talking with sales representatives and constructing marketing plans for various Bausch and Lomb products, such as ReNu, Purevision, and Ocuvite. Expanded knowledge of marketing, strategic planning, account management, and client relations. Nurtured project management, writing, communication, and team skills.

Chris Smith

123 Main Street • Hometown, NY 00000 • (555) 555-1234 • csmith@company.com

CONSULTING QUALIFICATIONS

- Specialized knowledge of e-business models and techniques related to market segmentation.
- Skills gained conducting real and academic focused case analyses related to Wal-Mart and Dell Computers and projects investigating marketing and distribution strategies.
- Capacities to research, analyze data, identify trends, and create proposals, plans, and documents.
- Word, Excel, Power Point, PageMaker, Netscape, Explorer, and Internet talents.
- German and English fluency and conversational French and Swedish talents.

ECONOMICS, BUSINESS, AND MATH STUDIES AND HONORS

UNIVERSITY OF ROCHESTER   Rochester, NY
Bachelor of Arts, Economics, with **Mathematics** minor   anticipated May 2003
Economics GPA of 4.0, **Overall** GPA of 3.92, and **Mathematics** GPA of 3.91
- Recipient of John Dows Mairs Economics Prize for a Junior achieving the best in the field.
- Golden Key International Honour Society and Omicron Delta Epsilon Economics Honor Society.

WILLIAM E. SIMON SCHOOL OF BUSINESS ADMINISTRATION   Rochester, NY
Management Studies Certificate, with Marketing Track   anticipated May 2003
- Courses include: Financial Accounting, Statistics, Principles of Economics, Intermediate Micro- and Macroeconomics, Economic Growth in America, Economic Thinking, Probability and Statistical Inference, Advanced Microeconomics, Econometrics, Marketing, and International Organizations.
- Recipient of Simon Scholar tuition scholarship applied to future enrollment at Simon School.

RESEARCH AND POLICY ANALYSIS EXPERIENCE

EUROPEAN PARLIAMENT   Brussels, Belgium
Intern   2002
- Supported efforts of German SPD delegation and 35 MEPs and performed competitive analysis of German parties impacting federal elections of 2002.
- Also, researched and wrote paper on topic of emissions trading from an environmental, economic, and industrial standpoint.

BUSINESS, STRATEGIC PLANNING, AND QUANTITATIVE EXPERIENCE

SAATCHI & SAATCHI ROWLAND   Rochester, NY
Freelance Media Assistant   Summer 2002
Account Management and Media Intern   Winter 2001
Account Management and Media Intern   Summer 2001
- Assisted media team with DuPont 2002 and 2003 media planning.
- Assisted with customer profiling and competitive ad spending runs for DuPont Teflon.
- Performed product research and customer profiling, and interviews with sales representatives to construct marketing plans for various Bausch and Lomb products, such as ReNu, Purevision, and Ocuvite. Expanded knowledge of marketing, strategic planning, account management, and client relations.

Chris Smith

123 Main Street • Hometown, NY 00000 • (555) 555-1234 • csmith@company.com

QUALIFICATIONS

- Specialized knowledge of e-business models and techniques related to market segmentation.
- Skills gained conducting real and academic focused case analyses related to Wal-Mart and Dell Computers and projects investigating marketing and distribution strategies.
- Capacities to research, analyze data, identify trends, and create proposals, plans, and documents.
- Word, Excel, Power Point, PageMaker, Netscape, Explorer, and Internet talents.
- German and English fluency and conversational French and Swedish talents.

EDUCATION

1999-2003   UNIVERSITY OF ROCHESTER, Rochester, NY
Bachelor of Arts, Economics, anticipated May 2003
Economics GPA of 4.0 and **Overall** GPA of 3.92
Minors: **Mathematics**, with a current GPA of 3.91
- John Dows Mairs Economics Prize for Junior achieving the best in the field
- Golden Key Honour Society and Omicron Delta Epsilon Economics Honor Society
- Courses at Uppsala University, Uppsala, Sweden, Fall 2001

1999-2003   WILLIAM E. SIMON SCHOOL OF BUSINESS ADMINISTRATION, Rochester, NY
Management Studies Certificate, with Marketing Track, anticipated May 2003
- Courses include: Financial Accounting, Statistics, Principles of Economics, Intermediate Micro- and Macroeconomics, Economic Growth in America, Economic Thinking, Probability and Statistical Inference, Econometrics, Marketing, Economics of the Organization, International Organizations
- Simon Scholar tuition scholarship applied to future enrollment at Simon School

EXPERIENCE

2002   EUROPEAN PARLIAMENT, Brussels, Belgium
Intern: Supported efforts of German SPD delegation and 35 MEPs. Performed competitive analysis of German parties impacting federal elections of 2002. Also, researched and wrote paper on topic of emissions trading from an environmental, economic, and industrial standpoint.

SAATCHI & SAATCHI ROWLAND, Rochester, NY
Summer 2002   **Freelance Media Assistant:** Assisted media team with DuPont 2002 and 2003 media planning.
Winter 2001   **Account Management and Media Intern:** Assisted with customer profiling and competitive ad spending runs for DuPont Teflon.
Summer 2001   **Account Management and Media Intern:** Performed product research customer profiling, and interviews with sales representatives to construct marketing plans for various Bausch and Lomb products, such as ReNu, Purevision, and Ocuvite.

CHRIS SMITH

123 Main Street • Hometown, NY 00000 • (555) 555-1234 • csmith@company.com

BUSINESS, ECONOMICS, AND LIBERAL ARTS STUDIES

UNIVERSITY OF ROCHESTER   ROCHESTER, NY
Bachelor of Arts, Economics   **anticipated May 2003**
- **Economics** GPA of 4.0 and **Overall** GPA of 3.92
- Minor: **Mathematics**, with a current Mathematics GPA of 3.91
- John Dows Mairs Economics Prize for a Junior achieving the best in the field
- Golden Key International Honour Society and Omicron Delta Epsilon Economics Honor Society
- Completed courses at Uppsala University, Uppsala, Sweden, Fall 2001

WILLIAM E. SIMON SCHOOL OF BUSINESS ADMINISTRATION   ROCHESTER, NY
Management Studies Certificate, with Marketing Track   **anticipated May 2003**
- Completed Financial Accounting, Statistics, Principles of Economics, Intermediate Micro- and Macroeconomics, Economic Growth in America, Economic Thinking, Probability and Statistical Inference, Advanced Microeconomics, Econometrics, and Marketing
- Recipient of Simon Scholar tuition scholarship applied to future enrollment at Simon School

BUSINESS AND POLICY ANALYSIS EXPERIENCE

EUROPEAN PARLIAMENT   BRUSSELS, BELGIUM
Intern   **2002**
- Supported efforts of German SPD delegation and 35 MEPs. Followed daily Parliamentary procedures and performed analysis of German parties impacting federal elections of 2002
- Also, researched and wrote paper on topic of emissions trading from an environmental, economic, and industrial standpoint

SAATCHI & SAATCHI ROWLAND   ROCHESTER, NY
Freelance Media Assistant   **Summer 2002**
Account Management and Media Intern   **Winter 2001**
Account Management and Media Intern   **Summer 2001**
- Assisted media team with DuPont 2002 and 2003 media planning
- Assisted with customer profiling and competitive ad spending runs for DuPont Teflon
- Performed product research, customer profiling, and interviews with sales representatives, creating marketing plans for Bausch and Lomb products, such as ReNu, Purevision, and Ocuvite

CONSULTING QUALIFICATIONS

- Specialized knowledge of e-business models and techniques related to market segmentation
- Skills gained conducting real and academic focused case analyses related to Wal-Mart and Dell Computers and projects investigating marketing and distribution strategies
- Capacities to research, analyze data, identify trends, and create proposals, plans, and documents
- Word, Excel, PowerPoint, PageMaker, Netscape, Explorer, and Internet talents
- German and English fluency and conversational French and Swedish talents

Jamie Brown

123 Main St. • Hometown, MN 00000 • (555) 555-1234 • jbrown@company.com

EXPERIENCE

**June 2001
to Present**

RBC Capital Markets (formerly Dain Rauscher Wessels), Minneapolis, MN
Analyst, Investment Banking, Healthcare Group
One of fifteen investment banking professionals serving life sciences companies worldwide. Advise clients on M&A candidates and perform strategic analysis; conduct due diligence; determine valuation parameters; evaluate pro formas; and identify potential acquirers/targets. Assist in the execution of equity, debt, and private placement offering process.
Identify potential clients; develop presentations; participate in introductory meetings; evaluate company, analyze sector and market-related issues affecting a transaction. Manage documentation; support Equity Research, Capital Markets, and Sales & Trading; and assist in transaction committee approval process. Perform company valuation including discounted cash flow analyses, comparable company analyses, and precedent transaction analyses. Develop financial models to analyze mergers, equity, debt, and private placement offerings. Assist Research Analysts and advise Investment Bankers on technology and product assessment, applying industry knowledge gained via education and professional experiences.

Summer 2000

Vaccinex Inc., Rochester, NY
Research Intern, Cellular and Molecular Immunology Department
Worked in a team with twenty professionals including summer interns, research associates, Ph.D. candidates, and Senior Scientists. Reported to the Director of Research & Development.

Summer 1999

University of Rochester Medical Center, Rochester, NY
Laboratory Assistant, Department of Pharmacology and Physiology Peracchia Lab
Worked in a laboratory with eight staff members including Ph.D. candidates, postdoctoral candidates, and the Principal Investigator. Developed cell colonies and oocytes for gap junction experiments.

**Summers 1997
and 1998**

Harvard Medical School, Brookline, MA
Department of Epidemiology Research Assistant
Supported three Principal Investigators and a Ph.D. candidate in the collection and organization of Physician and Nurse interviews and medical literature.

EDUCATION

1997-2001

University of Rochester, Rochester, NY
Bachelor of Science in Chemical Engineering, May 2001
Emphasis on Life Sciences systems; including courses in Biochemical Engineering, Biotechnology, Biochemistry, Clinical Diagnostics, Reactor Design, Separation Processes, and Organic Chemistry.

1997-2001

William E. Simon School of Business Administration, Rochester, NY
Management Studies Certificate, with Finance and Accounting Track, May 2001
Earned certificate for completion of courses in Financial Markets, Financial Accounting, Marketing Management, Economics, Computer Programming, and Statistics.

Jamie Brown

123 Main St. • Hometown, MN 00000 • (555) 555-1234 • jbrown@company.com

INVESTMENT BANKING EXPERIENCE

RBC Capital Markets (formerly Dain Rauscher Wessels) Minneapolis, MN
Analyst, Investment Banking, Healthcare Group June 2001–present
- One of fifteen investment banking professionals serving life sciences companies worldwide.
- Advise clients on M&A candidates and perform strategic analysis; conduct due diligence; determine valuation parameters; evaluate pro formas; and identify potential acquirers/targets.
- Assist in the execution of equity, debt, and private placement offering process.
- Identify potential clients; develop presentations; participate in introductory meetings; evaluate company, analyze sector and market related issues affecting a transaction.
- Manage documentation; support Equity Research, Capital Markets, and Sales & Trading; and assist in transaction committee approval process.
- Perform company valuation including discounted cash flow analyses, comparable company analyses, and precedent transaction analyses.
- Develop financial models to analyze mergers, equity, debt, and private placement offerings.
- Assist Research Analysts and advise Investment Bankers on technology and product assessment, applying industry knowledge gained via education and professional experiences.

RESEARCH EXPERIENCE

Vaccinex Inc. Rochester, NY
Research Intern, Cellular and Molecular Immunology Department Summer 2000
- Worked in a team with twenty professionals including summer interns, research associates, Ph.D. candidates, and Senior Scientists. Reported to the Director of Research & Development.

University of Rochester Medical Center Rochester, NY
Laboratory Assistant, Department of Pharmacology and Physiology Peracchia Lab Summer 1999
- Worked in a laboratory with eight staff including Ph.D. candidates, post docs, and Principal Investigator.

Harvard Medical School Brookline, MA
Department of Epidemiology Research Assistant Summers 1997 and 1998
- Supported three Principal Investigators and a Ph.D. candidate with collection of interviews and literature.

BUSINESS AND ENGINEERING STUDIES

William E. Simon School of Business Administration Rochester, NY
Management Studies Certificate with Finance and Accounting Track May 2001
- Earned certificate for completion of courses in Financial Markets, Financial Accounting, Marketing Management, Economics, Computer Programming, and Statistics.

University of Rochester Rochester, NY
Bachelor of Science in Chemical Engineering May 2001

Jamie Brown

123 Main St. • Hometown, MN 00000 • (555) 555-1234 • jbrown@company.com

BUSINESS AND FINANCE EXPERIENCE

June 2001–
present

RBC Capital Markets (formerly Dain Rauscher Wessels), Minneapolis, MN
Analyst, Investment Banking, Healthcare Group
- One of fifteen investment banking professionals serving life sciences companies.
- Advise clients on M&A candidates and perform strategic analysis; conduct due diligence; determine valuation parameters; evaluate pro formas; and identify potential acquirers/targets.
- Assist in the execution of equity, debt, and private placement offering process.
- Identify potential clients; develop presentations; participate in introductory meetings; evaluate company, analyze sector and market related issues affecting a transaction.
- Manage documentation; support Equity Research, Capital Markets, and Sales & Trading; and assist in transaction committee approval process.
- Perform company valuation including discounted cash flow analyses, comparable company analyses, and precedent transaction analyses.
- Develop models to analyze mergers, equity, debt, and private placement offerings.
- Assist Research Analysts and advise Investment Bankers on technology and product assessment, applying industry knowledge gained via education and experience.

RESEARCH EXPERIENCE

Summer 2000

Vaccinex Inc., Rochester, NY
Research Intern, Cellular and Molecular Immunology Department

Summer 1999

University of Rochester Medical Center, Rochester, NY
Laboratory Assistant, Department of Pharmacology and Physiology Peracchia Lab

Summers 1997
and 1998

Harvard Medical School, Brookline, MA
Department of Epidemiology Research Assistant

BUSINESS AND ENGINEERING STUDIES

1997–2001

William E. Simon School of Business Administration, Rochester, NY
Management Studies Certificate, May 2001
- Certificate for completion of courses in Financial Markets, Financial Accounting, Marketing Management, Economics, Computer Programming, and Statistics.

1997–2001

University of Rochester, Rochester, NY
Bachelor of Science in Chemical Engineering, May 2001
- Emphasis on Life Sciences systems; including courses in Biochemical Engineering, Biotechnology, Biochemistry, Clinical Diagnostics, Reactor Design, Separation Processes, and Organic Chemistry.

Jamie Brown

123 Main St. • Hometown, MN 00000 • (555) 555-1234 • jbrown@company.com

INVESTMENT BANKING QUALIFICATIONS

- Comprehensive Analyst experience within major regional bank.
- Confidence within research, analysis, due diligence, and deal support capacities, gained within experiences in Corporate Finance, M&A, Corporate Credit, Private Equity, and Sales and Trading areas.
- Specialized knowledge of healthcare, biotechnology, and pharmaceutical deals.

BUSINESS AND FINANCE EXPERIENCE

June 2001-
present

RBC Capital Markets (formerly Dain Rauscher Wessels), Minneapolis, MN
Analyst, Investment Banking, Healthcare Group
- Advise clients on M&A candidates and perform strategic analysis; conduct due diligence; determine valuation; evaluate pro formas; and identify potential acquirers/targets.
- Assist in the execution of equity, debt, and private placement offering process.
- Identify potential clients; develop presentations; participate in introductory meetings; evaluate company, analyze sector and market-related issues affecting a transaction.
- Manage documentation; support Equity Research, Capital Markets, and Sales & Trading; and assist in transaction committee approval process.
- Perform company valuation including discounted cash flow analyses, comparable company analyses, and precedent transaction analyses.
- Develop financial models to analyze mergers, equity, debt, and private placement offerings.
- Assist Analysts and advise Investment Bankers on technology and product assessment, applying industry knowledge gained via education and professional experiences.

RESEARCH EXPERIENCE

Summer 2000

Vaccinex Inc., Rochester, NY
Research Intern, Cellular and Molecular Immunology Department

Summer 1999

University of Rochester Medical Center, Rochester, NY
Laboratory Assistant, Department of Pharmacology and Physiology Peracchia Lab

Summers 1997
and 1998

Harvard Medical School, Brookline, MA
Department of Epidemiology Research Assistant

BUSINESS AND ENGINEERING STUDIES

1997-2001

University of Rochester, Rochester, NY
Management Studies Certificate for courses in Financial Markets, Financial Accounting, Economics, Computer Programming, and Statistics, May 2001
Bachelor of Science in Chemical Engineering, May 2001

Jamie Brown

123 Main St. • Hometown, MN 00000 • (555) 555-1234 • jbrown@company.com

education

WILLIAM E. SIMON SCHOOL OF BUSINESS ADMINISTRATION   ROCHESTER, NY
Management Studies Certificate   *May 2001*
- Earn certificate for completion of courses taught by College and Simon School faculty.
- Emphasis on Finance and Accounting; including courses in Financial Markets, Financial Accounting, Marketing Management, Economics, Computer Programming, and Statistics.

UNIVERSITY OF ROCHESTER   ROCHESTER, NY
Bachelor of Science in Chemical Engineering   *May 2001*

experience

RBC CAPITAL MARKETS (FORMERLY DAIN RAUSCHER WESSELS) MINNEAPOLIS, MN
Analyst, Investment Banking, Healthcare Group   *June 2001 to present*
- One of fifteen investment banking professionals serving life sciences companies worldwide.
- Advise clients on M&A candidates and perform strategic analysis; conduct due diligence; determine valuation parameters; evaluate pro formas; and identify potential acquirers/targets.
- Assist in the execution of equity, debt, and private placement offering process.
- Identify potential clients; develop presentations; participate in introductory meetings; evaluate company, analyze sector and market related issues affecting a transaction.
- Manage documentation; support Equity Research, Capital Markets, and Sales & Trading; and assist in transaction committee approval process.
- Perform company valuation including discounted cash flow analyses, comparable company analyses, and precedent transaction analyses.
- Develop financial models to analyze mergers, equity, debt, and private placement offerings.
- Assist Research Analysts and advise Investment Bankers on technology and product assessment, applying industry knowledge gained via education and professional experiences.

VACCINEX INC.   ROCHESTER, NY
Research Intern, Cellular and Molecular Immunology Department   *Summer 2000*

UNIVERSITY OF ROCHESTER MEDICAL CENTER   ROCHESTER, NY
Lab Assistant, Department of Pharmacology and Physiology Peracchia Lab   *Summer 1999*

HARVARD MEDICAL SCHOOL   BROOKLINE, MA
Department of Epidemiology Research Assistant   *Summers 1997 and 1998*

qualifications

- Unique blend of business and science studies as well as investment banking experience.
- Knowledge of investment banking, healthcare, biotechnology, and pharmaceutical industries.
- Confidence applying scientific method as well as financial analytical models to test hypotheses and support qualitative thinking with quantitative methodologies.

DANA JOHNSON

123 Main Street ■ Hometown, New York 00000 ■ 555.555.1234 ■ DJOHNSON@COMPANY.COM

OBJECTIVE

Pharmaceutical sales representative position.

QUALIFICATIONS

- Experience building and maintaining relationships with physicians, surgeons, and nurses.
- Ability to interface with individuals at all levels of health care organization.
- Results oriented and ready to implement marketing strategies that meet and exceed goals.
- Adept at processing and conveying complex terminology via written and verbal communication.
- Timely and assertive follow-up skills to handle inquiries and reinforce existing relationships.

MARKETING AND COMMUNICATION ACHIEVEMENTS

Albert Einstein Hospital   **New York, NY**
Assistant Director of Public Relations   May 1994 - present
Function as PR account representative for Medical Center and 750-bed Hospital. Develop and maintain relationships with physicians, surgeons, and nurses. Generate publicity for urology, orthopedics, neurology, neurosurgery, blood/marrow transplant, emergency medicine, dermatology, radiology, anesthesiology, and otolaryngology. Proactively and effectively pitch stories to news media. Serve as spokesperson and liaison to local/national news media, on-call 24/7 as needed. Write news releases and speeches. Assist news crews and direct press briefings. Develop text for brochures, fundraising pieces, and websites. Write op-ed pieces and letters to the editor. Direct, write, produce, and edit videos. Develop and implement strategic publicity plans.

New Jersey Corn Cooperative   **New Brunswick, NJ**
Communications Manager   June 1990 - December 1993
Directed all aspects of corporate communications/public relations for 600-member cooperative. Managed production of monthly member newsletter, quarterly employee newsletter, and annual report. Served as spokesperson and liaison to local and national news media. Wrote news releases, pitched stories, created print ads/brochures, and assisted with speech writing. Directed public relations events at fairs, schools, and festivals. Performed all in-house photography.

Princeton Vineyards & Winery   **Princeton, NJ**
Sales Representative   Summers 1988 and 1989
Served as tasting room sales representative and tour guide for 30,000 gallon winery. Managed all tasting room operations and represented winery at festivals and other events.

EDUCATION

New York University   **New York, NY**
Bachelor of Science, Communication   May 1990

DANA JOHNSON

123 Main Street ■ Hometown, New York 00000 ■ 555.555.1234 ■ djohnson@company.com

PHARMACEUTICAL SALES QUALIFICATIONS

- Comprehensive knowledge of health industry, ability to cultivate client relationships, industry contacts, goal-driven personality, and commitment to long-term profitability and productivity.
- Experience building and maintaining relationships with physicians, surgeons, and nurses.
- Ability to interface with individuals at all levels of health care organization.
- Adept at processing and conveying complex medical terminology via written and verbal communication.

ACHIEVEMENTS

- Increased number of proactive media hits by an average of 15% annually in designated clinical areas.
- Ninety-nine percent of proactive pitches are broadcast or printed by at least one media outlet.
- Assumed major responsibility planning, coordinating, and directing patient remotes for Children's Miracle Network Telethon from 1994 through 2002; events that raise nearly $2 million annually for hospital.
- PR department landed 2,400 media hits in 2002, 2,2000 in 2001, 1,300 in 2000, compared to 1,000 in 1999, and 800 in 1998.
- As a result of proactive media pitch on free skin cancer screening, over 1,000 patients were screened annually, detecting numerous deadly melanomas, basal cell carcinomas, and squamous cell carcinomas.

HEALTHCARE AND MARKETING EXPERIENCE

ALBERT EINSTEIN HOSPITAL   NEW YORK, NY
Assistant Director of Public Relations   **May 1994 - present**
- Function as PR account representative for Medical Center and Hospital.
- Develop and maintain relationships with physicians, surgeons, and nurses.
- Generate publicity for urology, orthopedics, neurology, neurosurgery, blood/marrow transplant, emergency medicine, dermatology, radiology, anesthesiology, and otolaryngology.
- Serve as spokesperson and liaison to local/national news media, on-call 24/7 as needed. Write news releases and speeches.
- Develop text for brochures, fundraising pieces, and websites and write op-ed pieces and letters to the editor.
- Direct, write, produce, and edit videos.

NEW JERSEY CORN COOPERATIVE   NEW BRUNSWICK, NJ
Communications Manager   **June 1990 - December 1993**
- Established new department and directed all corporate communications/public relations for 600-member cooperative.
- Directed all communications/public relations for 600-member cooperative.
- Managed production of monthly member newsletter, quarterly employee newsletter, and annual report.
- Served as spokesperson and liaison to local and national news media.
- Wrote news releases, pitched stories, created print ads, and assisted with speech writing.

EDUCATION

NEW YORK UNIVERSITY   NEW YORK, NY
Bachelor of Science, Communication   **May 1990**

DANA JOHNSON

123 MAIN STREET • HOMETOWN, NEW YORK 00000 • 555.555.1234 • DJOHNSON@COMPANY.COM

PHARMACEUTICAL SALES QUALIFICATIONS

- Experience building and maintaining relationships with physicians, surgeons, and nurses.
- Ability to interface with individuals at all levels of health care organization.
- Results-oriented and ready to implement marketing strategies that meet and exceed goals.
- Adept at processing and conveying complex terminology via written and verbal communication.
- Timely and assertive follow-up skills to handle inquiries and reinforce existing relationships.

MARKETING AND COMMUNICATION ACHIEVEMENTS

Albert Einstein Hospital, New York, NY
Assistant Director of Public Relations, May 1994 - present
Function as PR account representative for Medical Center and 750-bed Hospital. Develop and maintain relationships with physicians, surgeons, and nurses. Generate publicity for urology, orthopedics, neurology, neurosurgery, blood/marrow transplant, emergency medicine, dermatology, radiology, anesthesiology, and otolaryngology. Proactively and effectively pitch stories to news media. Serve as spokesperson and liaison to local/national news media, on-call 24/7 as needed. Write news releases and speeches. Assist news crews and direct press briefings. Develop text for brochures, fundraising pieces, and websites. Write op-ed pieces and letters to the editor. Direct, write, produce, and edit videos. Develop and implement strategic publicity plans.

New Jersey Corn Cooperative, New Brunswick, NJ
Communications Manager, June 1990 - December 1993
Directed all aspects of corporate communications/public relations for 600-member cooperative. Managed production of monthly member newsletter, quarterly employee newsletter, and annual report. Served as spokesperson and liaison to local and national news media. Wrote news releases, pitched stories, created print ads/brochures, and assisted with speech writing. Directed public relations events at fairs, schools, and festivals. Performed all in-house photography.

Princeton Vineyards & Winery, Princeton, NJ
Sales Representative, Summers 1988 and 1989
Served as tasting room sales representative and tour guide for 30,000 gallon winery. Managed all tasting room operations and represented winery at festivals and other events.

EDUCATION New York University, New York, NY
Bachelor of Science, Communication, May 1990

DANA JOHNSON

123 Main Street • Hometown, New York 00000 • 555.555.1234 • djohnson@company.com

PHARMACEUTICAL SALES QUALIFICATIONS

- Experience building and maintaining relationships with physicians, surgeons, and nurses.
- Ability to interface with individuals at all levels of health care organization.
- Results-oriented and ready to implement marketing strategies that meet and exceed goals.
- Adept at processing and conveying complex terminology via written and verbal communication.
- Timely and assertive follow-up skills to handle inquiries and reinforce existing relationships.

MARKETING AND COMMUNICATION ACHIEVEMENTS

1994 – present   ALBERT EINSTEIN HOSPITAL, New York, NY
Assistant Director of Public Relations
- Function as PR account representative for Medical Center and Hospital.
- Develop and maintain relationships with physicians, surgeons, and nurses.
- Generate publicity for urology, orthopedics, neurology, neurosurgery, blood/marrow transplant, emergency medicine, dermatology, radiology, anesthesiology, and otolaryngology.
- Proactively and effectively pitch stories to news media.
- Serve as spokesperson and liaison to local/national news media, on-call 24/7 as needed. Write news releases and speeches.
- Assist news crews and direct press briefings.
- Develop text for brochures, fundraising pieces, and websites.
- Write op-ed pieces and letters to the editor.
- Direct, write, produce, and edit videos.

1990 – 1993   NEW JERSEY CORN COOPERATIVE, New Brunswick, NJ
Communications Manager
- Directed all communications/public relations for 600-member cooperative.
- Managed production of monthly member newsletter, quarterly employee newsletter, and annual report. Served as spokesperson and liaison to local and national news media.
- Wrote news releases, pitched stories, created print ads/brochures, and assisted with speech writing.
- Directed public relations events at fairs, schools, and festivals.
- Performed all in-house photography.

Summers 1988 and 1989   PRINCETON VINEYARDS & WINERY, Princeton, NJ
Sales Representative

EDUCATION

NEW YORK UNIVERSITY, New York, NY
Bachelor of Science, Communication, May 1990

DANA JOHNSON

123 MAIN STREET • HOMETOWN, NEW YORK 00000 • 555.555.1234 • DJOHNSON@COMPANY.COM

PHARMACEUTICAL SALES QUALIFICATIONS

- Experience building and maintaining relationships with physicians, surgeons, and nurses.
- Ability to interface with individuals at all levels of health care organization.
- Results-oriented and ready to implement marketing strategies that meet and exceed goals.
- Adept at processing and conveying complex terminology via written and verbal communication.
- Timely and assertive follow-up skills to handle inquiries and reinforce existing relationships.

MARKETING AND COMMUNICATION ACHIEVEMENTS

Albert Einstein Hospital, New York, NY
Assistant Director of Public Relations, May 1994 - present
Function as PR account representative for Medical Center and 750-bed Hospital. Develop and maintain relationships with physicians, surgeons, and nurses. Generate publicity for urology, orthopedics, neurology, neurosurgery, blood/marrow transplant, emergency medicine, dermatology, radiology, anesthesiology, and otolaryngology. Proactively and effectively pitch stories to news media. Serve as spokesperson and liaison to local/national news media, on-call 24/7 as needed. Write news releases and speeches. Assist news crews and direct press briefings. Develop text for brochures, fundraising pieces, and websites. Write op-ed pieces and letters to the editor. Direct, write, produce, and edit videos. Develop and implement strategic publicity plans.

New Jersey Corn Cooperative, New Brunswick, NJ
Communications Manager, June 1990 - December 1993
Directed all aspects of corporate communications/public relations for 600-member cooperative. Managed production of monthly member newsletter, quarterly employee newsletter, and annual report. Served as spokesperson and liaison to local and national news media. Wrote news releases, pitched stories, created print ads/brochures, and assisted with speech writing. Directed public relations events at fairs, schools, and festivals. Performed all in-house photography.

Princeton Vineyards & Winery, Princeton, NJ
Sales Representative, Summers 1988 and 1989
Served as tasting room sales representative and tour guide for 30,000 gallon winery. Managed all tasting room operations and represented winery at festivals and other events.

EDUCATION

New York University, New York, NY
Bachelor of Science, Communication, May 1990

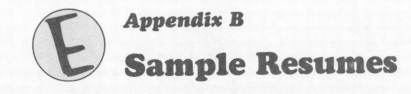

Appendix B

Sample Resumes

If imitation is the sincerest form of flattery, it is also the best resume-writing and job-search strategy. Sample resumes give you a great place to start, whether you're writing your resume from scratch, or making your existing resume more effective.

Getting Started

In Chapter 10, you reviewed and analyzed several sample resumes. You are now ready to do the same for many more. The following samples represent varied career fields, yet they possess characteristics common to all great resumes. Don't limit your review to resumes that match your goals. Find one or two that do, and then investigate a few more that strike you as particularly appealing.

ALERT!

Readers should note, font sizes and word counts were reduced slightly to allow sample resumes to fit on the illustration pages. When creating your resume, using these as guides, feel free to write as much as will fit, while maintaining a visually appealing document. Most resumes created on 8½" x 11" pages will contain more copy and lines than the samples.

Keep those pens, highlighters, and sticky notes handy! Buy more, if you must. You'll make the best progress, and get the most out of your reviews, if you take notes as you go. Circle elements you think are particularly effective. Query the elements that don't work for you. Later, as you start writing your own first draft, you'll use these gut reactions to make your own resume as powerful as possible.

Also keep track of words, phrases, designs, and details you find appealing. When looking at elements, consider how well these reflect who you are. If you pride yourself on being professional and slightly conservative, don't worry about adding lots of flash and style to your resume. Likewise, if you want to convey an attitude of being creative and edgy, don't structure your resume to look overwhelmingly professional and dry.

CHRIS SMITH

123 Main Street • Hometown, MT 00000 • (555) 555-5555 • csmith@company.com

ACCOUNTING EXPERIENCE AND ACHIEVEMENTS

ROSS PECOE, INC., Billings, MT
Senior Accountant, 1998–present
Oversee all accounting and payroll functions for a $20 million publicly held company that develops, manufactures, and markets proprietary X-ray systems.
- Assist controller in preparing financial statements and SEC reports.
- Prepare budgets and projections and monthly budget-to-actual reports and distribute to managers.
- Review work of staff accountant and approve journal transactions for data entry.
- Manage accounting duties of a venture-capital-funded start-up spin-off organization, Beta Technologies, including financial reporting and coordinating annual audit with external auditors.
- Interact with systems and payroll services professionals regarding problems and solutions.
- Assisted with analyzing implications, making final decisions, and completion of consolidation of three European subsidiaries.

Accountant, 1996–1998
- Assisted with monthly closings and financial reporting.
- Worked directly with controller to prepare primary and secondary public stock offerings.
- Implemented Solomon general ledger accounting package.
- Installed and set up modules, developed procedures for new system, and trained staff.

STEADFAST CORPORATION, Cheny Creek, MT
Staff Accountant, 1994–1996
- Monitored cash and accounts receivable for venture-capital-funded software development firm.
- Assisted in general ledger close, including foreign currency translation of foreign subsidiaries.
- Trained new employees to administer the accounts-payable and order-entry functions.

GRADUATE AND UNDERGRADUATE ACCOUNTING STUDIES

BRONTE COLLEGE, Newcastle, MT
Master of Science in Accountancy, expected completion May 2003

CARROLL COLLEGE, Helena, MT
Bachelor of Arts, Business Management, Accounting/Finance emphasis, June 1994

TECHNICAL ACCOUNTING SKILLS AND COMPETENCIES

- Skills associated with progressively responsible internal auditing, managerial accounting, budgeting, and financial analysis roles.
- Capacities to use and teach others Excel, Lotus 1-2-3, and QuickBooks.
- Experience interacting with external auditors, internal financial colleagues, as well as financial managers and senior executives.
- Capacities to draft, edit, and finalize detailed financial reports.
- Specialized knowledge of due diligence and risk analysis associated with venture capital funding and initial private offerings.

CHRIS SMITH

123 Main Street • Hometown, VA 00000 • (555) 555-1234 • Cell (555) 555-5678
csmith@company.com

QUALIFICATIONS

- Over 12 years of progressive sales and sales management responsibilities leading to current position as National Account Manager
- Experience developing and implementing marketing strategies, overseeing sales professionals, and developing effective sales relationships with direct users and resellers of personal computers and mainframes, as well as peripheral equipment, customer service contacts, and computer consulting services
- Capacities to hire, train, and motivate sales colleagues and to create reports identifying key profit areas and potential markets

ACHIEVEMENTS

- Progressive achievements within management and direct sales roles, directly contributing to expanded profits and sales
- A career averaging consistent percentage increases year after year, contributing to multi-millions of dollars in sales and profits
- Capacities to generate continued sales growth within an industry where competitors increased annually and market required sensitivities to pricing and service

SALES ACCOMPLISHMENTS

1997 to present

STARBUCK COMPUTERS INC., Richmond, VA
National Account Manager
Develop and implementing national sales strategy for computer and peripheral manufacturer, consultant, and support-service provider. Initiated, built, and nurtured relationships with several Richmond-based *Fortune* 500 corporations including Ackler Industrial, The Carnulton Group, Hanlon and Associates, and Polamin Company. Oversaw resale accounts as well as direct user accounts. Involves identification and analysis of potential business applications within target accounts and cultivation of key business relationships with senior management to facilitate sales.

- Average performance over five year period was 125%.
- Grew Starbuck profits 200% over 5 years to $15M amidst decreasing unit pricing, increasing sales goals, and enhanced competition.
- Completed all five years in the top 12% of the National Account Channel as Golden Star Award winner.
- Created new revenue streams resulting in an estimated $30M in Starbuck sales and $40M in new services for the company.
- Regularly report sales results and status of strategies to senior marketing executives and CEO.

CHRIS SMITH
Page Two

STARBUCK COMPUTERS INC., Richmond, VA

1994 to 1997

Dealer Account Executive

As team leader and dealer liaison, oversaw completion of relationship building, bidding, delivery, and all sales efforts required to market Starbuck products and services through dealer locations.

- Initiated cooperative sales strategy with reseller business owners.
- Designed marketing promotions and directed reseller's sales efforts into business and education accounts.
- Average performance over six year period was 110% and recognized by Golden Star Club Awards.
- Grew sales by 400% to $20M.
- Oversaw training and completed performance reviews of 10-15 Sales Representatives.

1992 to 1994

Corporate Chain Account Sales Representative

Provided administrative and technical sales support to Richmond corporate chain account locations, including Power Electronics, Computer Corral, and Circonne Computer.

- Regularly called upon accounts to maximize knowledge of retail personnel, address concerns, and promote in-store visibility.
- Developed marketing promotions and trained store personnel.
- Tracked individual store sales and profit data to determine efficient coverage schedule and recognize particular achievements.

Summers and Part-time 1990 to 1992

Customer Support Representative

- Resolved customer issues including invoicing discrepancies, shipping errors, and upgrades for hardware.

EDUCATION

1988 to 1992

RANDOLPH-MACON WOMAN'S COLLEGE, Lynchburg, VA
B.A., Communications and Political Science, May 1992

Dana Johnson

123 Main Street • Apartment 13 • Hometown, NY 00000 • (555) 555-1234 • djohnson@company.com

Physical Profile and Languages

Height and Weight: 6' 2" and 190 lbs.
Build: Muscular and Athletic

Hair and Eyes: Dark Brown and Brown Eyes
Languages: Bilingual English-French

Film, Commercial, and Theatre Training

Scene Study with Jean Shelton
Advanced program with personalization, imagery, and character development training. Fall 1996. Comprehensive program involved group and individual performance, scene studies, character creation, auditioning, and stage direction exercises. Spring 2002.

EVN TV and Film Studios
Comprehensive 10-week program with Earl Nanhu, Canadian Actor, Teacher, and Director. Working with camera, enhanced acting fundamentals and audition techniques through scene studies as well as interactive group and individual exercises. Spring 2001.

Acting for the Camera and Auditioning Techniques
Presented by Squire Fridell, commercial actor. On camera, enhanced interactive group and individual exercises. Spring 2000.

Improvisation Workshops
Presented by Joel Lerer, film and commercial actor. Improvisational exercises to develop performance skills. Summers 1999-2001.

Film, Commercial, and Theatre Experience

Reason #403 Levi's Jeans Commercial	**Actor**	**Tool Shed Productions**

Action role in commercial directed by David Fox.

Canadian Football League Commercial	**Actor**	**CBC of Toronto**

Action role depicting various football skills and positions. Filmed at CBC Studios in Toronto.

Decoy	**Actor**	**Prism Productions of LA**

Speaking role in action vehicle starring Peter Weller and Robert Patrick. Filmed in Regina, Saskatchewan.

I Have A Dream Tribute	**Actor**	**MTV Productions**

Non-speaking role in tribute to Martin Luther King filmed in San Jose, California.

Professional and Collegiate Athletics

Canadian Football League Toronto Argonauts, 1999-2001, and **Saskatchewan Roughriders,** 1998-1999. **University of Pennsylvania NCAA Division I Football and Track,** 1995-1998.

Education

University of Pennsylvania, Philadelphia, PA
Bachelor of Arts, International Relations, 1998

DANA JOHNSON

123 Main Street • Hometown, NY 00000 • (555) 555-6509 • djohnson@company.com

Administrative Qualifications

- Skills and perspectives gained through progressively responsible administrative roles.
- Abilities to prioritize tasks and complete tasks accurately and on time in deadline-sensitive settings.
- Professionalism required to address concerns of patients and clients while maintaining office efficiency and following standardized procedures and policies.
- Flexibility required to transform instructions and feedback of diverse supervisors into projects completed independently and thoroughly.
- Capacities to use, support, and train others to use Word, WordPerfect, Excel, Access, and FileMaker Pro.

Administrative and Office Management Experience and Achievements

LOYALTY INVESTMENTS, Albany, NY
Administrative Assistant, 1998–present
- Provide administrative support for new business development group; assist CFO with special projects.
- Ensure smooth workflow; facilitate effectiveness of 14 sales consultants.
- Direct incoming calls; initiate new client application process; maintain applicant record database.
- Aided in streamlining application process.
- Assisted in design and implementation of computer automation system.

JENNINGS HOSPITAL, Washington, D.C.
Radiation Therapy Department Secretary, 1996–1998
- Answered phones, scheduled appointments, greeted patients and visitors, and prepared and filed charts.
- Typed and printed invoices and requisitions.
- Supervised inventory and general office organization.
- Served as liaison between physicians, staff, and patients.

Additional Business Experience

GROVER FINANCE, Buffalo, NY
Telemarketing Sales Representative, Summers and Part-time 1993–1996
- Secured new business using customer inquiries and mass-mailing responses; provided product line information to prospective clients. Initiated loan application and qualifying processes.
- Maintained daily call records and monthly sales breakdown.
- Acquired comprehensive product-line knowledge and ability to quickly assess customer needs and assemble appropriate financial packages.

Education

HOFSTRA UNIVERSITY, Hempstead, NY
Bachelor of Arts, English, Concentration: Business 1996
- Dean's List 2 of 4 eligible semesters and overall GPA 3.3

TRIBORO JUNIOR COLLEGE, Denver, CO
Associate of Arts, Business, 1994–1996

Francis Williams

123 Main Street • Hometown, New Jersey 00000 • (555) 555-1234 • fwilliams@company.com

OBJECTIVE
Senior Admissions and Enrollment Management Position.

ADMISSIONS ACHIEVEMENTS

1999 to present **Seton Hall University Office of Undergraduate Admissions**, South Orange, NJ
Senior Assistant Director of Admissions – Director of International Recruitment and Admission

- Develop, implement, and assess the annual recruitment plans for international admissions.
- Assist with the coordination of the international student orientation programs.
- Develop new international recruitment publications and coordinate the mailing calendar.
- Coordinate international application review and foreign credit evaluation for 1100 applicants annually.
- Manage all need-based and merit-based scholarship programs for international students.
- Conduct regular training sessions for counseling staff on issues regarding international admissions.
- Plan and execute international travel including alumni events and student interviews.
- Update and revise the University's undergraduate international admissions Web site.

1997 to 1999 **Seton Hall University Office of Undergraduate Admissions**, South Orange, NJ
Assistant Director of Admissions – Director of Transfer Recruitment and Admission

- Developed, implemented, and assessed the annual recruitment plans for transfer admissions.
- Created and coordinated the transfer open-house and orientation programs.
- Developed new transfer publications and coordinated the transfer mailing calendar.
- Automated the transfer program to track potential applicants straight through conversion.
- Developed and maintained articulation agreements with several two-year institutions.
- Coordinated the training of all counseling staff on issues regarding transfer admissions.
- Created and updated a transfer reference manual to accurately reflect changing guidelines.

1995 to 1997 **Rutgers, the State University of New Jersey, Office of Admissions,** New Brunswick, NJ
Admissions Counselor

- Coordinated the student ambassador program and supervised its 65 volunteers.
- Developed an overnight hosting program for campus events administered by the Admissions Office.
- Assisted with international application review and credential evaluation.
- Organized several phone-a-thons to assist Admissions with its recruitment activities.
- Managed a significant travel region for domestic recruitment.
- Conducted on-campus interviews and large group information sessions.

EDUCATION
Rutgers, the State University of New Jersey, New Brunswick, NJ
Bachelor of Arts, Economics, with International Relations Minor, 1995

University of North London, United Kingdom
Overseas studies program involving economics, history, and culture courses, 1992

PROFESSIONAL MEMBERSHIPS
- National Association of College Admissions Counselors (NACAC)
- New Jersey Association for College Admissions Counselors (NJACAC)

Advertising Account Executive

JAMIE BROWN

123 Main Street • Hometown, NY 00000 • (555) 555-1234 • jbrown@company.com
987 Centre Avenue • Apartment 13 • New York, NY 10001 • (555) 555-5678

ADVERTISING ACCOUNT MANAGEMENT QUALIFICATIONS

- Marketing research, strategic planning, promotions, customer service, and sales talents nurtured by in-depth and diverse advertising, promotions, and retail internships and employment.
- Skills gained via courses including: Principles of Marketing, Marketing Projects and Cases, Psychology of Human Motivation, Public Relations Writing, Advertising, and Consumer Behavior.
- Blend of research, analysis, writing, and presentation talents.
- German, French, Dutch, and Farsi fluency, and conversational Spanish capabilities.
- UNIX, HTML, Word, WordPerfect, Excel, PageMaker, PhotoShop, Netscape, and Internet skills.

ADVERTISING, MARKETING, AND FINANCE EXPERIENCE

DAYS ADVERTISING, INC., Pittsford, NY
Intern/Assistant to an Account Manager: Assisted with design of television and radio ads and proposals for varied clients, including Wegmans and Bausch & Lomb. Developed customer database. Summer 2001

ADEFFECTS, Rochester, NY
Intern/Assistant to an Account Manager: Researched and developed promotional materials for retail, manufacturing, and restaurant clients. Gained knowledge of small business marketing. Suggested changes in advertising materials, consumer outreach strategies, and marketing literature. May 2000–July 2001

THE FINANCIAL GROUP, INC. DISCOUNT BROKERAGE FIRM, Pittsford, NY
Intern/Assistant to Operations Manager, January–May 2001

PEARLE VISION CENTER, Pittsford, NY
Sales Representative: Assisted customers and ordered inventory targeting upscale market. Summer 2001

IT HAPPENS, Antwerp, Belgium
Marketing Intern: Determined target markets and developed advertisement budget for concert and entertainment agency. Collected and analyzed financial and marketing data. Conducted market surveys to determine market penetration. Assisted graphic artists with ads, posters, and brochures. Summer 1998

BUSINESS, ECONOMICS, AND LANGUAGE STUDIES

UNIVERSITY OF ROCHESTER, Rochester, NY
Bachelor of Arts, French, with a major GPA of 3.5, May 2002.
Bachelor of Arts, Psychology, with a major GPA of 3.3, May 2002.
Minor: **Economics,** with a minor GPA of 3.4.

WILLIAM E. SIMON GRADUATE SCHOOL OF BUSINESS ADMINISTRATION, Rochester, NY
Management Studies Certificate, Marketing and Finance/Accounting Tracks, May 2002.

HOBART AND WILLIAM SMITH COLLEGES, Geneva, NY
Completed varied Economics and Liberal Arts Courses prior to transferring, 1998–1999.

JAMIE BROWN

123 Main Street • Hometown, PA 00000 • (555) 555-1234 • jbrown@company.com

MEDIA PLANNING QUALIFICATIONS AND ACHIEVEMENTS

- Area of expertise is advertising media planning, with special knowledge of television and magazine options.
- Ability to project and elicit client enthusiasm and drive using a quantitative, yet common sense approach.
- Adept at analyzing client needs, demographics, pricing and account team strategies, and then developing appropriate courses of action to yield desired results.
- 7 years advertising media planning experience; handling accounts with up to $7 million annual budgets.
- Strong service and interpersonal skills with clients, colleagues, and media sales professionals.
- Proven supervisory skills, effectively training staff in new concepts and procedures, monitoring performance and maximizing output.
- Expertise associated with use of Word, Excel, Access, and PowerPoint for development of plans, proposals, budgets, financial analyses and projections, as well as presentations.

MEDIA PLANNING EXPERIENCE

THE MERCER MEDIA GROUP   Philadelphia, PA
Senior Media Planner   1992 to Present
- Direct all phases of media planning services for national accounts, primarily based in Eastern Region.
- Plan media and placement for 5 of the firm's largest clients, with annual media budgets ranging from $1 million to $7 million, and total media budgets in excess of $15 million.
- Oversee efforts of 2 Media Coordinators, a Media Assistant and 2 support professionals.
- Created Excel and Access systems to track media plans and purchases, client quarterly sales and profits.
- Regularly interact with account services colleagues and with clients to address queries, determine commitment to existing plans, and redirect plans as needed.

Account Supervisor and Media Coordinator   1990 to 1992
- Trained, guided, and directed staff of five while monitoring ad placement system.
- Assisted in creation of advertising campaigns and acted as liaison between client, agency and media vendors, including selection, budget and advertisement placement.

MERTON KASS & HOWE   Philadelphia, PA
Advertising and Public Relations Internship   Summers and Part-time 1988 to 1990
- Conducted market research, wrote press releases, produced traffic reports, worked media events and assisted with advertising production.

EDUCATION

RUTGERS UNIVERSITY AT CAMDEN   Camden, NJ
B.A. in Mass Communication, with a minor in English   1990

PROFESSIONAL AFFILIATION

The Advertising Club of Pennsylvania

Dana Johnson

123 Main Street • Hometown, VA 00000 • (555) 555-1234 • djohnson@company.com

MEDIA SALES AND PRODUCTION ACHIEVEMENTS

WCVT-TV (Channel 3)   Wise, VA
Senior Sales Account Executive   *1994-present*
- Established and maintained national corporate accounts as well as regional and local accounts
- Interacted with national NBC Sales, regularly identifying and leveraging new packages based on demographics and ratings
- Utilized production experience to establish and grow *Advertising for All* strategy targeting regional and local revenues, primarily generated from independently owned retailers and service providers
- Developed relationships with regional ad agencies, specifically media planners, to establish client-focused team approach
- Accounted for over $2 million in new clients revenues over 4-year period, and average annual revenues of $500,000
- Initiated and developed marketing strategies and target grid for the second ranked TV station in fifth largest market for effective sales programs/promotions

Sales Account Executive   *1993-1994*
Sold time and production support to potential clients
- Assisted with establishment of all media and production plans, proposals, and budgets submitted to potential and existing clients
- Implemented existing local, regional, and national strategies and media sales programs
- Increased sales and production revenues

Associate Director/Stage Manager   *1992-1993*
- Production Department Stage Manager for Noon, Five O'Clock, and News at Ten newscast, all public affairs programs, editorials, and news cut-ins
- Assembled sets and operated chyron machine

VNBC-TV (Channel 8)   Charlottesville, VA
Assistant to the Advertising Manager for Good Morning Charlottesville   *1990-1992*
- Prepared statistical analyses of advertising lineage for use in assessing competitive ranking
- Provided resource contact and encouragement to Sales Staff

VNBC-TV (Channel 8)   Charlottesville, VA
Production Intern   *1988-1990 Part-time and Summers*
- Wrote hard news, feature stories, scheduled/interviewed guests
- Researched materials and packaged tapes for production
- Operated teleprompter

Dana Johnson
Page Two

WNUV-TV (Channel 62)   Charlottesville. VA
University of Virginia Campus Cable Television and Radio Station Producer   *1987-1990*
- Responsible for researching materials for mini-documentary
- Scheduled and interviewed guests for round-table discussions
- Wrote and edited scripts and edited master tape

University of Virginia Campus Cable Television Production Assistant   *1986-1987*
- Performed as camera technician, stage manager, and teleprompter operator
- Assembled lighting and audio equipment

EDUCATION

UNIVERSITY OF VIRGINIA   Charlottesville, VA
B.A., Economics, with Afro-American Studies minor, magna cum laude   *1990*

PROFESSIONAL AFFILIATIONS

National Association of Media Workers
National Association of Broadcast Journalists

QUALIFICATION SUMMARY

- Record of success sourcing new accounts and building sales of existing accounts
- Abilities to translate demographic and rating statistics into projections of potential revenues for clients and media buyers
- Confidence interacting with clients, media buyers, national corporate representatives, and network media sales executives
- Capacity to use production experience to enhance first time television advertisers to purchase time and production services

Francis Williams

123 Main Street • Apartment 13 • Hometown, NY 00000 • (555) 555-1234
fwilliams@company.com

APPLICATIONS PROGRAMMING EXPERIENCE

BENTLEY LIFE INSURANCE, New York, NY

1998–Present   **Programmer Analyst/Senior Programmer**

Supervised junior programmers on varied PC Illustration System Projects.
- Developed, maintained, and supported Sales Illustration Systems in "C."
- Wrote "Illustration Software Installation" routine in INSTALIT software.
- Designed file transfer process for Mainframe to PC using NDM software.
- Hands-on experience with PC hardware, WS, MS Windows, IBM, OS/2, NovellSoftware, Emulation Software (Rumba, Extra, etc.), Dial-In Software (SimPC, XTalk, etc.) and have understanding of Token Ring LAN.
- Wrote DOS Batch files for Illustration Software Installation routine.
- Developed an Executive Information System on the mainframe using COBOL 2. Became familiar with mainframe production environment.

MEDWARE CORPORATION, New York, NY

1995–1998   **Senior Programmer - Patient Scheduling System**

Served as senior member of programming and testing team for software company specializing in health care industry.
- Designed and implemented system enhancements and new products.

1993–1995   **Programmer/Analyst**
- Developed on-line message system for members of the programming group.
- Instituted utilities that aided detection and repairs of client bugs.

SHADOW ASSOCIATES, Hartford, CT

Summers 1991, 1992   **Co-op Computer Programmer**
- Developed and maintained program that monitored product availability and inventory for branch sites, displaying new product releases, and accessing updated information daily.

GRADUATE AND UNDERGRADUATE ENGINEERING EDUCATION

NEW YORK UNIVERSITY, New York, NY

MS Electrical Engineering, Software and Networks emphases, 1995
BS Engineering, 1993

QUALIFICATIONS

- Knowledge of C, COBOL, COBOL II, Pascal, FORTRAN, Visual Basic, Assembly, CC+, Cajon, Pascal, LISP, IBM, PL/I, Prolog, AION Databases: SQL/DS, Oracle
- Effective design, resource allocation, and status evaluation skills associated with large projects that shaped production testing and data collection processes.
- Proficient designing and implementing program enhancements, including an on-line message system, database repair/troubleshooting utilities, and release system to update clients.

Corey Davis

123 Main Street • Hometown, NJ 00000 • (555) 555-1234 • cdavis@company.com

PROFESSIONAL PROFILE

- Over seven years in Architecture and Facility Management-related industries with emphasis in Computer Design Base, Education, and Communication.
- Skilled in three-dimensional CADD modeling and rendering.
- Particular ability to visualize in three dimensions and utilize computer software for design, budgeting, estimating, and project management activities.

PROFESSIONAL ARCHITECTURE EXPERIENCE

Computer Design Software, Inc.   **East Brunswick, NJ**

1996–Present   *Architect*

Provide industry consultation and implementation expertise in architecture and Facilities Management for firm developing, distributing, and providing user support for specialized software used by architects, contractors, and property managers.

- Assisted with development and testing of Computer-Aided Design and Database software
- Provided demonstration and technical support for pre- and post-sales activity
- Acted as subject matter expert for future software enhancements and requirements
- Served in leadership roles for various joint studies teaming with IBM and other major corporations in the evaluation of CDB software for architecture

Hanna, Olin and Sherman Architecture   **Philadelphia, PA**

1990–1996   *Architect*

Participated in conceptual design, design development and construction documentation of architecture and landscape design.

- Created exploration, analytical and presentation models materially and on computers for residential and commercial projects
- Fabricated sculptural wood and bronze detail elements installed in varied projects
- Projects included private residences, multifamily units, and professional offices

City of Philadelphia   **Philadelphia, PA**

1988–1990   *Building Inspector*

PROFESSIONAL REGISTRATIONS

Licensed Architect State of New Jersey Certificate 2344888

EDUCATION

University of Pennsylvania   **Philadelphia, PA**

Master of Architecture   *1988*

Massachusetts Institute of Technology   **Cambridge, MA**

Bachelor of Science, Architecture   *1986*

Art Instructor

CHRIS SMITH

123 Main Street ■ Hometown, IN 00000 ■ (555) 555-1234 ■ csmith@company.com

AREAS OF INSTRUCTIONAL EXPERTISE

- Eclectic experience teaching studio art, art appreciation, and art history within elementary and secondary public schools.
- Experience teaching studio art, crafts, and mixed media as private instructor and as director of special recreation program.
- Confidence developing group curriculum and exercises for students of varied ability levels, from beginner to expert.
- Expertise associated with media including: oil, acrylics, water colors, ceramics, and airbrush.
- Experience supervising student teachers, developing district-wide curricula, and advocating for funding.
- Capacities to translate passion into effective learning plans, utilizing varied modalities, and instructional techniques.

SCHOOL-BASED INSTRUCTION

GARY REGIONAL SCHOOL DISTRICT
Secondary Art Instructor

GARY, IN
1990-present

- Developed new and updated existing curriculum regularly for Studio Art, Art History, and Art Appreciation courses.
- Studio Art focused on composition, color, and conceptual problem solving, requiring completion of projects using varied media, including: charcoal, pen and ink, acrylics, and airbrush.
- Inventoried, ordered, and controlled budget of approximately $10,000 annually.
- Implemented curriculum with classes for gifted art students, including a district-wide art competition and scholarship in 1988.

Elementary Art Instructor

1986-1992

- Visited school sites on a regular basis, implementing a creativity-focused curriculum.
- Teamed with teachers to incorporate art projects and related lessons into existing units.

STUDIO AND RECREATION-BASED INSTRUCTION

ART DUDE STUDIOS
Private Art Instruction

GARY, IN
1996-present

- Planned and implemented private instruction focusing on talented teens and adults.
- Address specific portfolio development needs of students seeking admissions to and scholarships to art schools.

GARY PARKS AND RECREATIONAL ASSOCIATION
Summer Art Institute Director

GARY, IN
Summers 1988-1998

- Created and facilitated arts and crafts activity programs offered at 6 sites throughout the city.
- Media included sewing, weaving, knitting, sculpting, clay, jewelry, painting, and drawing.
- Successfully hired, trained, and directed 15 Arts Aides to supervise each site.

EDUCATION AND CERTIFICATIONS

INDIANA UNIVERSITY
Bachelor of Fine Arts in Studio Art, *cum laude*

BLOOMINGTON, IN
1984

State of Indiana Secondary Education Certification in Art — **1986**
State of Indiana Elementary Education Certification — **1984**

A RESUME DOCTOR'S BIO

Burton Jay Nadler

88 Wood Creek Drive • Rochester, NY 14534

Home (716) 248-9743 • Office (716) 275-2366

Fax (716) 461-3093 • BNadler@aol.com

Burt Nadler has been Assistant Dean of the College and Career Center Director at University of Rochester since 1998. UofR is annually ranked as among the top Comprehensive Universities in the nation. Prior, he was director of University of the Pacific's Career Services from 1990 through 1998. He considers himself an experienced "job search coach" and "Resume Doctor." Burt has been assistant director, MBA placement coordinator, and career counselor at Southern Methodist University, and associate director of Dartmouth's Career and Employment Services. As Director of Recruiting for Strategic Planning Associates, a management consulting firm, Burt recruited MBAs from some of the most prestigious schools of business. As Manager of College Recruiting and College Relations for Merrill Lynch Consumer Markets he recruited undergrads and grads for one of the largest financial services firms in the world. For almost 25 years he has actively examined "why candidates get hired and who does the hiring" from both sides of the college recruiting process. Specifically, he has focused curiosity and creativity on the tools and techniques that enhance the efforts of college students, recent grads and experienced job seekers.

As a job search coach he teaches and reinforces skills required for successful search, including resume writing, correspondence, and interviewing. For those he coaches "job search is simple, not necessarily easy," because the process is broken down into easy to follow (yet challenging) behavioral steps and easy to accept motivational attitudes. To date, he has critiqued over 9,552 resumes (he does count) and worked with over 15,000 job seekers (he guesses, but doesn't exaggerate).

Also, as reflected in his writings, presentations, and counseling style, Burt believes job search doesn't have to be taken *too* seriously and that it is best undertaken with humor and positive affect. His most recent writing project is *The Everything® Resume Book, 2nd Edition,* published by Adams Media. This is one of the most comprehensive and up-to-date guides that empowers readers to create effective resumes and use these tools as cornerstones for dynamic job search efforts. Burt also authored *Liberal Arts Jobs* and *Liberal Arts Power,* two top selling Peterson's job search publications which were re-released in an updated and merged format in 1998. *Naked at the Interview: Tips and Quizzes to Prepare You For Your First Real Job,* is another of Burt's books, released by John Wiley. Burt has shared ideas with students, alumni, recruiters, career services professionals, and "anyone who will listen" in a variety of traditional, creative, and virtual venues. He has been the "Resume Doctor" and "Interview Guru" for University of Dreams *(www.uofdreams.com)*; he exchanged ideas via the Internet as an "On-line Expert" for Career City and StudentCenter.com; he hosted *Job-Shock,* a campus radio show; and he has written articles on career and job search, appearing in *California Job Journal, Delta Sky Magazine, Journal of College Placement, Wall Street Journal's Managing Your Career, Careers and the MBA,* and *Careers and the College Grad.*

Burt has presented at conferences hosted by National Association of Colleges and Employers, National Association of Job Search Trainers, Western Placement Association, California Career Development Association, Japanese Exchange and Teaching Program Alumni, and Western Regional Greek Council.

He has conducted seminars for job seekers, recruiters, and career services professionals, enhancing recruiting efforts and teaching job search approaches. He has spoken to human resources and college recruiting professionals and employees at CitiBank, Hewlett Packard, and Disneyland. This job search coach, educator, and counselor has taught *Job Search Made Simple, Weeks of Work,* and *Senior Job Search Survival* courses, and he has facilitated numerous topical seminars and delivered motivational presentations at a number of colleges, universities, and high schools. If you would like to discuss a potential speaking engagement, call or email Burt.

Burt graduated *cum laude* from University of Pennsylvania in 1975, with dual undergraduate degrees in Psychology and Sociology. In 1977 he earned a MS in Education from Stanford University and in 1978 he earned a MA in Psychological Services from University of Pennsylvania. From 1981-1982 he supplemented his academics with additional doctoral coursework at Penn. He is the proud father of a daughter who attends Cornell University and a son who dreams of someday playing in an NCAA lacrosse championship game. For obvious reasons, recent personal attention has focused on exploring college admissions and application processes and on first-year foundations for college success.

Corey Davis

123 Main Street • Hometown, Illinois 00000 • 555-555-1234 • cdavis@company.com

OBJECTIVE

Banking loan officer, branch management, or training position.

QUALIFICATIONS

- Outstanding record of achieving sales goals as Branch Manager; successfully conducting residential and commercial mortgage acquisition and personal and commercial loan transactions and marketing programs.
- Extensive experience developing commercial lending packages for private clientele, including financial restructuring, REFI, equipment financing; coordinating activities with COMIDA, GCIDA, IBDC, and ESCDC, and attorneys, appraisers, title companies, and governments.
- Capacity to train, supervise, and motivate others to achieve maximum performance.
- Experience as branch manager, business development, and commercial lending officer and training officer.
- Comprehensive knowledge of Cook County consumer, industrial, and commercial clientele.
- Expertise to develop marketing strategies and collateral, internal management programs, and professional business plans through utilization of Word, Excel, and PowerPoint.
- Successfully developed and implemented marketing strategies and collateral material.

BRANCH, LOAN, AND TRAINING ACHIEVEMENTS

BIG BANK OF ILLINOIS, Chicago, IL
Branch Manager/Commercial Business Development Officer, 1989-1994
- Co-Managed District Officer Call Program to retain, expand, and track commercial customer base.
- Instituted Branch Neighborhood Equity Call Program, which enhanced sales of Home Equity and first and second mortgage products 33% over a 6-month period.
- Designed and managed District Product Development Program which included development of H.E.L.O.C., Home Equity Loans, residential mortgage products (2-Year Fixed ARM, 5-Year Fixed ARM), Business Installment Loan (BIL), and marketing collateral.
- Served as one of two Chicago Area Sales Trainers, supervising professional sales training program for 23 branch network which included Train-the-Trainer, market identification and definition, needs analysis, program development, implementation, results assessment, and follow-up responsibilities.

UNIVERSITY SAVINGS AND LOAN ASSOCIATION, Evanston, IL
Branch Manager/Mortgage Development Specialist, 1980-1989
- Developed Branch Neighborhood Equity Call Program to introduce and expand Home Equity Programs resulting in a 16% increase in Lines and Loans in first month.
- Designed and managed Branch Product Development and Customer Information and Sales incentives.

SECOND CITY SAVINGS BANK, Chicago, IL
Branch Manager/IRA Specialist, 1970-1980
- Designed brochures for IRA Marketing Program and instituted model for customer focus groups.
- Co-designed and managed new IRA Marketing strategies through Customer/Client Focus Groups.
- Managed overall loan operations of 3rd largest branch, with transactions averaging over $10 million per year.

FINANCIAL SERVICES ACHIEVEMENTS

ILLINI LOANS FINANCIAL ASSOCIATES, Chicago, IL
Owner, Part-time 1990-present
- Integrated all management, marketing, and client services efforts, including: insurance, commercial mortgage/equipment financing, coordinating SBA programs, factoring, lines of credit, Letters of Credit, warehousing, floor plans, leasing.
- Successfully placed loans for businesses of varied sizes, and individuals with diverse scenarios; ranging from $5,000 LOC to $25 million development of fruit processing factory.
- Utilized knowledge of cash flow, capital formation, marketing analysis, and lending procedures, marketing skills to successfully address client needs and resolve issues.
- Originated, processed, and coordinated all closing activities related to residential mortgage/home equity loans. Established working relationships with attorneys, appraisers, borrowers, and title companies.

CONSULTING ACHIEVEMENTS

UNITED WAY OF GREATER COOK COUNTY, Chicago, IL
Office Manager/United Airlines, January-September 2000
Area-Wide Interim Director/Cook and Area Counties, January-September 2000
- Served within Train-the-Trainer capacities, training selected individuals to perform United Way presentations, track results, and input payroll deduction data.
- Implemented IT Systems for input format and follow-up procedures.
- Scheduled and performed group presentations.
- Organized and facilitated board meetings and "Cabinet" meetings for both United Airlines, Cook, and neighboring counties.
- Established formal 3-Year Business Plan for each county to increase overall total annual contributions.
- Served as Business Development Officer.

PROFESSIONAL DEVELOPMENT AND EDUCATION

- Illinois Credit School; AIB/IFE courses in credit, insurance of accounts, mortgage, consumer and commercial lending principles, real estate law; Chicago Association of Agents and Brokers; Illinois State Certified Instructor/Sales; State of Illinois Notary Public
- University of Chicago, Bachelor of Science, 1970

JAMIE BROWN

123 Main Street • Hometown, MD 00000 • (555) 555-1234 • jbrown@company.com

BANKING QUALIFICATIONS

- Experience in customer service-focused teller roles, completing personal and commercial banking transactions.
- Confidence training and motivating teller colleagues.
- Specialized accounting courses supported by business curriculum.
- Knowledge of Excel, Lotus 123, Creative Solutions, Word, PowerPoint, as well as Tax and Internet applications.

BUSINESS, FINANCE, AND ACCOUNTING EDUCATION

UNIVERSITY OF MARYLAND, University Park, MD
Bachelor of Science in Business Administration, with Finance and Accounting emphases, anticipated May 2003

- Overall GPA: 3.7 and Finance and Accounting GPA: 3.7 (out of 4.0) and Dean's Honor Roll All Semesters
- Beta Gamma Sigma Business Honor Society President and Member
- Phi Kappa Phi Honor Society, Accounting Society, and Delta Sigma Pi Business Fraternity

SELECTED FINANCE, ACCOUNTING, AND BUSINESS COURSES

Money, Credit and Banking, Introduction to Marketing, Tax Accounting, Advanced Accounting, Intermediate Accounting, Auditing, Strategic Management, Cost Accounting, Financial Management, and Operations Management

BANKING AND ACCOUNTING EXPERIENCE

BANK OF MARYLAND, College Park, MD
Teller, Part-time 2000–present
Process account transactions, reconcile and deposit daily funds. Inform customers of bank products, refer public to designated personnel, provide account status data, and handle busy phone. Orient, train, supervise, and delegate tasks for new hires. Assisted with planning and implementing extended hours customer service strategies.

GORDON, ODOM & DAVIS, INC., Baltimore, MD
Accounting Intern, Spring 2002 and Fall 2002
Completed compilations, reviews, audits, and tax returns for individual and corporate clients. Created financial schedules and reports using Excel spreadsheet programs.

TRADER PUBLICATIONS, San Diego, CA
Accounting Assistant, Summer 2002
Compiled daily reports for magazine and advertising revenues. Completed Accounts Receivable and Payable efforts.

LEGAL AID SOCIETY, San Diego, CA
Bookkeeping Volunteer, Summer 2001

LAW RELATED EXPERIENCE

SULLIVAN, DELAFIELD, ET AL, San Diego, CA
Legal Assistant, Summer 2002–present

Francis Williams

123 Main Street, Apartment 13 • Hometown, CA 00000 • (555) 555-1234 • fwilliams@company.com

Bilingual Japanese-English Qualifications

- Bilingual Japanese-English talents gained working and studying Japan and via comprehensive academics.
- Research, data and trend analysis, report writing and presentation skills targeting bilingual audiences.
- Abilities to teach and tutor English as a Second Language to students of varied ages, ability levels.

Bilingual Experience and Achievements

2000-present   JAPAN EXTERNAL TRADE ORGANIZATION, San Francisco, CA
Analyst
- Conduct research for Information Alliance Technology Program, identifying and examining potential US-Japanese hi-tech firm linkages.
- Assist with annual and monthly Japan-US and Japan-California publications.
- Established and oversaw all efforts associated with monthly topical seminars addressing Japan-US commerce issues and featuring internationally recognized speakers.
- Serve as translator, transcribe documents, write correspondence, and complete projects.

1997-2000   ASIAN MARKETING RESEARCH, Belmont, CA and Tokyo, JAPAN
Bilingual English-Japanese Telephone Researcher
- Conducted surveys regarding views of Japanese executives on airline services, advertising options, computer hardware and services, and other topics.

Part-time 1996-2000   INTERNATIONAL INSTITUTE OF JAPAN, Tokyo, JAPAN
English Instructor for Non-English Speakers
- Taught high school and college students basic and advanced English conversation skills.

Summers 1998-1994   ASIAN MARKETING COMMUNICATION RESEARCH, Belmont, CA
Bilingual English-Japanese Telephone Researcher

1994-2000   INDEPENDENT LANGUAGE INSTRUCTION, Yokohama and Tokyo, JAPAN
English Tutor

Bilingual Education and Specialized Training

UNIVERSITY OF ARIZONA, Tucson, AZ
Graduate Coursework in Teaching English as a Second Language, 1993-1995

UNIVERSITY OF THE PACIFIC, Stockton, CA
Bachelor of Arts, Japanese, January 1994

UNIVERSITY OF CALIFORNIA SANTA CRUZ, Santa Cruz, CA
Intense Japanese Language Program, Summer 1992

KEIO UNIVERSITY, Tokyo, JAPAN
Completed Japanese Language Courses, 1992-1994

(Note: Resume in Japanese appears on reverse side.)

DANA JOHNSON

123 Main Street • Hometown, MN 00000 • (555) 555-1234 • djohnson@company.com

BOOKKEEPING QUALIFICATIONS

- Over 12 years of bookkeeping experience within progressively responsible roles.
- Experience overseeing comprehensive bookkeeping, including supervision of clerks and support staff.
- Capacities to address organizational finance related issues as well as those of individuals.
- Skills to develop financial data and summary findings on monthly, quarterly, and annual basis.
- Expertise associated with use of QuickBooks, Excel, TurboTax, and other financial software.

BOOKKEEPING EXPERIENCE

ASSOCIATES, INC.   EDEN PRAIRIE, MN
Senior Bookkeeper   **1994–Present**
- Oversee bookkeeping for mortgage and home equity loan firm, specializing in addressing first home purchases, debt consolidation, educational payment needs of clients from diverse financial backgrounds.
- Generate and present general ledger and investors' monthly reports for firm that generates over $10 million in mortgage and loan portfolios annually.
- Oversee A/R and A/P staff to ensure accuracy of accounts.
- Monitor efforts of third-party payroll services, checking accuracy of scheduled payments.
- Personally manage multiple accounts for major investor, real estate developer with commercial and residential properties in several states.
- Effectively interact with all finance savvy senior managers, specifically reporting to CFO.
- Support annual auditing and tax efforts of CPA firm.

MORNINGSIDE CO.   HOPKINS, MN
Bookkeeper   **1990–1994**
- Supervised general ledger through trial balance, as well as A/P, payroll, and payroll tax returns for construction and home improvement firm with annual revenues in excess of $2 million.
- Converted bookkeeping procedures from written documents to in-house computer system.
- Coordinated department's work flow, supervising A/R and A/P Clerks.
Accounts Receivable Clerk   **1989–1990**

THE DARNELL BANK   EDEN PRAIRIE, MN
Teller   **1985–1989**

EXCELSIOR CORP.   MANKATO, MN
Administrative Assistant   **1982–1985**

EDUCATION

SOUTHWEST STATE UNIVERSITY   MARSHALL, MN
Accounting and General Business Courses   **1985–1989**

FRANCIS WILLIAMS

123 Main Street, Apartment 13 • Hometown, CA 00000 • (555) 555-1234 • fwilliams@company.com

BUDGET ANALYSIS AND FINANCE ACHIEVEMENTS

1996-Present   Golden Life Insurance Company   Los Angeles, CA
Budget Analyst
- Balance $1.3 billion budget using internally developed and regularly revised software
- Reconcile accounts on ISA/ABC system to other financial systems
- Assist management in budget preparation
- Conduct training classes on the financial system for upper-level management
- Prepare comparison of expense to budget reports for executives on demand and on weekly, monthly and quarterly basis
- Submit accounts and IRS filing for the Political Action Committee.
- Generate financial analysis and reporting projects using Focus Report Writing and Lotus 1-2-3, including macro programming, and WordPerfect
- Contribute annually to budget development and strategic planning processes

1990-1996   The Pacific Group   Los Angeles, CA
Auditing Analyst
- Prepared contract proposals and illustrative cost calculations
- Constructed Actuarial Valuation and analyzed actuarial gains and losses
- Independently generated regular reports for 40 individual clients and oversaw development of reports for 60 corporate clients
- Determined the minimum and maximum contribution allowable by law for the IRS
- Assured accuracy of comprehensive financial information data base

1987-1990   *Accounting Technician*
- Maintained and reported on financial records and created financial statements associated with money market mutual fund for 60 corporate clients
- Balanced Trial Balance and generated journal entries
- Maintained, compared and reconciled the fund on three computer systems
- Assisted system analysts in preparation and implementation of new computer system

FINANCE AND BUSINESS EDUCATION

University of Washington   Seattle, WA
1987   *Bachelor of Science Degree in Finance*

QUALIFICATIONS SUMMARY

- Competencies required to track and balance a $1.3 billion budget
- Record of developing, utilizing and training others to use proprietary software and internalized systems for budget monitoring purposes
- Capacities to support executive decision making on budgeting
- Experience as regular contributor to groups making strategic financial plans
- Creativity associated with generating and explaining financial reports

COREY DAVIS

123 Main Street • Hometown, CO 00000 • (555) 555-1234 • cdavis@company.com

CASE MANAGEMENT AND ADVOCACY EXPERIENCE

THE WOMEN'S SAFE PLACE   GOLDEN, CO
Director of Case Management Services and Legal Advocate   *1990-Present*
- Provide counseling and referral services for residents of shelter for abused women and their children.
- Train and regularly interact with 24-hour hot line volunteers, supporting telephone crisis counseling and authorizing admission of residents on an emergency basis and for long-term transition periods.
- Conduct individual and group orientations, take case histories, and facilitate counseling sessions.
- Assist women completing Temporary Restraining Orders and serve as liaison with legal counsel.
- Provide expert testimony during domestic violence legal cases and report outcomes to staff.
- Assist with public relations and fundraising and regularly contribute to grant writing activities.

FAMILY SERVICES OF DENVER   DENVER, CO
Social Worker   *1985-1990*
- Provided services for clients and families with medical, psychological, housing, and financial needs.
- Supervised agency volunteers and graduate student interns.
- Worked collaboratively with various community agencies to provide needed serves.
- Conducted in-service training offered staff and those from other agencies.

GREATER GOLDEN SCHOOL DISTRICT   GOLDEN, CO
Case Manager   *1980-1985*
- Served within counseling and referral roles for at-risk students and their families.
- Coordinated outreach, intake, and referrals for those with financial, educational, and medical issues.
- Maintained detailed case records and statistics for reports distributed to district and state officials.

LIVINGSTON HIGH SCHOOL   GOLDEN, CO
School/Family Counselor   *1976-1980*
- Provided individual counseling related to scheduling, college applications, and behavioral issues.
- Coordinated parent-teacher conferences and conducted family conferences and counseling sessions.

SOCIAL WORK AND COUNSELOR TRAINING

COLORADO STATE UNIVERSITY   FORT COLLINS, CO
Master of Arts, Social Work   *1980*
Master of Arts, School Counseling   *1976*
Bachelor of Arts, Sociology, with a minor in Education *1975*

COLORADO COMMUNITY COLLEGE   DENVER, CO
Associate of Arts, Sociology   *1973*

CREDENTIALS, LICENSURE, AND AFFILIATIONS

- State of Colorado Licensed Social Worker and State of Colorado Counseling Certification
- American Association of Social Workers and State of Colorado Association of Social Workers

Certified Public Accountant

CHRIS SMITH, CPA

123 Main Street • Hometown, TX 00000 • (555) 555-1234 • csmith@company.com

ACCOUNTING QUALIFICATIONS

- Comprehensive experience in public and private accounting roles.
- Background in varied industries and specialized knowledge of engineering and oil and gas areas.
- Skills gained via audit, tax services, supervisory and training accomplishments.
- Specialized accounting degree supported by general business curriculum and updated by ongoing professional development.
- Knowledge of Excel, Supercalc, Lotus 123, Creative Solutions, Lacerte Tax Program, QuickBooks, Word, Access, FileMaker Pro, and WordPerfect.

ACCOUNTING EXPERIENCE

MASTERMIND ENGINEERING, Houston, TX   1992 to present
Accounting Manager: Complete SEC Reporting and Disclosure forms. Manage general ledger closing and maintenance. Supervise and review all accounting and finance areas. Administrate 401(K) pension plan. Implement accounting, payroll, and manufacturing software. Report directly to CFO, providing financial data and analytical reports to maximize profits and support managerial decisions. Hire, train, evaluate, and supervise accounting, bookkeeping, and analyst professionals.

DUNPHY & REILLY, INC., Houston, TX   1988 to 1992
Senior Internal Auditor: Conducted operational and financial audits of manufacturing subsidiaries. Designed and implemented audit programs to test the efficiency of all aspects of accounting controls. Recommended changes and improvements to corporate and divisional management. Trained and supervised staff auditors in all aspects of the audit engagement. Involved with corporate management in areas of acquisition and corporate development.

CHURCHILL NORTH, Houston, TX   1982 to 1988
Supervising Senior Accountant: Supervised, planned, and budgeted audit engagements. Oversaw and completed checks of audit reports, financial statements, and tax filings. Recruited, trained, supervised, and evaluated staff accountants. Gained experience from client assignments, including those in oil and gas, manufacturing, real estate, and nonprofit arenas. Proficient training use of spreadsheet packages. 1984 to 1988.
Senior Accountant: Served as liaison between Supervisor, Staff Accountants and clients. Assisted with preparation of financial statements, tax filings, and audit reports. 1982 to 1984.

GORDON, ODOM & DAVIS, INC., Austin, TX   1980 to 1982
Staff Accountant: Completed compilations, reviews, audits, and tax returns for individual and corporate clients. Created financial schedules and reports using Excel and Supercalc spreadsheet programs. Passed Audit, Law, and Theory portions of CPA exam at first sitting.

ACCOUNTING EDUCATION

UNIVERSITY OF TEXAS, Austin, TX
Bachelor of Science, Accountancy, May 1980

Jamie Brown

123 Main Street ■ Hometown, OR 00000 ■ (555) 555-1234 ■ jbrown@company.com

Professional Profile

- Over a decade of positions as pastry chef, bakery manager and related roles in varied venues.
- Thorough knowledge in the preparation of an extensive assortment of baked goods, including pastries, cookies, puddings, muffins, breads and specialties.
- Creative talents to develop attractive thematic, customer and event-inspired presentations.
- Experience addressing needs and budgets of restaurant, catering and retail bakery.
- Competencies to organize production and personnel to maximize use of space and finances.
- Recipient of numerous Culinary Awards for superior creations inspired by passion for excellence.

Pastry Chef Achievements

THE BEVENSHIRE HOTEL, Eugene, OR
Pastry Chef and Bakery Manager, 1999-present
- Plan and prepare desserts on a daily basis for restaurant patrons.
- Oversee all operations of retail bakery and prepare desserts and breads for catered functions.

DELTA PINES BAKERY & CAFE, Corvallis, OR
Pastry Chef, 1996-1999
- Prepared an extensive assortment of desserts, rotating on a weekly basis, including cakes, cookies, cobblers, puddings, tarts, special-order desserts and wedding cakes.
- Created breakfast pastries and breads for lunch specials.

THE PLUMROSE RESTAURANT, Corvallis, OR
Pastry Chef, 1994-1996
- Planned and executed monthly menu which included six desserts, two sorbets, two ice cream dishes and two fresh breads daily for lunch and dinner.
- Ordered all bakery and dairy supplies, and prepared desserts for retail store and special orders.

THE WILLARD HOTEL, Boston, MA
Assistant Pastry Chef, 1990-1994
- Work with executive pastry chef, monitoring baking, mixing and finishing of cakes, pastries and a full range of bakery products on an as-needed basis.
- Completed special orders for banquets, catered functions and Hotel Restaurant.

LE HOTEL DE VIVRE, Bangor, ME
Pastry Cook, 1988-1990

Culinary and Pastry Training

AMERICAN PASTRY ARTS CENTER, Medford, MA
Course in Chocolates and Candy, 1988-1990

GOURMET INSTITUTE OF AMERICA, Boston, MA
Associate of Culinary Arts, with Certificates in Food Services and Catering Management, 1988

Chris Smith

123 Main Street • Hometown, NY 00000 • (555) 555-1234 • csmith@company.com

Chemical and Environmental Engineering Qualifications

- Strong problem-solving skills acquired via engineering curriculum including varied special projects.
- Capacities to plan, implement, and report on the findings of individual or group projects.
- Confidence within engineering and science-focused settings, transforming instructions into detail-focused and accurately completed projects and reports.
- Academic and professional interest in energy efficiency, environmental issues, and quality assurance.
- Familiarity with Mathematica, MathCAD, Visual Basic, Excel, Word, Lotus.

Chemical Engineering Education

UNIVERSITY OF PENNSYLVANIA, Philadelphia, PA
Bachelor of Science in Chemical Engineering, minor in Environmental Engineering, with a cumulative GPA of 3.3, December 2001

Engineering Courses and Design Projects

Organic Chemistry, Quantum Chemistry, Atmospheric Chemistry, Physical Geology, Environmental Geology, Energy Resources & Utilities, Physics, Engineering Mechanics, Calculus, Multi-Dimensional Calculus, Differential Equations, Chemical Process Analysis, Thermodynamics, Chemical Reactor Design, Fluid Dynamics, Heat & Mass Transfer, Separation Processes, Process Control, Process Design

- **Steam heating system:** In group, designed steam heating system from a centralized power plant to a block of four buildings. Enhanced capacities to work in groups and apply concepts of fluid mechanics. Presented plan in written report. Spring 2000
- **Solar box cooker:** In group, designed and tested two solar box cooker prototypes. Refined capabilities to design, troubleshoot and test prototype, assessing the most efficient of two designs. Fall 2001
- **Geothermal heating system:** In group, developed paper design for residential home geothermal heating system. Fall 2001
- **Catalytic disproportionation process:** With partner, completed flow sheet design for a catalytic disproportionation process, identifying areas of potential energy savings. Presented findings in written report. Fall 2000

Engineering Experience

PENNSYLVANIA ENERGY RESEARCH AND DEVELOPMENT AUTHORITY, Harrisburg, PA
Energy Resources Division Intern, Summer 2001
- Examined petroleum and natural gas industry within NY State to determine appropriate allocation of funds to regional studies and projects.
- Visited various energy source sites including a wind plant, solar collection site, natural gas drilling site, and a biofuel plant.
- Collected, analyzed, and reported on results of survey of potential Appalachian natural gas supply.

Chris Smith **Page Two**

Collegiate Awards and Activities

- University of Pennsylvania Benjamin Franklin and Moore School of Engineering Scholarship
- National Merit Scholarship
- Social Chair of University of Pennsylvania Chapter of the American Institute of Chemical Engineers

Employment

H. L. GAGE SALES INC., Albany, NY
Office Assistant, Summer 1997-2000

UNIVERSITY OF ROCHESTER FITNESS CENTER, Rochester, NY
Student Supervisor/Fitness Instructor, 1998-2001

EAST GREENBUSH HEALTH & FITNESS, East Greenbush, NY
Fitness Instructor, Summer 1997-2000

Coach

Dana Johnson
123 Main Street • Hometown, NJ 00000 • (555) 555-1234

Field Hockey Coaching Profile

- Successful coaching experience at high school, collegiate, and US Olympic Developmental levels.
- Capabilities gained as Division III Head Coach and Division I Assistant Coach.
- Skills to plan practices, recruit, assess talent, enhance individual and team performance, and raise funds.
- Desire to utilize teaching techniques in practice and game situations.
- Abilities to develop popular and profitable camp programs.

Coaching Experience

2000 – Present
U.S. Futures Program – New Jersey and Delaware
2002 and 2001 Head Coach and 2000 Assistant Coach

1998 – 2002
United States Olympic Sports Festival, Minneapolis, MN and Los Angeles, CA
2002 Head Coach and 2000 Assistant Coach

1998 – Present
University of Delaware, Newark, DE
Assistant Field Hockey Coach and Assistant Field Hockey Camp Director
2002 Record 14 wins and 4 losses and 2001 Record 12 wins and 6 losses

1998 – Present
USA Olympic Developmental Camp
Coaching Staff D, C, and B Levels

1994 – 1998
Bentley College, Waltham, MA
Head Field Hockey Coach
1998 NCAA Division III Northeast Regional Champions, 1997 NCAA Final Four, and 1996 NCAA Division III Regional Finals

1994 – 1998
Waltham Academy, Waltham, MA
Varsity Field Hockey Coach
1998 Central Mass Division I Champions and Massachusetts State Semi-Finals and l987 Central Mass District III Quarterfinals and Wachusett League Champion

Education

2000
University of Delaware, Newark, DE
M.A. in Sport Sciences

1990 – 1994
Springfield College, Springfield, MA
B.S. cum laude in Health, Physical Education, and Recreation
Member of 1994 and 1993 USA Field Hockey Squad, Outstanding College Athletes of America 1994, Captain, 1993 – 1994, and Member, 1990 – 1993, Field Hockey Team

Teaching Experience

1994 – 1996
Waltham Public Schools, Waltham, MA
Physical Education Instructor

1993 – 1994
Student Teacher

Chris Smith

123 Main Street • Hometown, NY 00000 • (555) 555-1234 • csmith@company.com

EDUCATION, CO-CURRICULARS, AND HONORS

ALLENDALE COLUMBIA SCHOOL, Rochester, New York
Senior Year, 2000-2001
- Yearbook Editor-in-Chief
- Upper School Chorus
- Pittsford Crew Club Varsity Crew Team Member
- Varsity Swimming Team Member and Captain

Junior Year, 1999-2000
- Yearbook Sports/Special Events Editor
- Explorers Post Program in Psychology
- Upper School Chorus
- *Cum laude* Society and High Honor Roll
- Varsity Swimming Team Member and Captain and Varsity Crew Team Member
- Della Simpson Book Award for Excellence in English and History
- Student Life Committee Class Representative

Sophomore Year, 1998-1999
- Co-chair Holiday Bazaar—raised $1500 for Strong Children's Hospital
- Pittsford Crew and Varsity Swimming Team Member
- High Honor Roll
- Upper School Chorus
- Sophomore Class Forum Speaker

THE SANTA CATALINA SCHOOL, Monterrey, California
Freshman Year, 1997-1998
- Gold Cord Honor Roll and Top 10% of class
- Varsity Swimming Team Member
- Amnesty International
- Lower School Volunteer Aide
- Co-chair St. Patrick's Day Dance

THE MABEL BARRON SCHOOL, Stockton, California
2nd through 8th Grade, 1990-1998
- Student Council President, 1998, Council Secretary, 1997, Council Treasurer, 1996 and PTSA Student Member, 1997-98
- Amy Lina Award Winner, 1998

EMPLOYMENT

HARLEY SCHOOL, Pittsford, New York
Day Camp Counselor, Summers 2000 and 1998
- Planned and led activities and games for 5-6 year old campers
Youth Swim Instructor, Part-time 1998-present
- Prepared lessons, taught basic breathing and strokes and motivated 6-9 year old students

EDDIE BAUER, Victor, New York
Sales Associate, Summer 1999

HARRO EAST ATHLETIC CLUB, Rochester, New York
Lifeguard, Summer 1998

ATHLETICS ACHIEVEMENTS

ALLENDALE COLUMBIA SCHOOL, Pittsford, New York

Pittsford Crew, 2000-present
- Pittsford Crew, Founded Fall 1998, William C. Warren Boathouse, constructed 1999 by donations, team fundraisers and community support
- Compete in Western New York area regattas, Tail of the Fish, Cascadilla Invitational, New York State Scholastic Rowing Championships
- Port Side, Stroke, Club 4 New York State Scholastic Rowing Championship Gold Medal Winner
- Northeast Rowing Camp, Raymond, Maine, summer 2000; worked with Yale University and University of Miami coaches focused on rowing posture, connection, and slide control
- 8:19, 2k erg score
- 21.15.77 5k erg score

Varsity Swimming Team Member, 1998-present
- Section Five Athletic League, Male Season
- 500, 200, freestyle, 100 breaststroke
- school record, 400 freestyle relay, 200 medley relay, 200 freestyle relay

Captain, 1999-2000, 2000-2001
- Organized Team Activities Dinners, Served As Liaison Between Team And Coach, Helped Organize Fundraisers For Florida Training Trip

THE SANTA CATALINA SCHOOL, Monterrey, California

Varsity Swimming, 1997-1998
- 500, 200, freestyle, 100 breaststroke
- 3rd place, 100 breaststroke, league championships

TIGER ACQUATICS, Stockton, California

USS Swim Club Team Member, 1990-1997
- Age group, year round swim club
- Traveled throughout California for competitions

PERSONAL PROFILE

Born March 17th, 1984, in Hanover, New Hampshire. Lived in Washington, D.C.; Princeton, New Jersey; Stockton, California; and Rochester, New York. Attended all-girls boarding school freshman year. Traveled to Spain, France, and Italy. Enjoy reading, politics, sports, and music.

College Internship Resume

Corey Davis
123 Main Street • Hometown, NY 00000 • cdavis@company.com
987 Centre Avenue • Homeville, NJ 10001 • (555) 555-1234

OBJECTIVE

Summer Internship in biotechnology or biomedical engineering utilizing and expanding upon:
- Knowledge of and experience using basic physics and chemistry laboratory techniques and procedures.
- Skills gained from research project on the ethics of the human genome project.
- Abilities to conduct library research and document lab research efforts in detailed or summary notes.
- Experience with: spectrometer, oscilloscope, super conducting materials, and varied lab equipment.
- Word, Excel, Publisher, Mathematica, Works, Quicken, Medline, C++, DOS, UNIX, FTP, and Internet Skills.

BIOMEDICAL ENGINEERING AND SECONDARY EDUCATION

UNIVERSITY OF ROCHESTER, Rochester, NY
B.S. Biomedical Engineering, with concentration in Mechanical Engineering **Expected May 2004**
- Overall GPA: 3.58/4.0, Engineering GPA: 3.72/4.0, and Dean's List 3 Semesters.

COLUMBIA HIGH SCHOOL, Maplewood, NJ
High School Diploma, with Honors **June 2000**
- Graduated in top 10% with an overall GPA of 3.8/4.0, **and** SAT scores of 720 Verbal and 760 Math.
- Varsity Track-and-Field Team Member and Letter Recipient.

BIOMEDICAL ENGINEERING COURSES

Introduction to Biomedical Engineering, Introduction to Computer Programming, Engineering Mechanics I, Statics, Engineering Thermodynamics, Principles of Biology, Chemistry, and Physics

COLLEGIATE AWARDS AND ACTIVITIES

- Bausch and Lomb Scholarship for Science and Rush Rhees Scholarship for Secondary Achievement.
- Biomedical Engineering Society Member and Blood Drive Committee Chair.
- Men's Varsity Indoor/Outdoor Track and Field Team Member.

TECHNICAL AND MEDICAL EXPERIENCE

UNIVERSITY OF ROCHESTER MEDICAL CENTER, Rochester, NY **1999-2000**
E.G. Miner Library Computer Assistant: Address Windows and MacOS software and hardware issues.

TOWN OF SOUTH ORANGE, South Orange, NJ **1997-1999**
Emergency Medical Technician: Licensed to practice emergency medicine at the ambulatory level.

EMPLOYMENT

ACE HARDWARE, South Orange, NJ **1997-2001**
Sales Associate

FRANCIS WILLIAMS

123 Main Street • Hometown, PA 00000 • (555) 555-1234 • fwilliams@company.com

PROFESSIONAL PROFILE

- Instructional expertise at law school and undergraduate levels.
- Instruction and Research interests: Business Administration, Legal Studies, Criminal Law and Procedures, Supreme Court Rulings, Legal Trends and History
- Research, writing and presentation skills nurtured as author, lecturer, teacher, clerk debater, and mediator.

TEACHING AND LEGAL EXPERIENCE

DREXEL UNIVERSITY, Philadelphia, PA
Professor, 1998–Present
- Teach undergraduates Criminal Law, Criminal Procedures, Crime in America, and Business Law.
- Stimulate class involvement through use of case studies, mock trials, and law-school simulation.
- Annually serve as Freshman Advisor to diverse students and Faculty Advisor to Pre-law Majors.

UNIVERSITY OF PENNSYLVANIA SCHOOL OF LAW, Philadelphia, PA
Adjunct Professor, 1998–Present
- Teach Criminal Procedures to First-Year Students enrolled in the Evening Studies Program.

DICKINSON COLLEGE AND DICKINSON SCHOOL OF LAW, Carlisle, PA
Assistant Professor, 1995–1998
- Taught undergraduate courses in Business Administration and Law, including: Criminal Law, Crime in America; Courts and Criminal Law; Criminal Procedures; Crime in America; and The Courts.
- Taught First Year Law students Criminal Procedures and Juvenile Procedures.

JOHN CARROLL UNIVERSITY, University Heights, OH
Adjunct Professor, 1992–1995
- Taught Legal Writing, Criminal Procedures, and Legal Reasoning, to First-Year Students.

SUPREME COURT OF THE STATE OF OHIO, Columbus, OH
Clerk to the Honorable Justice Stanford Harvard, 1990–1992

SELECTED WRITINGS

- *Many Mondays in October: Supreme Court Trends in Criminal Rulings,* Law Texts Publishers, 2000
- *Undergraduate Studies of Criminal Procedures,* Law Texts Publishers, 1998

PROFESSIONAL, GRADUATE, AND UNDERGRADUATE STUDIES

JOHN CARROLL UNIVERSITY, University Heights, OH
Juris Doctor Degree 5th in a Class of 300, with Highest Honors, 1990
- Editor Law Review, 1992–1993, Law Review Staff, 1991–1992 and T.A. for Criminal Procedures, 1991–1993

CASE WESTERN RESERVE UNIVERSITY, Cleveland, OH
Master of Arts in Business Administration, with Honors, 1987
Bachelor of Science in Criminal Justice, *summa cum laude,* 1985

JAMIE BROWN

123 Main Street • Hometown, AR 00000 • (555) 555-4432 • jbrown@company.com

OBJECTIVE

Computer Programmer

PROFESSIONAL EXPERIENCE

1999–present   PUBLIC AUTHORITY FOR CIVIL INFORMATION, Little Rock, AR
Technical Manager
- Maintained over 300 assembler modules and developed 75.
- Formulated screen manager program, using Assembler and Natural languages, to trace input and output to the VTAM buffer.
- Developed program to monitor complete security control blocks, using Assembler and Natural.
- Produced a standalone IPL and created a backrest on IBM 3380 DASD.

1991–99   STATE OF ARKANSAS, Fayetteville, AR
Systems Programmer
- Initiated start-up and implemented operations.
- Designed and managed implementation of a network providing the legal community with a direct line to Supreme Court cases.
- Developed a system that catalogued entire library's inventory.
- Used C++ to create a registration system for a university registrar.

EDUCATION AND PROFESSIONAL DEVELOPMENT

ARKANSAS TECH UNIVERSITY, Russellville City, AR
Completed varied programming courses, 1997-present

UNIVERSITY OF ARKANSAS AT PINE BLUFF, Pine Bluff, AR
Bachelor of Science, Mathematics and Computer Science, 1997

CODING AND COMPUTER SCIENCE COURSES

Advanced IBM 370 Assembler, SNA Fundamentals, MVS/ESA Architecture, Natural 2 Programming Language, MVS/XA Concepts and Facilities, MVS/XA Job Control Language, MVS/XA System Problem Determination, ACFNTAM Concepts, MVS/XA Using Utility Programs, MVS/XA Using and Creating Procedures

OPERATING SYSTEMS, LANGUAGES AND SOFTWARE

DOS, Windows, UNIX, C++, Java, Visual Basic, Assembler. Database: Access, Oracle, dBASE, RoboHELP. Other: Word, Excel, Lotus 1-2-3

Dana Johnson, Psy.D.

123 Main Street • Hometown, FL 00000 • (555) 555-1212 • djohnson@company.com

PROFESSIONAL PROFILE

Bilingual English-Spanish psychologist who has served youth and adult populations within agency, clinical, and school settings. Experienced individual and group therapist within community programs offering services to clients from diverse socioeconomic and psychosocial backgrounds. Assessment, training, and referral professional; school counselor; and teacher of English as a Second Language.

QUALIFICATIONS, CLIENTELE, AND THERAPEUTIC STRATEGIES

Eclectic graduate and undergraduate studies focusing on family dynamics, rationale, emotive, and behavioral strategies. Background in family therapy, general psychotherapy, and assessment and treatment of behavioral and deficit disorders. Skilled developing and implementing treatment plans in social service and educational arenas. Experience coordinating service networks and collaborating with health-service professionals. Completed case management training with the Department of Social Services.

DOCTORAL, MASTERS, AND UNDERGRADUATE STUDIES

Nova University, Fort Lauderdale, FL
Psy.D., Counseling Psychology, 1995
MA, Counseling Psychology, with Community Clinical Concentration, 1992

Barry University, Miami Shores, Florida
BA, with Developmental Psychology and Human Development dual majors, cum laude, 1983

CLINICAL EXPERIENCE

1996-present   **Mental Health Services of Ft. Lauderdale,** Ft. Lauderdale, FL
Counseling Psychologist: Facilitate individual and group counseling for clients diagnosed with varied neurotic, psychotic, developmental, and behavioral disorders. Collaborate with health-service professionals to development treatment plans for emotionally disturbed adolescents. Assist clients in developing survival skills to aid transition from residential to independent living. Coordinate service networks for academic, psychological, and social assistance.

1994-1996   **Tyler Adoption Agency,** Miami Beach, FL
Counselor: Served as assessment, recruitment, and referral specialist. Traveled to community sites and executed presentations to recruit prospective parents for minority children. Conducted testing and home studies of prospective parents to determine eligibility. Followed up for evaluation purposes 3 months, 6 months, 1 year, and 2 years post-adoption. Served as referral source to private and public mental health services as needed.

1990-1994   **Dade County, Department of Social Services,** Miami Beach, FL
Bilingual Case Worker: Assessed client needs, developed treatment plans, and managed cases. Communicated with court officials. Served as child advocate for court proceedings.

Dana Johnson, Psy.D.
Page Two

MULTICULTURAL SCHOOL COUNSELING AND TEACHING EXPERIENCE

1987-1990   **American School of Recife,** Recife, Brazil
International Primary School Counselor: Administered psychological and educational testing for students ranging from prekindergarten to 5th grades. Counseled students, families, and teachers. Designed remedial and therapeutic plans. Led group activities for self-image enhancement and behavior modification. Worked with teachers on preventive strategies for social and disciplinary problems.

Institute of America, Sao Paulo, Brazil
1984-1987   *Guidance Counselor and English as a Second Language Instructor:* Counseled students and families for clientele ranging from prekindergarten to 12th grade. Administered psychological and educational testing. Designed complete record-keeping system for all students. Implemented behavior modification programs. Administered achievement, vocational, and college prep tests. Made policy on admissions and discipline. Worked with teachers on individual educational and behavioral programs. Taught English as a Second Language to students in grades 3 through 6.

Credit Analyst

Corey Davis
123 Main Street • Hometown, OH 00000 • (555) 555-1234 • cdavis@company.com

CREDIT ANALYSIS AND FINANCE QUALIFICATIONS

- Over 10 years' experience in retail banking and commercial lending.
- Specialized expertise associated with credit and financial analysis and use of modeling and regression analysis to assess risk and project rates.
- Proficient analyzing financial statements, assessing risk, and evaluating credit worthiness.
- Experience using Excel, Lotus 1-2-3, and internal systems for analyses and creating supporting illustrations for credit reports and presentations to colleagues and board.
- Experience using Dutch fluency and German conversation skills in business contexts.
- Naturalized U.S. Citizen.

FINANCE, ACCOUNTING, AND BUSINESS DEGREES

OHIO STATE UNIVERSITY GRADUATE SCHOOL OF MANAGEMENT, Columbus, OH
Master of Business Administration, with Finance Concentration, May 1998
- Completed Executive MBA Program with Honors, for Finance and Overall GPAs of 4.0.
- Courses included: International Finance, Money and Capital Markets, Investment, Corporate Finance, Corporate Financial Reporting, and Global Macroeconomics.

OHIO STATE UNIVERSITY, Columbus, OH
Bachelor of Science, Business Administration, with Accounting Concentration, 1990

BANKING AND CREDIT ANALYSIS ACCOMPLISHMENTS

WISTERIA BANK, Grace City, OH
Senior Credit Analyst, 1998-Present
- Oversee efforts of 8 Analysts working on commercial and personal lending teams.
- Review all documentation and recommendations before final determinations are rendered.
- Calculate and track positive and negative yield statistics, reporting findings to management.

Commercial Loan Credit Analyst, 1995-1998
- As member of lending team, analyzed and evaluated financial statements.
- Developed proforma statements and cash-flow projections.
- Documented findings; prepared independent recommendations on advisability of granting credits for corporate lenders.

Senior Personal Banker, 1992-1995
- Monitored overdraft reports, reviewed and executed consumer loans, supervised vault area, audited tellers, and provided customer service.

Personal Banker, 1990-1992
- Established and serviced professional clientele accounts. Expedited investments in treasury bills, repurchase agreements, CD's, retirement accounts, and discount brokerage for bank clients. Assisted branch corporate lender weekly on a revolving commercial loan.

Chris Smith

123 Main Street • Hometown, CO 00000 • (555) 555-5555 • Cell (555) 555-9999

DAY CARE QUALIFICATIONS AND COMPETENCIES

- Over 9 years of experience within home and school settings, teaching and caring for children aged 2 months to 7 years.
- Commitment to needs of infants, preschoolers, and kindergarteners and record reflecting learning and loving.
- Background including courses in Childhood Development, Early Childhood Education, and Educational Psychology.
- CPR/First Aid certified and valid driver's license, with perfect driving record.

DAY CARE, TEACHING, AND CHILD CARE EXPERIENCE

1999–present PRIVATE RESIDENCE, Livermore, CO
Nanny: Care for twin boys from the age of two months through two years. Provide environmental enrichment, personal care, and play supervision.
- Accompanied family on numerous trips and cared for children during illnesses.

1997–1999 BABY BEAR PRESCHOOL, Keystone, CO
Teacher: Taught infant, preschool, and after-school programs. Planned curriculum, organized activities, communicated with parents and staff regarding children's growth and development.
- Responded to annual increase in students and move to new facility.
- Worked with owner on goals and assisted with annual licensing documentation and visitation.

1995–1997 THIS LITTLE PIGGY DAYCARE CENTER, Dove Creek, CO
Teacher: Planned and implemented infant program, blending developmental with custodial needs. Communicated with parents and colleagues regarding daily progress of children.
- Enhanced skills development through interactive play and song.

1993–1995 THE KID CORRAL, Wild Horse, CO
Teacher: Planned and implemented curriculum for toddler program. Enriched children's experiences through play, music, and art.

SPECIAL CARE EXPERIENCE

1995–present COALITION FOR RETARDED CITIZENS, Ivywild, CO
Volunteer

EDUCATION

1990–1993 METROPOLITAN STATE COLLEGE, Denver, CO
- Completed 30 credits in Education, with an emphasis on the day care setting.

REFERENCES

William and Sarah Smithers, (555) 555-4444, smithers123@company.com
Sue Bear, Owner, Baby Bear Preschool, (555) 555-1244, bbear@company.com

Dental Hygienist

Francis Williams

123 Main Street • Hometown, NJ 00000 • (555) 555-1234

DENTAL HYGIENIST QUALIFICATIONS

- Progressively responsible experience as a Hygienist, Assistant, and Office Administrator.
- Sound knowledge of medical terminology and clinical procedures.
- Certified in first aid, cardiopulmonary resuscitation, and electrocardiography.
- Additional experience as receptionist/secretary with an executive search/management consulting firm, financial management company, and realty firms.

LICENSURE

- New Jersey Dental Hygiene License National Board Dental Hygiene Exam (Written: 90)
- N.E.R.B. Dental Hygiene Exam (Clinical: 93; Written: 90)

DENTAL HYGIENE AND OFFICE MANAGEMENT EXPERIENCE

HERBERT DICKEY, D.D.S.   Brooklyn, NY
Dental Hygienist, Surgical Dental Assistant, and Assistant Office Manager   1999–present
- Provide state-of-the-art individualized prophylaxis treatment to adult and adolescent patients.
- Administer teeth cleaning, gum massage, oral hygiene education, and periodontal scaling procedures and supervise interns undertaking similar procedures.
- Schedule patients for appointments for surgical procedures and provide presurgical preparation.
- Record temperature and blood pressure, insert intravenous units, and administer sedatives.
- Provide postoperative care in person and via telephone follow-up.
- Record vital signs every 10 minutes until patient is conscious; establish patient comfort; provide necessary information to patients regarding new medications and possible side effects.
- Handle accounts payable and receivable and health insurance transactions.

DR. RETTMAN, D.M.D.   Upper Montclair, NJ
Dental Hygienist   1998–99
- Provided prophylaxis treatment, teeth cleaning, oral hygiene education, and periodontal scaling.
- Administer Novocain prior to painful procedures.
Dental Assistant   1996–98
- Assisted dentist in prophylactic procedures: provided necessary tools, sterilized equipment, comforted patients.
- Provided secretarial assistance, same as above.
Dental Trainee/Extern   1994–96
- Initially, served in rudimentary observation and support roles, then advanced to Dental Assistant.
- Sterilized instruments, processed X rays, scheduled appointments, maintained patient relations.

PROFESSIONAL TRAINING

KELLY SCHOOL OF DENTAL HYGIENE, New York, NY
A.S. in Dental Hygiene   June, 1996
Coursework included Radiology, Periodontology, Pathology, Dental Equipment, Oral Biology, and Pharmacology.

Dentist

Chris Smith, D.D.S.

123 Main Street • Hometown, WA 00000 • (555) 555-1234 • csmith@company.com

PROFESSIONAL DENTISTRY EXPERIENCE

1990-Present   PAYNE DENTAL ASSOCIATES, Bellingham, WA
Owner—General Practice
- Purchased large dental practice through a leveraged buy-out.
- Determined and successfully implemented long-term growth strategies.
- Supervised a staff consisting of two other dentists and six support personnel.
- Provided comprehensive care for over 2000 patients.
- Lead the office in steadily increasing production and revenues.
- Updated practice and computerized equipment.
- Presently facilitating transition of practice to new owner.

1988-1996   SEATTLE UNIVERSITY DENTAL SCHOOL, Seattle, WA
Clinical Instructor and Assistant Dental Clinic Director
- Supervised clinic with rotating groups of dental students and support personnel.
- Evaluated student performance via videotape voice-overs and written reports.
- Annually analyzed financial viability of clinic, instituted regularly revised plans to increase profitability, and managed business related activities.

1986-1988   UNIFIED DENTAL CENTERS, Moses Lake, WA
Dentist
- Provided comprehensive dental care and trained staff members.
- Developed marketing plan, established and allocated marketing budget, and oversaw business operations of practice composed of one dentist, one hygienist, and one support professional.

1981-1986   UNIVERSITY OF WASHINGTON, Seattle, WA
Instructor of Clinical Periodontics
- Supervised small groups of students during their first contact with patients.
- Developed lessons, demonstrated periodontal procedures, and evaluated students.

PROFESSIONAL AND UNDERGRADUATE EDUCATION

UNIVERSITY OF WASHINGTON SCHOOL OF DENTISTRY, Seattle, WA
Doctor of Dental Surgery, 1981
- Completed comprehensive studies, including 2000 hours of clinical experience.
- Graduated 10th in a class of 400.
- Served as Mentor for 1st and 2nd Year Students.

SEATTLE INSTITUTE OF TECHNOLOGY, Seattle, WA
Bachelor of Science Degree, Biology, 1977

Corey Davis

123 Main Street • Hometown, CA 00000 • (555) 555-5340 • cdavis@company.com

Editing, Writing, and Reporting Qualifications

- Research, writing, and editorial talents for interviewing, fact checking, script writing, and proofreading.
- Book, magazine, newspaper, and broadcast writing and editing experience.
- Confidence drafting, editing, and finalizing news, features, and sports stories.
- Production experience within varied print and broadcast media.
- Abilities gained through graduate studies and positions within magazine, newspaper, and television.
- Bilingual Spanish-English skills as well as MacOS, Windows, Internet capabilities.

Editorial, Writing, and Reporting Experience

BOOKS R COOL, INC., Long Beach, CA
Senior Editor, 2002-Present
- Evaluate general trade reference titles and assess profit potential, acquire titles, and negotiate contracts.
- Oversee publication, from development and editing to production, publicity, and marketing.
- Serve as in-house editor for internal and external newsletters and Web documentation.

BOP and BB MAGAZINES, Studio City, CA
Staff Writer, 2000-2002
- Wrote and researched music- and celebrity-related stories.
- Interviewed various celebrities and wrote and maintained a monthly column.

TEEN MAGAZINE, Los Angeles, CA
Editorial Assistant, 1999-2000

THE BEACON HILL TIMES, Boston, MA
Reporting Intern, 1998

WHDH CHANNEL 7 NEWS, Boston, MA
Reporting and Production Intern, 1997

Professional Development

- New York University Graduate Publishing Program, 1997-Present.
- American Society of Magazine Editors Junior Editorial Seminar Series, Summer 1999.
- American Society of Newspaper Editors Training Seminars, 1997-Present.

Graduate and Undergraduate English and Communication Degrees

SIMMONS COLLEGE, Boston, MA
Master of Arts, English, January 1998

UNIVERSITY OF THE PACIFIC, Stockton, CA
Bachelor of Arts, Communication, with English minor, May 1996

Jamie Brown

123 Main Street • Hometown, Texas 00000 • (555) 555-9873 • jbrown@company.com

ELECTRICAL ENGINEERING QUALIFICATIONS

- Success leading product development efforts for commercial, OEM, and government markets.
- Experience administering research and development activities, managing vendor and partner technology relationships, and satisfying customer expectations.
- A decade of project management, design, testing, and troubleshooting experience.
- Specialized knowledge of microprocessor development, marketing, and implementation.

ELECTRICAL ENGINEERING ACCOMPLISHMENTS

AEROSPACE SYSTEMS, Dallas, Texas
Systems Engineering OEM Section Manager, 1994–present

- Managed development of customized versions of personal computer products meeting requirements of OEM customers, Japanese, and United States government agencies.
- Supplied personal computer products with customized security and networking functionality.
- Provided OEM customers with problem-solving support and systems integration engineering.
- Managed development of laptop PC in support of US Navy Lightweight Computer Unit.

Design Evaluation Manager, 1990–1994

- Managed development support engineering group established to complete personal computer competitive analysis and design verification testing.
- Developed competitive analysis process resulting in more compact computer designs.
- Initiated test processes including electrostatic discharge; conducted susceptibility, emissions, and related problem solving to meet regulatory requirements.
- Developed test plans and processes to verify functionality of computer products.

BELL SYSTEMS, Arlington, Texas
Senior Principal Design Engineer, 1986–90

- Developed bus architecture enhancements to a Goldstone 10000-based in-store processor to meet customer performance requirements.
- Developed Goldstone 15000 based cluster terminal controller, emulating an IBM 3050.
- Developed a PCL 2/6 Channel interface in partnership with Expectations, Inc.

MITASHA CORPORATION, Galveston, Texas
Microcontroller Operations Product Engineer, 1984–1986

- Designed wafer-sort production test hardware for the 6235 microcontrollers, incorporated as a plug-in card to a test system.
- Developed test process improvements, resulting in 85% gross margin and less returns.

AIR DESIGN CORPORATION, Houston, Texas
Electrical Engineer Coop Student, Summer 1983

ENGINEERING EDUCATION

MASSACHUSETTS INSTITUTE OF TECHNOLOGY, Cambridge, MA
Bachelor of Science, Electrical Engineering, *cum laude,* June 1984

Chris Smith

123 Main Street • Hometown, MA 00000 • (555) 555-9873

Teaching Qualifications and Achievements

- Certification in Elementary Education, Music, and Secondary English.
- Experience teaching Elementary, Junior High, and High School Students.
- Competencies teaching choral and instrumental classes and directed choirs and bands.
- Success developing youth music programs by creating musicals tailored to student abilities.
- Musicals involved students composing, acting, choreographing, playing instruments, and singing.
- As classroom and private teacher, used audio-visual and electric piano computer systems.
- Formed **Music & More,** a civic musical theater company composed of multicultural youth.
- Accomplished pianist, singer, accompanist, conductor, composer, and writer.

Music Teaching Experience

1977-present   E.M. VOICE AND PIANO, Boston, MA
                Voice and Piano Teacher
- Instruct approximately 70 voice, piano, and composition students.
- Present 6 recitals annually, working with students to select and prepare performance pieces.
- Regularly use video and electronic piano computer system to provide audio and visual feedback.
- Students applied for admissions, auditioned for, and attended selective music programs; then progressed to professional performance and composition.

1985-94   MASSACHUSETTS METHODIST CHURCH, Boston, MA
                Director of Youth Choirs
- Prepared and conducted weekly rehearsals and performances for students grades K-12.
- Composed and directed 8 Christmas Pageants televised on local station.

1987-89   "MUSIC AND MORE," Boston, MA
                Musical Director
- Founded after-school musical theater company for students grades 2-12.
- Composed, directed, and accompanied original scores and scripts for various productions.

1972-77   CHESTNUT HILL SCHOOLS, Chestnut Hill, MA
                Primary Schools Choral Director/Show Choir Director
- Directed choral groups associated with 6 elementary schools.
- Introduced students kindergarten through 2nd grades to music appreciation and vocal performance.
- Nurtured vocal performance skills within students 3rd grades through 6th grades.
- Oversaw extracurricular Show Choir composed of approximately 175 students grades 9-12.
- Coached students in composing, choreographing, and performing original musicals.

Education and Credentials

Berklee College of Music, Boston, MA
Master of Music, 1978, and Bachelor of Music, 1970

Massachusetts Elementary and Secondary Teaching Credentials with certification in Music and English

Dana Johnson

123 Main Street • Hometown, CA 00000 • (555) 555-5543 • djohnson@company.com

EMERGENCY MEDICAL QUALIFICATIONS

- Knowledge of and experience implementing state-of-the-art Emergency Medical procedures.
- Proven capabilities assisting in emergency childbirth and heart attacks.
- Familiar with procedures for critical burns, shock, gunshot wounds, physical manifestations of child abuse, and spousal battering.
- Provide emergency treatment for rape victims while staying within the guidelines of the law.
- Certified to teach and administer CPR.

EMERGENCY MEDICAL EXPERIENCE

DOLAN AMBULANCE SERVICES, Visalia, CA
Head Emergency Medical Technician, 1998-present

RUSSELL AMBULANCE SERVICES, Modesto, CA
Emergency Medical Technician, 1996-1998

MEDICAL LICENSES, CERTIFICATIONS, AND EDUCATION

- Certified, EMT License Visalia Hospital, 1996
- License # 4490223 State of California, 1996

MODESTO JUNIOR COLLEGE, Modesto, CA
Emergency Medical Technician Certification Program, 1995-1996

ATHLETIC TRAINING EXPERIENCE

UNIVERSITY OF THE PACIFIC ATHLETIC TRAINING INTERNSHIP, Stockton, CA
Sports Medicine Clinic, 1992-1995
Men's and Women's Tennis, Spring 1994 and 1995
Men's Basketball, Fall 1994 and 1995

- California Interscholastic Federation Wrestling Tournament, Spring 1993, 1994, and 1995
- Northern California Sectional High School Basketball Tournament, Spring 1993, 1994, and 1995
- Nike Volleyball Festival, Spring 1993, 1994, and 1995

ATHLETIC TRAINING EDUCATION

UNIVERSITY OF THE PACIFIC, Stockton, CA
Bachelor of Arts, Sport Sciences, with Biology minor, June 1995

Executive Assistant

Chris Smith

123 Main Street • Hometown, PA 00000 • (555) 555-1234 • csmith@company.com

OBJECTIVE

Executive Secretary Position

QUALIFICATIONS AND CAPABILITIES

- Extensive knowledge of bank administrative policies and procedures through six years of experience.
- Able to supervise employees and work with all levels of management in a professional, diplomatic, and tactful manner. Rapidly analyze/recognize department problems and solutions.
- Work on multiple projects under pressure and meet strict deadlines and budget requirements.
- Literate in WordPerfect, Word, Excel, PowerPoint, MultiMate, Sidekick, Spotlight, and Symphony.
- Confidence drafting and proofreading correspondence.
- Proficient using shorthand, dictation machines, and multifunction calculators.

ADMINISTRATIVE SUPPORT EXPERIENCE

ERIE SAVINGS BANK, Erie, PA
Administrative Assistant to the Chief Executive Officer, 1998-present
Coordinated and prioritized daily activities of Board Chairman. Performed administrative functions in support of CEO. Required an in-depth knowledge of the bank, financial community, investors, and customers. Assisted with preparation for Board of Directors and Shareholder meetings. Recorded and distributed minutes of Board, Shareholder, and Executive Committee meetings. Maintained CEO's travel and appointment schedule, using computerized scheduling system.
Executive Secretary to the Senior Vice Present Commercial Division, 1994-1998
Set up Commercial Loans on System. Prepared monthly reports for Board of Directors. Updated financial statements. Maintained appraisal files. Coordinated loan renewals.

SPARTAN TRUST COMPANY, Erie, PA
Administrative Assistant to the President and Chief Executive Officer, 1990-1994
Prioritized daily activities of CEO. Set up and maintained "tickler system." Composed, and edited correspondence for President. Assisted CEO with sensitive customer and employee relationships. Recorded and distributed Management Committee minutes. Maintained and distributed monthly department reports.
Executive Secretary to Executive Vice-President and Senior Loan Officer, 1986-1990
Managed secretarial staff supporting Commercial Loan Officers. Coordinated staff meetings and presentations to Board of Directors. Prepared monthly departmental and divisional reports for distribution. Updated and maintained Policy and Procedure Manual on a timely basis.
Commercial Finance Assistant, 1983-1986
Prepared daily client loan advances and payment activity. Maintained client loan/collateral statements. Assisted with preparation of departmental reports and loan agreements.

EDUCATION

PENNSYLVANIA STATE UNIVERSITY PITTSBURGH CAMPUS, Pittsburgh, PA
Continuing Education Program Participant, 1981-1986

ERIE INSTITUTE OF BUSINESS STUDIES, Pittsburgh, PA
Associate of Arts, Administrative Studies, 1981

Chris Smith

123 Main Street • Suite 234 • Hometown, NE • (555) 555-1234 • csmith@company.com

OBJECTIVE

Financial Analyst Position

FINANCE, ACCOUNTING, AND RELATED QUALIFICATIONS

- Experience working as liaison with accounting, treasury, and finance professionals.
- Confidence collecting and analyzing data to identify trends, make projections, and assist with managerial decision making.
- Specialized knowledge of banking industry, regulations, and auditing techniques.
- Abilities to use and teach others Excel, Lotus 1-2-3, Word, WordStar, and Lotus Macros.

FINANCE AND BANKING EXPERIENCE

September 2000 to Present

BRIDELL BANK AND TRUST CO., Omaha, NE
Comptrollers Division Corporate Accounting Analyst
- Prepared and analyzed income statements, balance sheets, and earnings schedules for $9 billion corporation.
- Compiled 10k federal reserve, management, and analyst reports.
- Utilized trend reports to analyze balance sheet and income statement key ratios.

September 1997 to August 2000

CARTEL BANK, Wayne, NE
Intern Audit Trainee
- Conducted audits to complete Federal and State regulatory documentation associated with the FDIC.
- Assessed efficacy of policies and procedures related to fiscal, regulatory, and customer service standards.
- Gained knowledge of operating procedures associated with departments including Personal Banking, Small Business Banking, and Home Equity Loans.

Summers 1995 and 1997

Account Group Intern
- Supported efforts of Relationship Managers, servicing depositors with accounts in excess of $500,000.
- Supported transactions and addressed inquiries, developed reports and assisted colleagues and customers.

FINANCE AND BUSINESS EDUCATION

UNIVERSITY OF NEBRASKA AT OMAHA, Omaha, NE
Bachelor of Science, Finance, May 1997
Selected Courses: Tax Accounting, Advanced and Intermediate Accounting, Auditing, Strategic Management, Cost Accounting, Financial Management, International Business, and Operations Management.

UNIVERSITY OF ROCHESTER'S EUROPEAN INTERNSHIP PROGRAM, Rome, Italy
Completed banking internship while studying Italian language, economics, and history.

Financial Planner

Francis Williams

123 Main Street • Hometown, New Jersey 00000
(555) 555-0987 • fwilliams@company.com

Financial Planning Qualifications and Credentials

- Over a decade of progressively significant roles and achievements within planning, portfolio management, and client services.
- Personal responsibilities for more than $210 million in client assets.
- Recognized for outstanding asset-based performance and customer service.
- After completion of ABC Financial Consultant Sales Training and Advanced Training, served as trainer and curriculum developer.
- Licensed Series 6,7,63 and health and life insurance.

Financial Planning Accomplishments

ABC FINANCIAL CONSULTANTS, Princeton, NJ

1990–present **Financial Consultant/Financial Planner**

Serve in comprehensive financial planning and roles. Oversee individual and group portfolios. Serve as manager, supervisor, and trainer within corporate headquarters of firm responsible for over $800 million in client assets.

- Developed $210 million client asset base through aggressive prospecting and targeting campaign.
- Successfully built portfolio that includes stock, bonds, options, and insurance products for more than 450 clients.
- Gained expertise associated with estate planning, asset allocation, and wealth succession.

1988–1990 **Sales Associate**

- Worked directly with firm's top producer, profiling high net worth individuals for future business.
- Generated $90,000 for top producer through new account openings.
- Analyzed existing portfolio, assisting in development of accounts.

1987–1988 **Account Executive Trainee/Intern**

- Completed more than 35,000 account transactions annually.
- Completed comprehensive training related to trade settlement, NASD regulations, and customer service.
- Acted as liaison between sales force and New York operations.

Summers 1986 and 1987 MAPLEWOOD INVESTMENTS, Maplewood, NJ
Prospecting Intern

Education IONA COLLEGE, Iona, New York
Bachelor of Arts in Economics, with Concentration in Management, 1988

CHRIS SMITH

123 Main Street • Hometown, TN 00000 • (555) 555-1234 • csmith@company.com

HUMAN RESOURCES EXPERIENCE

TENNESSEE MUTUAL INSURANCE   MEMPHIS, TN
Director of Human Resources and Staff Development   **1997-Present**
Develop and implement overall human resource policies. Provide leadership in the areas of personnel, payroll, labor relations, training, and affirmative action for operations with over 2,000 employees. Administer personnel and payroll procedures, policies and systems to meet management and employee needs. Consult with Chairman, Executive Board, managerial staff, and supervisors to ensure policy compliance with applicable statutes, rules, and regulations. Advance agency Affirmative Action Plan. Determine appropriate grievance procedures required to resolve labor disputes. Act as liaison for regulatory agencies: EOHS, OER, DPA, State Office of A.A., and PERA. Maintain staff training program. Interface with Legal Staff when addressing discipline and grievances.

WILMONT INSURANCE CO.   NASHVILLE, TN
Director of Human Resources   **1987-1997**
Oversaw hiring, training, and all personnel responsibilities for insurance broker with 400 employees. Determined technology and procedures related to maintaining and updating personnel files, ensuring compliance with federal and state regulations pertaining to benefits and wages. Supervised grievance adjudication. Performed claim payment internal audits. Coordinated activity with reinsurance carriers.
Central Personnel Administrator   **1985-1987**
Coordinated statewide reclassification study. Organized questionnaires and individual interviews. Evaluated, analyzed and rewrote job descriptions; prepared study package for senior management approval. Established related managerial files. Dealt with diverse personnel-related projects.

DEPARTMENT OF EMPLOYMENT AND TRAINING   NASHVILLE, TN
Supervisor   **1982-1985**
Claims Adjudicator   **1980-1982**

HUMAN RESOURCE AND BUSINESS EDUCATION

MILLIGAN COLLEGE   MILLIGAN, TN
Course work in Personnel Management and Human Resources   **1990-Present**

TENNESSEE WESLEYAN COLLEGE   NASHVILLE, TN
B.A. Management, with Personnel Track   **1980**

PROFESSIONAL PROFILE

- Over 15 years of human resource experience; 5 as a Director of comprehensive programs.
- Expertise recruiting, training, performance reviews, compensation and affirmative action.
- Capacities to work with senior management to develop, implement and monitor HR strategies.
- Specialized knowledge of issues, policies and procedures associated with the insurance industry.
- Commitment to ongoing professional development through continued courses and seminars.

Jamie Brown

123 Main Street • Hometown, IL 00000 • (555) 555-1234 • jbrown@company.com

OBJECTIVE
Human Services Counselor/Administrator Position.

QUALIFICATIONS
- Comprehensive case management experience for juveniles and families.
- Expertise assessing cases, developing treatment plans, facilitating crisis intervention procedures and family therapy.
- Diverse counseling skills applicable to developmental and physical disabilities, and substance abuse.
- Experience with child abuse and neglect cases, as well as the needs of developmentally disabled youth.

EXPERIENCE

1988 to Present   SOCIETY FOR PREVENTION OF CRUELTY TO CHILDREN, Chicago, IL
Investigator/Case Manager
- Conduct assessments and develop treatment plans for family caseload.
- Maintain documentation of contracts and provide crisis intervention and family therapy.
- Serve as advocate for clients in court and with community agencies.

1986 to 1987   FARMINGTON JUVENILE COURT, Farmington, IL
Intern
- Tracked abuse/neglect cases to ensure that status reports and petitions were filed accurately and on time.
- Observed court hearings and trials and established court expectations.

1985 to 1986   PEORIA JUVENILE COURT, Peoria, IL
Intern
- Provided individual and group counseling for juvenile offenders in detention.
- Reviewed, updated, and cited findings of case files and incident reports.

1997 to Present   TEMPORARY RESOURCES, Peoria, IL
Human Service Worker
- As "temp," served clients in hospitals, day programs, and private residences.
- Counseled and supervised adolescents in group homes and serve as substitute teacher at institutions such as the Stafford School for the Deaf.

1995 to 1998   ALLIED GROUP HOMES, Columbus, IN
Residential Manager
- Worked in several residential programs for all levels of developmentally delayed clients.
- Counseled and taught daily living, hygiene, and community awareness skills.

Summers 1993 to 1995   DEPARTMENT OF MENTAL HEALTH, Gardena, IL
Intern
- Assisted developmentally delayed adults, encouraging development of self-sufficiency.

EDUCATION
BRADLEY UNIVERSITY, Peoria, IL
Bachelor of Science, Human Services, 1995

Corey Davis

123 Main Street • Hometown, AZ 00000 • (555) 555-8767 • cdavis@company.com

Underwriting Qualifications

- Underwriting and analytical skills, sales and marketing knowledge, and technical skills exhibited throughout past 20 years.
- Record of productivity and profitability in progressively responsible positions.
- Efficient supervisor, planner, organizer, and manager of time, projects, and professional peers.

Underwriting and Marketing Experience and Achievements

SCRIMSHAW INSURANCE CO., Tempe, AZ

1998-present **Personal Lines Insurance Underwriter**
- Analyzed all personal lines of business to determine acceptability and to control, restrict, or decline, according to company guidelines.
- Supervised all personal lines of business for Arizona and New Mexico.
- Kept current with changing policies, rates, and procedures, explaining coverage, rules, forms, and decisions to agents, staff, and insured.

1996-98 **Manual Rating and Policy Writing Supervisor**
- Delegated responsibilities, set objectives, and monitored work.
- Evaluated performance, established supervisory controls, and conducted audits.
- Implemented staff briefings, ongoing training, and updating materials.

CALIFORNIA INDEMNITY INSURANCE COMPANY, Sacramento, CA

1991-96 **Senior Marketing Representative**
- Managed assigned territory including prospecting new distribution sources, rehabilitating nonperforming agencies, and terminating relationships.
- Served in lead role for all insured sales presentations by conducting strategy negotiations, making presentations, and facilitating actual presentation.

1989-91 **Underwriting Manager-Commercial and Special Accounts**
1987-89 **Senior Underwriter**
- Developed book of $25,000 to $1,000,000 SIR deductible contracts.
- Served as Property/Inland Marine Specialist for Division by handling all referrals, audits, and facultative reinsurance negotiations.

FIREMAN'S FUND INSURANCE COMPANY, Sacramento, CA

1984-87 **Commercial Underwriter/Inland Marine Specialist**
1980-84 **Personal Lines Underwriter/Client Customer Service Representative**

Professional Development, Seminars, and Education

- Insurance 21, 22, and 23 Courses, Underwriting School (6-week program), Senior Underwriting Seminar, Listening Seminar, Supervisory Seminar.
- Bachelor of Arts, University of Phoenix, 1988

Laboratory Technician

Chris Smith

123 Main Street • Hometown, Ohio 00000 • (555) 555-6654 • csmith@company.com

Laboratory and Technical Expertise

- Proven ability in analysis, scientific theories, and procedures.
- Experience collecting and studying data from various biological sources.
- Proficient at producing and processing blood components.
- Skilled at performing tissue experiments using electron microscopy.
- Quickly and accurately learn and perform complicated tasks.
- Understanding of the differences between research within biotechnology and academic research.
- Knowledge and experience implementing SEC-HPLC techniques with Millennium software.
- Experience organizing, writing, and editing detailed reports and research papers.
- Trainer for biochemists in routine blood-banking procedures.
- Experience within Web design, graphic arts, layout, and related roles.
- Capacities to use, teach others, and support: Excel, Word, PowerPoint, PhotoShop, PageMaker, In Design, Omni Page Pro, Director, Flash, DreamWeaver and Internet applications.

Laboratory and Technical Experience

American Red Cross, Cleveland, OH
Laboratory technician: produce and process blood components. Label and release for transfusion and manufacture. Perform viral immunology testing and irradiation of blood products. 2001-present

Biogen Inc., Cambridge, MA
Analytical Development Department Intern: qualified an SEC-HPLC method with subtraction of a tween peak in an Avonex formulation for use in the Quality Control Department. Edited images using PhotoShop to illustrate a PowerPoint presentation delivered to corporate colleagues and internship peers. Summer 2001

Case Western Reserve University Hospital, Cleveland, OH
Department of Biochemistry and Molecular Biology Intern: Expressed proteins in E. Coli for use in protein translocation projects. Performed SDS-Page gels and Western blots to test protein expression. Summer 2000

Teaching and Computer Experience

Case Western Reserve University, Cleveland, OH
Biochemistry Laboratory Teaching Assistant: Assisted students in biochemistry laboratory. Worked with professors to prepare materials for use in the laboratory and graded quizzes and laboratory reports. Created web page allowing students access to test results, 2001-2002
Educational Technology Consultant: Assisted faculty and students with computer related problems with scanning and photographic manipulations. 2000-2002

Biological Sciences Education

Case Western Reserve University, Cleveland, OH
Bachelor of Science, Biology/Chemistry, with a major GPA of 3.3, May 2001
Courses include: Organic Chemistry I and II, Molecular Cell Biology, Biochemistry, Molecular Biology, Anatomy, Physiology, Biochemistry Laboratory, Immunology, and Topics of Biological Macromolecules.

DANA JOHNSON

123 Main Street • Hometown, NM 00000 • (555) 555-1234 • djohnson@company.com

LOCAL AREA NETWORK AND TECHNICAL COMPETENCIES

- Expertise designing and developing multi-user database management systems on Local Area Networks.
- Skilled in LAN management and USER training.
- Skills gained from post-baccalaureate courses including: Advanced Digital Electronics, C Language Hands-On Workshop, Visual BASIC programming, and Structured Analysis and Design Methods.
- Knowledge of IBM PC Compatibles, Tape Backup, Local Area Networks, MS-DOS, Lotus 1-2-3, dBase III, DBXL\Quicksilver, Clipper, C, Netware 3.11, Windows, Visual BASE, and SQL.

TECHNICAL EXPERIENCE AND ACHIEVEMENTS

JEFFERSON MANUFACTURING CORP., Albuquerque, NM
LAN Coordinator, 1998-Present
- Analyze, develop, and maintain application software for engineering LAN.
- Provide training and user support for all applications to LAN users.
- Maintain departmental PC workstations including software installation and upgrades.
- Reduced data entry errors and process time by developing an online program allowing program manager to submit model number information.
- Replaced time-consuming daily review board meetings by developing a program which allowed engineers to review and approve model and component changes online.
- Developed an on-line program which reduced process time, standardized part usage, and which allowed engineers to build part list for new products and components.

Computer Systems Analyst, 1994-1998
- Completed database management, systems analysis and design, workstation maintenance and repair, and LAN management tasks.
- Reduced process time and purchasing errors by developing an on-line program which allowed the purchasing department to track the status of all purchasing invoices.
- Developed purchase order program for that improved data entry speed and reduced data entry errors.

LAFAYETTE, INC., Albuquerque, NM
Engineering Technician, 1989-1994
- Prototyped and tested new PC products, drawing schematics and expediting parts for these new PC products. Designed and coded multi-user database management software for engineering use.
- Expedited the parts for 25 or more telecommunications terminal prototypes. Built, troubleshot, and transferred those prototypes to various departments for testing.

ELECTRONICS AND TECHNICAL EDUCATION

UNIVERSITY OF NEW MEXICO, Albuquerque, NM
Bachelor of Science, Electronics, 1994

SAN THOMAS COMMUNITY COLLEGE, Albuquerque, NM
Associate of Arts, Electronics Technology, 1990

Francis Williams

123 Main Street • Hometown, VT 00000 • (555) 555-1234 • fwilliams@company.com

PROFESSIONAL PROFILE

- Library professional with community, secondary school and university experience.
- Capacities to translate services, policies and procedures into patron focused and educational outcomes.
- Specialized focus on community outreach, patron education, program planning and public speaking roles.
- Experience using and instructing peers and patrons to use NLM Classification System, ALA filing rules as well as various indexes and Internet resources.

LIBRARY EXPERIENCE AND ACHIEVEMENTS

KATHRYN F. BELL LIBRARY, Burlington, VT
Librarian, 1996 to present
- Provide excellent patron services when covering circulation and reference desks.
- Give instructional guidance to patrons, including use of computerized and manual index tools and catalogs.
- Focus interactions on empowering and instructing patrons while creating positive relationships.
- Address reference questions by demonstrating proper Internet and printed resources.
- Plan and present regular community education programs.
- Record incoming periodicals and journals on computerized system and strip resources for security.
- Compile statistics on door count, circulation, photocopies, and reference activities.
- Serve on Acquisition Committee and provide quarterly and annual recommendation to Budget Committee.

Evening Librarian, 1994 to 1996
- Performed overall patron services and library operations, and supervised the evening clerk.
- Compiled and circulated specialized reference packet for series of community health seminars.

EAST CATHOLIC HIGH SCHOOL, Rutland, VT
Librarian/Audio Visual Coordinator, 1990 to 1994
- Supervised comprehensive secondary school library, overseeing volunteer, professional and student staffs.
- Established annual educational plans and regularly supported instructional efforts of teachers.
- Completed daily patron services and operations efforts and supervised student study periods.
- Interacted with Budget Committee to establish and monitor annual budgets.
- Ordered publications as well as software, and maintained audio-visual equipment.

SIMMONS COLLEGE, Boston, MA
Library Graduate Intern, 1989 to 1990
- Via supervised rotations, learned about reference, periodical, acquisition, and special collection areas.
- Researched, wrote and presented four special reports to library professionals and graduate student peers.

EDUCATION

SIMMONS COLLEGE, Boston, MA
Masters of Library Science, 1990

UNIVERSITY OF VERMONT, Burlington, VT
Bachelor of Arts in English, 1988

Management Consultant

Jamie Brown

123 Main Street NW • Apartment 12 • Hometown, VA 00000 • (555) 555-6777 • jbrown@company.com

Consulting
Experience

American Management Systems
Washington, D.C.

Senior Consultant Government Practice
2000–Present

- Ensured operational readiness of a division of the Internal Revenue System by preparing a staffing gap analysis and developing a database to record staffing demand of new organization; prepared package to submit new organizational design charts and functional statements to Commissioner.
- Developed operational policies, procedures, and responsibilities handbook for IRS management.
- Developed survey tool to baseline office characteristics.

Consultant
1998–2000

- Evaluated underutilization of grant funds for Housing and Urban Development program. Analyzed grant expenditure data, developed hypotheses, led interviews, and wrote sections of final report.
- Provided analytical and technical support to Department of Energy, Office of Environmental Management. Tracked appropriations legislation, managed the research, maintenance, and production of a portion of EM's FY 2000 Budget Request that was submitted to Congress.

Research Analyst
1997–1998

- Developed organizational redesign and change management initiatives for the District of Columbia, Metropolitan Police Department. Facilitated client team working groups, conducted best practices research, developed data collection and analysis tools, and developed new process diagrams.

Computer
Experience

University of Rochester Press
Rochester, NY

Web Developer
Fall 1996

- Developed first ever Web page, including HTML tool, provided general public access to UR Press publication profiles and order forms, and enabled authors and editors to submit work.

Government
Experience

Labour Party Headquarters
London, England

Intern
Spring 1966

Democratic Congressional Campaign Committee
Washington, D.C.

Intern
Spring 1995

Education

University of Rochester
Rochester, NY

Bachelor of Arts in Political Science, with Concentration in Journalism, cum laude *1997*

European Programs Abroad
London, England

Overseas Studies Program Participant
1996

Qualifications

- Ability to manage cases from evaluation and data collection to analysis, presentation, and implementation.
- Significant knowledge of government systems, structures, funding, and organizational oversights.
- Ability to use Excel and Access to create financial models and related databases and Word, PowerPoint, Project, WordPerfect, Visio, LexisNexis for research, presentation development, and report writing.

Dana Johnson

123 Main Street • Hometown, NC 00000 • (555) 555-3456 • djohnson@company.com

Management Information Systems Profile

- Extensive and diverse computer hardware and software knowledge related to personal computer usage within business and educational settings.
- Expertise assessing hardware and software needs, estimating costs, purchasing, and installing.
- Capacities to hire, train, and monitor performance of Information Systems professionals.
- Experience working with outside consultants, service and product vendors, and third-party temporary and permanent placement agencies.
- Ability to use, teach, and support programming languages, operating systems, network configurations, as well as word-processing, Internet, database, and spreadsheet applications.

Technical Qualifications

- Programming Languages: Borland C, C++, Qbasic, FORTRAN, and WordBasic.
- Operating Systems: Windows and DOS, MacOS, and Novell Netware.
- Database: FoxPro, askSAM, Access, and FileMaker Pro.
- Spreadsheet: Lotus 123 and Excel.
- Word Processing: WordPerfect, Word for Windows, and Word for Mac.
- Presentation and Publishing: Quark Xpress, PageMaker, PowerPoint.
- Web Page Development: PageMill and Fireworks.

Summary of Achievements

- Researched, wrote, and edited proposal used to identify needs and fund networks and desktop configurations composed of 8 personal computers and two printers.
- Supervise 3 Technology and Systems Consultants for office with 30 full-time employees.
- Planned and oversaw completion of special project teams related to existing and future technology needs and potential purchases.
- Regularly conduct software- and hardware-related troubleshooting and audit activities.
- Interact with product vendors and customer service and technology support professionals.
- Designed 24/7 backup and retrieval system for accounting databases and word-processing data.

Management Information Systems Experience

Maximum Data Systems, Charlotte, NC
Information Systems Manager, 1996-present

Touchestone Systems, Inc., Charlotte, NC
Computer Consultant, 1994-1996

Gilford College, Greensboro, NC
Introduction to Computer Science Instructor, Part-time and Summers 1993-1995

Information Technology Consultant, Part-time 1992-1994

Education

Duke University, Durham, NC
Bachelor of Science, Computer Science, June 1994

COREY DAVIS

123 Main Street • Hometown, OR 00000 • (555) 555-1234

Brand Management Accomplishments

- Accountabilities include P&L for $500 million covering 100+ film products and 80+ cameras.
- Developed and implemented comprehensive annual marketing and strategic plans covering 150 products.
- Delivered and executed 5 national marketing plans and 25 new product launches.
- Created 4 new imaging categories and negotiated $40 million in first year sales with a projected 20% increase in high tech market sales in newly established distribution.
- Fully profiled and conducted outreach to 30 multi-location customers and won them back to Cressidine, securing $20 million in sales.
- As Product Manager of the International Division, traveled for 5 years between 5 South American countries and 10 European subsidiaries building product launch plans and developing relationships and knowledge of foreign customs and business protocols.
- Provide leadership for national sales force of 500+.
- Mentored and promoted numerous managers into key positions.

Brand Management and Marketing Experience

CRESSIDINE CORPORATION   Corvallis, OR
Brand Manager and Director of Marketing Operations for Technical Imaging   *1992-Present*
- Spearhead implementation of corporate objectives within the Technical Imaging Division.
- Conceive and energize all marketing strategies and provide feedback on program performance and recommendations to corporate senior managers.
- Direct and supervise staff of 10 with responsibilities for generating $250 million in sales with a $150 million margin for core products.
- Prepare and effectively control a $7 million marketing expense and a $4 million advertising budget.
- Created first end-user direct mail strategy generating a 30% response rate and selling 400,000 units in first year.
- Mounted trade show exhibitions including designing booths, collateral materials, and advertisements. Secured $200,000 in pre-booked sales within a month of trade show presentations for 4 new products.

Group Marketing Manager for Technical Imaging   *1988-1992*
- Responsible for developing relationships with major imaging companies and securing long term contracts for core products within a vertical market framework.
- Directed and monitored new product launch programs: developed pricing and selling strategies.
- Fostered and maintained key account relations.

Business, Marketing, and Management Studies

UNIVERSITY OF OREGON   Eugene, OR
Masters of Business Administration   *1990*
Bachelor of Science in Business Administration   *1988*

CHRIS SMITH

123 Main Street • Hometown, NH 00000 • (555) 555-1234 • csmith@company.com

PROFESSIONAL PROFILE

- Expertise conducting research required to develop strategically sound business plans and used to generate capital.
- Confidence addressing consumer product, health care, government agencies, and non-profit issues.
- Capacities to develop state-of-the-art statistically viable projects and cite findings in comprehensive reports.

MARKET RESEARCH ACHIEVEMENTS

2001-Present SEARCHER ASSOCIATES, Ossipee, NH

Market Research Consultant: Established firm, conducted client outreach, recruited 3 associates, and oversee all operations activities. Build consumer behavior models using multivariate techniques, including regression and discriminate analysis, and cluster analysis. Analyze data from national survey to identify purchase intents and patterns for business to consumer direct marketers. Present information to senior management of client organizations. Specialized in entrepreneurial start-up activities, business plan development, and venture capital solicitation.

1998-2001 STEVEN ICE, INC., Derry, NH

Vice President of Marketing: Identified target markets, constructed complex questionnaires, conducted telephone interviews, compiled and analyzed data for research activities associated with entrepreneurial start-up. Conducted focus groups to identify market segments and penetration. Wrote and presented report to management including strategic recommendations. Addressed all marketing research needs. Gathered data to develop comprehensive business plan and marketing reports.

HAWTHORNE MANAGEMENT, Washington, D.C.

1990-1998 **Market and Strategic Management Research Consultant:** Conducted large-scale quantitative research projects based in customer satisfaction measurement and total quality implementation, including design, coordination, statistical analysis, and report generation. Specialized in business-to-business services, e-commerce, and health care.

1986-1990 **Research Associate:** Managed behaviorally-based research projects including proposal writing; methodology, instrument and sample development; field coordination; data coding, analysis; and report writing. Included customer and employee studies, communication audits, market analysis, name/logo testing, constituency relations, positioning, and consumer studies.

INTERNATIONAL RESEARCH GROUP, Miami, FL

1983-1986 **Management Consultant:** Provided Marketing, Behavior, and Research counsel for advertising, public relations, and marketing consulting firm. Participated in internal and external strategic planning for *Fortune* 500 firms, government agencies, non-profits, and health-care providers.

WEBBER AND SONS, INC., Washington, D.C.

1978-1983 **Research Assistant:** Completed projects for insurance providers, hospitals, and private practices.

EDUCATION GEORGETOWN UNIVERSITY, Washington, D.C.

Master of Arts, Applied Psychology, with concentration in Health Care Research, 1980
Artes Baccalaureate, Psychology, *cum laude,* 1978

Military to Business Transition

Jamie Brown

123 Main Street • Hometown, CA 00000 • (555) 555-1234 • jbrown@company.com

BUSINESS QUALIFICATIONS

- Knowledge gained from comprehensive business courses, including accounting and economics.
- Capacities to conduct topic specific or problem focused research and analysis.
- Confidence presenting research results verbally and via detailed reports and illustrated presentations.
- Experience prioritizing tasks and completing assignments accurately and on time.
- Comfortable within reporting hierarchies and motivating peers.
- Strong task management and personnel motivation capabilities gained through military training.
- Cross cultural skills enhanced through travel in Africa and Asia.
- Technical and mechanical aptitude applicable to manufacturing, trouble-shooting and technical settings and projects.
- Basic Russian language abilities.

EDUCATION

SACRAMENTO STATE UNIVERSITY, Sacramento, CA
Bachelor of Arts, Liberal Studies, anticipated June 2003.

AMERICAN RIVER COLLEGE, Sacramento, CA
Completed general education courses, 1991-93.

BUSINESS RELATED COURSES

Macro and Micro Economics
Managerial Accounting
Public Speaking

Financial Accounting
Contemporary World Issues
Social Research Methods

MILITARY EXPERIENCE AND TRAINING

1998-present EXPLOSIVES DISPOSAL UNIT, Mare Island, CA
US Navy EOD Diver
- As Bomb Disposal Unit team member, give and receive briefings to task related personnel, maintain and updating classified publications, procure operations related equipment, and process after-action documentation such as Dive logs, and equipment usage reports.

1995-1998 USS BERGALL (SSN-667) SUBMARINE SQUADRON
Submariner, Machinist Mate 2nd Class and *Operations-Diver*
- Operated and maintained submarines atmosphere control equipment, such as breathing air/gas mixture levels, and potable water.
- Ordered and kept accounting of repair parts and supplies for both Auxiliary Division and Dive locker.
- Nuclear Weapons Armed Security Guard. Security Swimmer.

Dana Johnson

123 Main Street • Hometown, CA 00000
(555) 555-1234 • djohnson@company.com

Education

2000-2002	**University of California Los Angeles (UCLA),** Los Angeles, CA Masters of Music, with a major in Conducting, June 2002
1998-2000	**University of the Pacific (UOP),** Stockton, CA Bachelor of Music, with a major in Music Education, May 2000
1996-1998	**California State University, Northridge (CSUN),** Northridge, CA Completed Music and General Education Courses

Music Performance Experience

	University of California Los Angeles, Los Angeles, CA
2000-2002	Conductor, Pianist, Composer, Studio Vocalist
2001-2002	Gospel Choir Accompanist and Vocalist
	University of South Carolina, Columbia, SC
Summer 2000	Conductors Institute Participant
	University of the Pacific, Stockton, CA
1998-2000	Trumpeter, Pianist, and Vocalist
	California State University, Northridge, Northridge, CA
1996-1998	Trumpeter, Pianist, and Vocalist
	Morris Chapel and St. Mary's Church, Stockton, CA
1998-2000	Conductor, Pianist, Organist, and Vocalist

Conducting and Music Teaching Experience

	Marymount High School, Los Angeles, CA
2000-present	Conductor and Teacher of Music Theory
	UCLA Music Department, Los Angeles, CA
2000-2002	Choral Ensembles Student Conductor
	Presentation Elementary School, Stockton, CA
1998-2000	Instrumental Music Teacher
	Central Valley Youth Orchestra, Stockton, CA
1998-2000	Assistant Conductor
	UOP Morris Chapel, Stockton, CA
1998-2000	Choir Director for Catholic Mass

Dana Johnson

Employment History

2000-present	**Marymount High School,** Los Angeles, CA Director of Music
2000-present	**Audiences Unlimited, Inc.,** Los Angeles, CA Studio Audience Coordinator

Honors and Affiliations

2000-present	Conductor's Guild
1996-present	California Music Educators Association, Southern California School Band and Orchestra Association, International Association of Jazz Educators, California Music Educators Conference, and International Trumpet Guild

Works Conducted

Beethoven's Symphony #8, First Movement

Mayer's Andante for Strings

Hindemith's Five Pieces for String Orchestra

Haydn's Symphony #49, "La Passione"

Elgar's Serenade for Strings

Grieg's Holberg Suite

Mozart's Symphony #29

Sibelius's Andante Festivo for Strings

Bizet's Carmen Suite

Conducting Instructors

Steven Smithers, Stockton, CA
Dr. Mitchell Pearson, Los Angeles, CA

Trumpet Instructors

Peter Smith, Northridge, CA
Robert Horn, Los Angeles, CA

Jazz and Classical Piano Instructors

Stephanie Best, Los Angeles, CA
Patricia Peterson, Pasadena, CA

Nanny

Jamie Brown

123 Main Street • Hometown, CA 00000 • USA
Phone (409) 555-1234 • Fax (409) 555-5678 • jbrown@company.com

Objective	Live-in Nanny/Au Pair Position.
Qualifications	

- Ability to develop trusting relationships with children and parents.
- Certified Teacher with strong classroom and private tutoring experience.
- Skills to plan educational and recreational activities.
- Command of teaching conversational English.
- Cross cultural and European travel experiences, with passport, international driver's license and working papers, and conversational abilities in Italian.
- Experience supporting children with special needs.

Childcare Experience

ROBERT AND THERESA SANTANA, Santa Clara, CA

2000 to present — *Nanny:* Provide live-in childcare for two boys, currently ages 2 and 4. Supervise play, transport children to preschool and other activities, and assist with meals. Reinforce parental rules and values. Accompany family on short and long trips and vacations.

Teaching Credential and Training

NATIONAL UNIVERSITY, San Jose, CA
California Multiple Subject Credential, June 1999
Curriculum included: whole language instruction, curriculum, and instruction, and literature based integrated language arts.
Courses included: Foundations of Education, Curriculum and Instruction, Literature Based Integrated Language Arts, and Exceptional Children in the Classroom.

Teaching and Tutoring Experience

CATHOLIC DIOCESE OF SANTA CLARA, Santa Clara, CA

Summer 1999 — *Summer School English Teacher:* Planned and implemented lessons focusing on literature, grammar, writing, and research. Addressed remedial needs of students.

PRESENTATION SCHOOL, Cupertino, CA

Spring 1999 — *3rd Grade Student Teacher:* Independently established and presented lesson and unit plans. Created specific inter-disciplinary Reading and Work unit, focusing on reading skills for varied jobs, and including visiting career field representatives.

1996 to 1998 — 1st, 2nd, and Kindergarten *Teacher's Aide*

Education — UNIVERSITY OF SANTA CLARA, Santa Clara, CA
Bachelor of Arts, English, May 1989

References and Letters of Recommendation Upon Request

FRANCIS WILLIAMS

123 Main Street • Hometown, Michigan 00000 • (555) 555-2322 • fwilliams@company.com

OBJECTIVE

Nurse Practitioner in a clinical, educational, research, or administrative setting

QUALIFICATION SUMMARY

- Eighteen years as an Adult Nurse Practitioner in Primary Care and Women's Health Care
- Skilled in medical histories, physical exams, microscopy, laboratory testing, and medical prescription
- Expertise evaluating and managing wide scope of acute, chronic, and complex problems, and preventive and routine medical care
- Strong interpersonal/communication skills with patients and colleagues
- Skilled with elderly, adults, teens, mentally retarded, and the hearing impaired (using medical Sign Language)
- Provide counseling for mood problems and other health issues
- Abilities to develop health education materials; teach in-service lessons; and act as preceptor
- Experienced in committee leadership and participation

NURSING EXPERIENCE AND ACHIEVEMENTS

Ann Arbor Gynecologic & Obstetric Associates, P. C., Ann Arbor, MI
Nurse Practitioner, 1991–present
- Provide gynecologic, obstetric, and primary care in collaboration with physicians in private practice
- Evaluate and manage acute and chronic gynecologic and obstetric problems, including: abdominopelvic pain, genitourinary problems, infections, breast concerns, endocrine-related problems, osteoporosis, and postoperative and pregnancy complications
- Evaluate and manage wide array of primary care problems including EENT, allergic conditions, dermatological problems, infectious diseases, chest pain, and respiratory, gastrointestinal, and musculoskeletal problems
- Perform annual and employment exams and prenatal and postpartum care
- Counsel and prescribe for cholesterol and weight management, contraception, menopause, osteoporosis, and mood disorders
- Developed health education handouts and presented staff in-service training
- Performed periodic Quality Assurance review for on-site laboratory
- Acted as preceptor for nurse practitioner and physician assistant students

University of Michigan University Health Service, Ann Arbor, MI
Senior Nurse Practitioner, 1987–1990
- Evaluated and managed health problems including: infectious diseases, allergic conditions, dermatological problems, respiratory, gastrointestinal, genitourinary, endocrine, and musculoskeletal problems, traumatic injuries, and occupational health issues
- Provided routine and preventive care, employment and sports physical exams
- Initiated gynecologic services for Eastman School of Music
- Made health education presentations, acted as preceptor, and served on Training and HIV Task Force
- Coordinated University Health Services Library used by nurses, nursing students, and patients

FRANCIS WILLIAMS
Page Two

University of Michigan University Health Service, Ann Arbor, MI
Nurse Practitioner, 1984–1987
- Evaluated and managed wide variety of health problems for students
- Performed routine and preventive care and sports physical exams
- Became proficient in Sign Language used in medical context
- Made health education presentations to staff and students, acted as preceptor for students, and served on various committees

NURSING EDUCATION AND LIBERAL ARTS STUDIES

University of Michigan School of Nursing, Ann Arbor, MI
MS, Family Health Nurse Clinician, 1990, and *BS, magna cum laude, Nursing,* 1983

Ann Arbor County Community College, Ann Arbor, MI
Completed prerequisite science and pre-nursing courses, 1980–1981

Albion College, Albion, MI
BA, Religion, 1980

CREDENTIALS AND AFFILIATIONS

- American Nurses' Association Certification, Adult Nurse Practitioner
- Michigan State Certification, Family Health Nurse Practitioner with Prescription Privilege
- Michigan State License, Registered Professional Nurse
- Certified in CPR, most recent update 2001

COREY DAVIS

123 Main Street • Hometown, NM 00000 • (555) 555-5555 • cdavis@company.com
345 Mission Boulevard • Hometown, CA 12121 • (555) 555-0987

PARALEGAL QUALIFICATIONS AND ACHIEVEMENTS

- Outstanding case research, client relations, document management, and writing skills gained in progressively responsible positions over a 13-year period.
- Expertise gained as law office manager, compiling a training manual and supervising administrative support personnel, revamping accounting, debit and credit systems.
- Trained and accomplished interviewer, negotiation, and mediation.
- LexisNexis, WestLaw, Word, FileMaker Pro, Excel, QuickBooks, and Internet skills.

PARALEGAL AND MANAGEMENT EXPERIENCE

LAW OFFICES OF BRENDAN ELLIS — Santa Fe, NM
Civil Litigation Specialist/Office Manager — 1990-present
- Manage office and staff of 3 secretaries, ensuring smooth operation of firm with 3 attorneys and billings in excess of $1.5 million and awards of over $10 million annually.
- Interview clients; prepare files and discovery; handle multiple cases.
- Request and review medical documentation; ascertaining evidence from appropriate parties.
- Negotiate and settle cases with defense attorney and insurance companies.
- Attend mediations and conciliations.
- Prepare clients for depositions and trials.
- Control and maintain law office accounts, utilizing accounting and billing software.
- Regularly attended seminars on personal injury law.

SANTA FE DISTRICT ATTORNEY'S OFFICE DOMESTIC VIOLENCE UNIT — Santa Fe, NM
Witness Advocate — Spring-Summer 1990
- Interviewed victims and witnesses, prepared documents, and organized information for court appearances.
- Assisted attorneys during trials, taking notes and facilitating access to evidentiary documents.

NEW MEXICO PUBLIC DEFENDER'S OFFICE — Santa Fe, NM
Legal Intern — Summers 1988 and 1989
- Researched and drafted motions on criminal law and procedural issues. Interviewed clients at New Mexico correctional institutions.
- Argued bail motions in several state district courts.
- Negotiated plea and bail agreements for defendants accused of misdemeanors. Attended criminal trials and depositions.

ATTORNEY DANIEL GALL — Santa Fe, NM
Legal Secretary/Legal Assistant — 1986-1990
- Greeted clients, maintained files, and completed administrative tasks.
- Prepared documents for legal proceedings involving real estate transactions.
- Entered client information into Excel- and Access-driven computer system.

EDUCATION

SAINT JOHN'S COLLEGE — Santa Fe, NM
B.S., Human Resource Management, with Honors — 1990
- Completed degree while employed and served as peer advisor to nontraditional students.

Dana Johnson

123 Main Street • Hometown, CA 00000 • (555) 555-1234 • djohnson@company.com

OBJECTIVE   Pharmacist Position

EDUCATION   UNIVERSITY OF THE PACIFIC SCHOOL OF PHARMACY, Stockton, CA
Pharm. D., May 1995
Pre-Pharmacy Studies, 1989-1991

PHARMACY ACCOMPLISHMENTS

1995-present   DAVID GRANT MEDICAL CENTER, Travis Air Force Base, Fairfield, CA
Pharmacist: Provide comprehensive pharmaceutical services for patients, assist physicians with identification of appropriate drug regiments, and support educational efforts targeting health care professionals and patients.

Spring 1995   *Internal Medicine Rotation:* Attended rounds with physicians; assisted physicians selecting proper drug regiments; monitored drug-to-drug interactions and patient lab results.

Fall 1994   *Clinical Psychiatric Rotation:* Monitored patient charts for drug-to-drug interactions; enhanced patient medication compliance; instructed patients regarding medication; and consulted with patients regarding discharge medications.

Winter 1995   VETERANS ADMINISTRATION OUTPATIENT CLINIC, Martinez, CA
Ambulatory Care Rotation: Monitored PT/INR in anticoagulation clinic; monitored patient status in cardiovascular and hypertension clinic; evaluated proper medication renewal in pharmacy refill clinic.

Winter 1994   LONGS DRUGS CORPORATE OFFICE, Walnut Creek, CA
Community Pharmacy Management Rotation: Undertook inventory control efforts and RXD orders; updated prices; completed key tagging for billing purposes; and developed positive customer service approaches and attitudes.

Summer 1994   WALGREENS PHARMACY, Cupertino, CA
Community Pharmacy Rotation: Processed new prescriptions and refills; took new prescriptions from physicians; processed 3rd party claims to AETNA, Blue Shield, and Foundation; labeled and organized inventory; assisted customers with OTC purchases and prescriptions.

June 1993-
June 1994   SMART FOOD PHARMACY, Stockton, CA
Pharmacy Intern

PROFESSIONAL AFFILIATIONS

California Pharmacists' Association
American Pharmacists' Association
Kappa Psi Pharmaceutical Fraternity

Chris Smith

123 Main Street • Hometown, IN 00000 • (555) 555-5094 • csmith@company.com

Physical Therapy, Sports Medicine, and Massage Therapy Qualifications

- Background in physical therapy and sports medicine, and clinical experience with adults, student athletes, and pediatric patients.
- Over 2,000 hours as Physical Therapist; 1,000 hours as Athletic Training; 4,000 hours as Physical Therapy Aid; 200 hours as Nurse; and 350 hours as certified Massage Therapist.

Physical Therapy, Massage Therapy Experience

MIDWEST MEMORIAL HOSPITAL, Indianapolis, IN
Orthopedic In- and Outpatient Clinic Therapist, 1999-present
- Develop treatment plans for chronic-pain and cardiac patients.
- Present regular in-service on hip and knee prostheses.

DEARBORN COUNTY HOSPITAL, Richmond, IN
Cardiac Rehabilitation Therapist, 1998-1999
- Acted as program coordinator for exercise regimen and provided treatments using ultrasound, electric stimulation, massage therapy, and stretching/strengthening exercises.
- Coordinated aquadynamics program for chronic-pain patients.

CINNAMON MOUNTAIN, Mishawaka, WI
Pediatric Rehabilitation, Summers 1996-1998
- Coordinated treatment of amputee children and children with congenital birth defects.
- Created "Alive with Pride" program now functional at 30 national hospitals.
- Developed child-oriented play program and trained teachers via elementary school seminars.

XCEL ORTHOPAEDIC PHYSICAL THERAPY, Bloomington, IN
Physical Therapy Aid, Spring 1997-Spring 1998
- Assisted with ultrasound, muscle stimulation, massage, and interferential treatments.
- Served as translator, using Spanish language skills with selected patients.

INDIANA UNIVERSITY, Bloomington, IN
Student Trainer, Spring 1994
Massage Therapy Intern, Fall 1994

Physical Therapy, Sports Medicine, and Nursing Training

INDIANA UNIVERSITY, Bloomington, IN
Bachelor of Science in Physical Therapy, May 1998
Performed independent research evaluating back and shoulder strength of musicians suffering from tendonitis. Presented findings to department and published in Indiana Journal of Medicine.

BLOOMINGTON COMMUNITY COLLEGE, Bloomington, IN
General Education Nursing, and Science Courses, 1994-1996
Massage Therapy Certificate, Summer 1996

FRANCIS WILLIAMS

123 Main Street • Hometown, MD 00000 • (555) 555-1234 • fwilliams@company.com

PROFESSIONAL PROFILE

- Over a decade of progressive responsible roles in private and municipal law enforcement.
- Specialized skills associated with community relations and maintenance of positive and professional attitudes among colleagues.
- Proven abilities to hire, train, evaluate, and motivate officers and support staff.
- Trained and certified law enforcement professional in front line and management roles.
- License to carry firearms. Emergency Medical Technician. Certification in Radar Usage, Breathalyzer, and Identi-Kit Systems.

LAW ENFORCEMENT AND SECURITY EXPERIENCE

JOHNS HOPKINS UNIVERSITY POLICE DEPARTMENT　　　Baltimore, MD
Assistant Chief of Campus Police　　　1998-present
- Assist with personnel, budget and procedural oversights associated with a department of 20 full-time and 20 part-time security professionals.
- Recruit, train and review performance of professional and administrative personnel.
- Protect life and property on and about the campus of Johns Hopkins University.
- Patrol on foot and via automobile, using strong observational and interaction skills.
- Uphold laws and codes of the State of Maryland and Johns Hopkins University.
- Cooperate with law enforcement agencies, regularly interacting with Deputy Sheriff.
- Conduct community outreach and educational efforts, focusing on alcohol use and abuse, safe dating, and property protection.
- Serve on Student Life Committees and assist with judicial investigations.

BUCKMAN ASSOCIATES　　　Bethesda, MD
Head of Security　　　1995-1998
- Managed all aspects of security for hotels and adjoining properties.
- Hired, scheduled, supervised, and evaluated personnel.
- Provided all policing functions, with emphasis on defusing potentially violent situations.
- Cooperated extensively with Baltimore and Bethesda Police Departments.

TOWN OF ROCKVILLE POLICE DEPARTMENT　　　Rockville, MD
Patrolman　　　1990-1995
- Performed all standard policing functions, earning excellent ratings annually.
- Interacted and communicated with town officials regarding proactive and reactive efforts.

LAW ENFORCEMENT TRAINING

BALTIMORE POLICE ACADEMY　　　Baltimore, MD
Graduate　　　1995

ROCKVILLE POLICE ACADEMY　　　Rockville, MD
Graduate　　　1990

COREY DAVIS

123 Main Street • Hometown, WA 00000 • (555) 555-1234 • cdavis@company.com

PROFESSIONAL PROFILE

- Experience as publicist, media consultant, publicity professional, and television booker.
- Extensive contacts within broadcast and print media, yielding successful placements of stories as well as interviews.
- Talents to establish and implement strategic media and promotional campaigns to generate multi-media coverage.
- Capacities to work with clients to attain marketing, attendance, and general publicity goals.

PRESS RELATIONS AND PROMOTIONS ACHIEVEMENTS

COVERAGE CONCEPTS CONSULTING, Pullman, WA

Personal Publicist and Consultant: Personally support media relations, campaign development, and implementation efforts associated with professional athletes, education, and not-for-profit clients. Interact with clients regularly to address needs and fine-tune annually updated strategic media plans. Draft, edit, and finalize news releases, speeches, and press packets. Develop and maintain relationships with regional and national print and broadcast media, supporting efforts to maximize desired coverage. Serve as client spokesperson and as press conference coordinator. *1998-present*

CNBS TELEVISION, Pullman, WA

Production Assistant for "Confrontations": Booked main guests and panelists for weekly topical talk show. Generated and researched story ideas. Conducted video research. Edited teasers for show. Organized production details for studio tapings. Coordinated publicity ads in local newspapers. *1995-1998*

BARSTOW PUBLISHING COMPANY, Seattle, WA

Publicity Assistant: Publicized new books and authors. Assisted with television, radio, and print media tours and individual appearances. Created and implemented author questionnaire to maximize publicity generated through professional contacts. Wrote press releases and designed press packets. Responded to review copy requests. *1993-1995*

WNBN-TV, Tacoma, WA

Production Intern for "Sports Talk": Assisted producers of live, daily sports interview, and call-in show. Researched and generated story ideas. Pre-interviewed guests. Covered shoots and wrote promos. Produced 5 segments. *1995-1996*

UNIVERSITY OF WASHINGTON, Seattle, WA

Sports Information Promotional Assistant: Implemented promotional campaigns, wrote copy, and designed advertisements. Enhanced attendance via creative competitions and corporate sponsored give-aways. *1994-1995*

THE CHERRY HAIKU, INC., Seattle, WA

Art Assistant: Produced paste-ups and mechanicals for full service advertising agency. Operated Photostat camera and coordinated logistics for photo shoots. Brainstormed with creative team. Summers and Part-time *1992-1994*

EDUCATION

UNIVERSITY OF WASHINGTON, Seattle, WA

B.A. in Communications, cum laude, with a Minor in English, 1995

JAMIE BROWN

123 Main Street • Hometown, NY 00000 • (555) 555-5555 • jbrown@co

PUBLIC RELATIONS EXPERIENCE

SYRACUSE HEART ASSOCIATION, Syracuse, NY
Public Relations Manager, 2000-present
- Serve as consultant to 7 state chapters regarding campaign problems and activities.
- Organize regional campaign meetings; speak at several campaign conferences.
- Review legislation and bring specific bills to the attention of the proper committee or individual.
- Staff the Legislative Advisory Committee and follow-through on specific bills.
- Develop fundraising programs.
- Conducted the previous two annual campaigns for the newly merged Central Chapter.

Campaign Assistant for Greater Syracuse Chapter, 1995-1997
- Supervised chapter campaign duties and assisted the Executive Director with administrative responsibilities, such as personnel and budget.

BIG APPLE NATURAL FOODS, Syracuse, NY
Special Events Coordinator, 1998-2000
- Created and coordinated special events and promotions, within $425,000 marketing budget.
- Selected and wrote event advertising, promotional materials, and publicity copy.
- Handled charity fundraising, corporate image positioning, and community outreach efforts.

Assistant to the Director of Public Relations, 1997-1998
- Assisted in promotion and publicity of special events.
- Developed press kits and releases to initiate, maintain, and maximize media relations.
- Compiled easy to access and update computerized publicity files using FileMaker Pro.
- Researched prospective consumer markets using Internet and direct contact techniques.
- Created direct-mail lists, updated media lists, and maintained task priority lists.

SYRACUSE UNIVERSITY, Syracuse, NY
Teacher's Assistant, Fall and Spring 1998

COMMUNICATION AND PUBLIC RELATIONS EDUCATION

SYRACUSE UNIVERSITY, Syracuse, NY
Bachelor of Arts in Public Relations, *magna cum laude,* June 1998

QUALIFICATIONS

- Ability to plan and direct successful fundraising, public relations, and promotions programs.
- Campaign development and implementation experience with major health agency.
- Extensive volunteer recruitment experience and success motivating diverse teams.
- Supervisory experience with both professional and nonprofessional staffs.
- Capacity to use Word, WordPerfect, Lotus 123, PageMaker, and FileMaker Pro for drafting and editing features and promotional materials, for budgeting tasks, and for graphics projects.

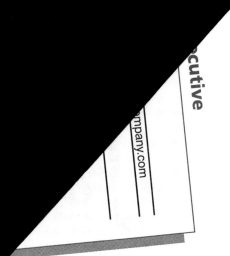

...a Johnson

...)00 • (555) 555-2311 • djohnson@company.com

...ENCE AND ACHIEVEMENTS

...)ANS, San Jose, CA

...to expand business in Santa Clara County.
...mortgage broker packets, complete individual and
...Conventional, FHA/VA, PERS, JUMBO, and

...rketing plan to expand business in Santa Clara

...........d mortgage broker packets, completed individual
... group presentations designed to generate loan business, and implemented first-ever real estate expo promotional event.

HOUSING LENDING, Fresno, CA
Wholesale Account Executive, 1996-1998
- Marketed loan and financing programs to financial institutions and mortgage brokers in San Joaquin, Merced, Fresno, and Stanislaus counties.

CALIFORNIA MORTGAGE SPECIALISTS, INC., San Mateo, CA
Professional Real Estate Loan Auditor, 1992-1996

SANTA CLARA SAVINGS, Santa Clara, CA
Loan Officer in Residential Lending Department, 1986-1992
Loan Underwriter/Processor in Residential and Government Loan Departments, 1982-1986
Loan Underwriter in Secondary Market Department, 1980-1982
Loan Packager in Loan Processing Department, 1978-1980

BUSINESS AND FINANCE DEGREE

SANTA CLARA UNIVERSITY, Santa Clara, CA
Bachelor of Science in Business Administration, 1980

PROFESSIONAL PROFILE

- Over 20 years of experience in mortgage banking and finance, with emphasis on customer service loan qualifications and accurate risk analysis.
- Experience as loan consultant enhancing qualification potential and prospective customers.
- Expertise with Conventional, FHA/VA, PERS, JUMBO, Community Home Buyer, and CHAFA loan programs for homes in Santa Clara, San Joaquin, Merced, and Stanislaus counties.

Real Estate Sales Professional

Chris Smith
123 Main Street ■ Hometown, CA 00000 ■ (555) 555-1234 ■ csmith@company.com

Real Estate Sales Qualifications

- Record of productivity and profitability as real estate sales professional.
- Proven accountability, dependability, and decisiveness, servicing needs of buyers and sellers.
- Sales and marketing talent gained via experience, achievements, and customer relationships.
- Efficient planner, organizer, and effective manager of time and territory.
- Self-starter, tenacious with ability to service existing business while prospecting new accounts.
- Competencies from Century 21 Sales Curriculum, Dale Carnegie's Face-to-Face Selling Skills, Xerox Selling Skills, Creating Customer Focus, and other varied seminars and training courses.

Real Estate Sales Achievements

1998-present CENTURY 21, Walnut Creek, CA
Residential and Commercial Associate

- Serve in comprehensive sales as well as mortgage and lease advisory capacities for residential and commercial clients for one of the Bay Area's largest branch office.
- Prospect new buyers and sellers via monthly seminars, direct mail, and e-mail campaigns, appearances on radio programs, and printed and television ads.
- Regularly exceeded sales goals, twice receiving national Gold Jacket recognition for top 10% production, three times receiving $100 million Club recognition for annual sales and leases, and annually receiving Top Producer recognition for regional and state sales figures.
- One of three "interdisciplinary producers," licensed in residential and commercial sales, property management, and financing and leasing.

General Sales Achievements

1992-1998 AMERICAN COMMERCIAL COMPANY, Walnut Creek, CA
Commercial Insurance Product Services for Northern California

- Developed internal structures for prospecting new production sources.
- Generated territory volume of $10 million from $3 million.

1990-1992 CENTURION INSURANCE COMPANY, San Francisco, CA
Territory Manager for Northern California

- Recruited to open and develop Bay Area for multi-line commercial accounts.
- Generated territory volume of $4 million from $250,000.

1987-1990 INDUSTRIAL INDEMNITY, Sacramento, CA
Marketing Representative

1977-1987 FIREMAN'S FUND INSURANCE COMPANY, Sacramento, CA
Commercial Lines Underwriter

Education UNIVERSITY OF THE PACIFIC, Stockton, CA
Bachelor of Arts, Communication, May 1977

JAMIE BROWN

123 Main Street • Hometown, CT 00000 • (555) 555-1234 • jbrown@company.com

Recruiting Qualifications

- Experience developing and implementing comprehensive college recruiting program.
- Capacities to source, screen, and select candidates based upon strategic qualification criteria.
- Abilities to conduct interviews, train interviewers, and facilitate decision-making regarding offers.
- Developed recruiting, selection, and training associated with internship program.
- Broad-based human resources knowledge to effectively interact with senior management.

Recruiting, Human Resources, and Management Achievements

NORMAN'S DEPARTMENT STORES   NEW LONDON, CT
Manager of Executive Recruitment   *1996-2000*

Oversee all logistical and financial aspects of program recruiting 20 Management Development Program participants annually for regional chain of 15 stores. Involves on-campus interviews, career fairs, and information sessions held at 7 target schools and participation in three multi-school consortium events.

- With VPs of Human Resources, Merchandising, and Operations, review and revise annual college recruiting strategies and yield targets.
- Develop, propose, and monitor annual college recruiting budgets of approximately $75,000.
- Regularly review and establish target school listings, contacts, and recruiting dates.
- Train college team liaisons and leaders to make effective campus recruitment presentations.
- Organized senior executive involvement in Career Days second interview processes.
- Facilitate College Recruiting Team discussions regarding Management Development Program offers.
- Recruit for, hire, and oversee 15 Summer Interns and 10 Academic Year Interns annually.
- Assist training staff with planning educational and social activities associated with initial portions of a 10 week program that blends classroom instruction with career networking and skills training.

Assistant Store Personnel Manager   *1996-2000*

- Hired, reviewed, and supported the needs of full-time and part-time sales professionals.
- Tracked daily, weekly, and monthly coverage data, to minimize costs and maximize coverage and service.
- Conducted various training sessions including: customer service, register operations, and security.
- Received award for overall achievement and outstanding performance in human resources.

Children's Department Manager   *1994-1996*

- Merchandised children's clothing and accessories, analyzing and marketing a $2 million inventory.
- Trained and developed staff of 15 sales associates in customer-service skills and selling techniques.
- Achieved 20% sales increase over one-year period and chosen manager of the year in 1995.

Education

CONNECTICUT COLLEGE   NEW LONDON, CT
B.A., Spanish Modified with Government Studies   *June 1995*

Francis Williams

123 Main Street • Hometown, CA 00000 • (555) 555-8876 • fwilliams@company.com

Restaurant Management and Service Experience

NORDSTROM, San Francisco, CA
Champaign Exchange Café Manager, 1999–present
- Oversee operations of 250-seat facility averaging over $10,000 daily sales, offering American cuisine luncheon and dinner service to store patrons.
- Schedule, motivate, and supervise staff of 25 full-time and part-time servers per shift.
- Monitor daily and monthly receipts and expenditures.
- Communicate with store and corporate management regarding sales targets and profit strategies.

SHAKESPEARE'S TAVERN, London, ENGLAND
Assistant Manager, 1997–1999
- Oversaw operations of 175-seat facility averaging over £2,000 daily food sales and £2,000 wine and alcohol sales, offering luncheon, dinner, and after-dinner service.
- Supervised staff of 30 employees per shift.
- Monitored food costs, effectively communicated with chef and prep staff regarding costs.
- Prepared and submitted weekly, monthly, and quarterly reports to owners.
- With chef, planned weekly menus.

CLUB METROPOLIS, Montreal, CANADA
Assistant Manager, 1995–1997
- Scheduled and supervised staff, controlled inventory, deposited cash, maintained physical plant, and completed daily and weekly reports for after-hours club catering to elite patrons.
- Supervised up to 20 employees per shift.
- Completed management training program.

Bartender and Bar Manager, 1994–1995
- Served patrons, purchased wine, alcohol, beer, and mixes.

Food Services Training and Experience

CALIFORNIA SCHOOL OF CULINARY ARTS, San Francisco, CA
Restaurant Management Certificate, 1999

PROFESSIONAL BARTENDING SCHOOL OF MONTREAL, Montreal, CANADA
Certificate, 1994

ROYAL CANADIAN AIR FORCE, Toronto and Montreal, CANADA
Completed Class A & C Cooking School, 1991–1994

Languages

Bilingual French-English

DANA JOHNSON

123 Main Street • Hometown, MD 00000 • (555) 555-1234 • djohnson@company.com

BUYING EXPERIENCE AND ACCOMPLISHMENTS

CALVIN CLOTHES COMPANY, Baltimore and Bethesda, MD and Washington, D.C.

1997-present *Baltimore Junior Apparel Department Buyer*
- Developed sales volume from $5.5 million to $7.5 million, 1997-99.
- Consistently achieved net operating profit of 50%, highest in company.
- Implemented promotional strategies and developed key classifications directly responsible for volume increase.
- Developed electronic and direct communication networks supplying product knowledge to sales staff and impacting strategic planning of vendor programs.
- Instituted e-mail communication strategies and status-tracking efforts.
- Chosen as Merchant of the Year 1998, 2000, and 2001.

1995-1997 *Bethesda Divisional Sales Manager*
- Handled furniture, electronics, and basement store, with 1995 volume of $5.6 million.
- During mall expansion, held store sales volume within plan by achieving 12% increase.
- Priorities included constant evaluation of stock levels and content, goal setting, development of key personnel, and achieving a high motivational level.

1993-1995 *Washington Assistant Buyer*
- Acted as liaison with vendors and warehouse to assure timely merchandise delivery of men's coordinates, coats, swimwear, and activewear.
- Interpreted, analyzed, and responded to OTB, selling reports, and seasonal plans.

1991-1993 *Washington Assistant Store Manager*
- Promoted from trainee to Assistant Manager within 12 months.
- Conceptualized and implemented employee training and effectiveness program.

1990-1991 *Executive Trainee*

PROFESSIONAL DEVELOPMENT AND EDUCATION

CALVIN CLOTHES COMPANY EXECUTIVE TRAINING SEMINARS, Baltimore, MD
Computerized Buying Techniques, Loss Prevention, Sales Motivation, Buyer-Store Communication Skills, Retail Mathematics and Quantitative Techniques, Buying Segmentation and Consumer Behavior, Merchandising, Personnel Management and Profits

UNIVERSITY OF DELAWARE, Newark, DE
Bachelor of Science in Marketing, 1990

QUALIFICATION SUMMARY

- Capacities to translate strategic plans into profitable purchases and merchandizing plans.
- Experience using communication programs and talents to maximize sales at store level.
- Quantitative skills required to establish market segmentations, maximize profits, and analyze sales figures.
- Commitment to understanding consumer attitudes, developing relationships with suppliers, and reinforcing positive achievements of sales professionals and operations personnel.

Corey Davis

123 Main Street • Hometown, CA 00000 • (555) 555-1234 • cdavis@company.com

Retail sales position using:

- Experiences within retail sales in diverse department and specialty store settings.
- Curiosity regarding consumer attitudes and behaviors and desire to sell based upon product qualities.
- Marketing and consumer behavior skills gained via business and psychology courses and projects.
- Outgoing personality, persuasive skills, and excitement about meeting sales goals.
- Time and task management and leadership skills nurtured as campus office holder.
- Knowledge of computerized registers and inventory control, and abilities to use Word, PowerPoint, and Excel to create sales materials and reports.

Sales, Marketing, and Customer Service Experience

NORDSTROM, San Mateo, CA
Salesperson, Seasonally 1997-present and Summers 2000 and 2001

NATIONAL SHOPPING SERVICE, Los Angeles, CA
Mystery Shopper, Part-time 1998-present

THE LIMITED, San Mateo, CA
Salesperson, Part-time and Summers 1996-1998

CRYSTAL MOON JEWELRY, San Mateo, CA
Stockperson and Administrative Support Person, Part-time 1995-1998

WEINSTOCKS, Sacramento, CA
Sales Associate, Part-time 1993-1996

Education

SAINT MARY'S COLLEGE, Miraga, CA
Bachelor of Arts, anticipated May 2003
Major in Psychology and minors in Business and Studio Art
Delta Gamma Sorority Treasurer, 2002-2003 and Activities Committee, 2001-2002

CALIFORNIA STATE UNIVERSITY HAYWARD, Hayward, CA
Completed psychology and business courses, Summer 1994

Marketing and General Business Courses and Projects

Marketing Management, Management and Organizational Behavior, Financial Accounting, Consumer Behavior, and Designing Effective Organizations

- Create hypothetical business to assess and create overall marketing plan.
- Developed, administered, and interpreted survey distributed at St. Mary's athletic events to determine target market profiling.
- Examined organizational structure of QVC Shopping Network.

Retail Store Manager

Francis Williams

123 Main Street • Apartment 13 • Hometown, CA 00000 (555) 555-1234 • fwilliams@company.com

RETAIL MANAGEMENT AND SALES ACHIEVEMENTS

SPINNER RECORDS CORPORATION   LOS ANGELES, CA
Manager   **1999-present**
- Manage Spinner's largest-volume store, with sales of approximately $30,000 per week.
- Handle all merchandising, inventory control, ordering, cash control, and maintenance.
- Oversee store opening and closing procedures.
- Direct sales floor activities, assist customers and address customer concerns.
- Input data to prepare daily sales reports and regularly use weekly and monthly data to develop sales and promotional strategies.
- Hire, train, and coordinate a staff of 26.
- Work with Spinner corporate colleagues as well as record company professionals to develop local marketing and advertising strategies, supplementing national campaigns.
- Inspire sales staff to develop and implement special promotions and events.
- Won two merchandising display contests.
- Received the "Super Spinner" Sales Award for exceeding sales goals

Assistant Manager   **1997-1999**
- Fulfilled all management responsibilities in absence of manager.
- Opened and closed store, handled customer service issues, and oversaw cash control.
- Supervised and motivated employees.
- Assisted with merchandising and promotions efforts.

SANTA ANA MEN'S SHOPPE   SANTA ANA, CA
Assistant Manager   **1992-1997**
- Hired, trained, and supervised staff of six serving customers of specialty men's clothing store.
- Provided exceptional customer services to high end consumers, regularly including direct email and phone contact, and relationship building.
- Tallied daily receipts and made bank deposits.
- Maintained inventory levels, monitored merchandise, provided feedback to owner/buyer regarding trends and need for reorders.

LENNY'S TOYS   SANTA ANA, CA
Assistant Manager   **Summers and Part-time 1988-1992**
- Hired, trained, and supervised three shifts of four sales associates daily.
- Tallied daily receipts and made bank deposits.
- Maintained inventory levels, ordered merchandise, and independently tracked all special orders.

BUSINESS AND RETAIL EDUCATION

COMMUNITY COLLEGE OF LOS ANGELES   LOS ANGELES, CA
Associate of Arts, Business Administration, with Retail Management Certificate   **1997**

SANTA ANA COMMUNITY COLLEGE   SANTA ANA, CA
Completed General Education and Business Courses Part-time   **1990-1994**

Chris Smith

123 Main Street • Hometown, New York 00000 • 555-555-1234 • csmith@company.com

Graduate and Undergraduate Counseling and Psychology Education

LOYOLA MARYMOUNT UNIVERSITY, Los Angeles, California
Ph.D., Counseling and Human Development, Dissertation to be defended, January, 2003
- Dissertation: "Ethnic Identity Development of Multi-ethnic College Students"
- As Rotary Scholarship Recipient received Full Tuition Award and Counseling Assistantship Stipend

M.A., School Counseling, May 1998

TOWSON UNIVERSITY, Towson, Maryland
B.S., Psychology, August 1994

College Counseling and Teaching Experience

LOYOLA MARYMOUNT UNIVERSITY, Los Angeles, California
Counseling and Mental Health Services Intern, September 2000–July 2001, January 2002–May 2002
- Counseled undergraduate and graduate students with personal, academic, and career issues.
- Addressed psychological and developmental needs of multicultural and diverse 3600 undergraduates and 1000 graduate students.
- Assessed and diagnosed clients on the basis of presenting problem, history, and rating on Personality Assessment Inventory (PAI).
- Participated in two hours of individual supervision and one hour of group supervision per week.
- Served as a liaison between Counseling Center and University Health Services through involvement in the development of "Feel Fit in February" speakers series and outreach program designed to meet the health needs of student populations.

Graduate Assistant, September 1999–May 2002
- Facilitated the CACREP accreditation process by designing program curriculum to meet standards by researching programs, developing and presenting graphs and charts, and attending faculty meetings.
- Designed the Counseling Student's Handbook for the Master's and Doctoral programs.
- Researched trends in Client-Centered Therapy, examining the influence of Carl Rogers on the field of professional counseling.
- Contribute to the enhancement of the Counseling and Human Development program by attending faculty meetings related to the development of the program, and by investigating new ideas to strengthen the curriculum and overall structure of the program.

Instructor/Supervised Intern in School and Community Counseling Course, September 2001–May 2002
- Planned and presented lectures, hosted guest speakers, and facilitated weekly discussions based on topics relevant to students' internship experiences in either a school setting or a community agency setting. Topics included diversity, confidentiality and ethics, eating disorders, and crisis intervention.
- Supervised students individually and in group via taped sessions and experiences at internship sites.

Counselor Supervisor for Practicum Course, January 2001–May 2001 and January 2002–May 2002
- Supervised four Masters' students individually who were counseling students within a K–12 school setting.

Counselor Supervisor for Professional Orientation and Practice, January 2001–May 2001
- Supervised Masters' students learning counseling techniques through the use of role-plays.

Chris Smith
Page Two

School Counseling and Teaching Experience

TORRANCE UNIFIED SCHOOL DISTRICT, Torrance, California
School Counselor, September 1998–June 1999
- Counseled students individually and in groups; designed specific counseling programs to meet needs.
- Responded effectively to various on-campus crises via crisis intervention strategies.
- Coordinated and oversaw IEP meetings and specific meetings designed to help high-risk students become more successful in school.
- Consulted daily with teachers and parents regarding student performance.
- Teamed with psychologist presenting information for special education students to parents and teachers.
- Facilitator of workshops, presentations, and programs for students, teachers, and staff.

WISEBURN SCHOOL DISTRICT, Hawthorne, California
School Counselor Intern, December 1997–June 1998
- Developed and implemented guidance services in a multicultural setting; included social skills groups, divorce groups, and disability awareness program.
- Conducted individual and group counseling for students in grades K–5.

CULVER CITY HIGH SCHOOL, Culver City, California
School Counselor Intern, January 1998–June 1998
- Counseled students on personal, educational, and career issues.
- Worked with the "Latinos Unidos" club to improve cultural awareness.
- Developed and implemented preschool curriculum to enhance language skills of developmentally delayed students.
- Coordinated with parents on designing an educational plan to facilitate the development of their children.

REDONDO BEACH UNIFIED SCHOOL DISTRICT, Redondo Beach, California
Substitute Teacher, September 1996–January 1998
- Instructed academic lessons to K–12 population; lesson development and classroom management.
- Worked with developmentally challenged students.

Professional Affiliations

Member, American Counseling Association
Member, Association for Counselor Education and Supervision
Member, Association for Multicultural Counseling and Development
Member, American College Counseling Association

Language Development

Spanish Grammar Course, University of Rochester, January 2002–present
Spanish Language Course, University of Navarra, Spain, August 2001–September 2001
Spanish Language Course, Eurocenters Salamanca, Spain, July 2000–August 2000

COREY DAVIS

123 Main Street • Hometown, WA 00000 • (555) 555-1234 • cdavis@company.com

TEACHING ACCOMPLISHMENTS

Tacoma High School, Tacoma, WA

Chairperson, Mathematics Department, 1998-present
- Serve as math instructor and Director of the Math Evaluation Committee.
- Develop report for submission to the National Association of Schools and Colleges.
- Develop and monitor budgets, assess goals, programs, plans, and professional performance.
- Select and approve departmental texts, and write and upgrade course descriptions as necessary.
- Evaluate instructional staff, advise on contract renewal, and evaluate candidates for new hires.

Mathematics Instructor, 1994-present
- Instruct grades 9-12 in trigonometry, algebra I & II, geometry, pre-calculus, and business math.
- Develop curricula and lesson plans, select texts, and design tests.
- Initiated remedial math program and after-school tutorial sessions for problem math students.
- Conduct summer-school sessions in remedial math and SAT preparation.

Stagg High School, Stockton, CA

9th - 12th Grade Mathematics Student Teacher, Fall 1994
- Implemented lessons for and assessed students in Honors Algebra, and Honors Trigonometry.

9th - 10th Grade Algebra and Geometry Mathematics Field Work Teacher's Assistant, Spring 1993

TUTORIAL EXPERIENCE

Private Tutoring, Stockton, CA and Tacoma, WA

Tutor for Middle and High School Mathematics Students, 1992-present
- Helped students with homework assignments and enhanced general understanding of concepts and approaches associated with Algebra, Trigonometry, Calculus, and General Math.

University of the Pacific, Stockton, CA

Mathematics Department Grader for Inferential Statistics, 1993-1994
Mathematics Resources Center Proctor for Algebra and Trigonometry, 1993-1994
Mathematics Department Grader for Finite Mathematics, Statistics, and Calculus, 1992-1993

Parklane Elementary School, Stockton, CA

Teacher's Aide for Summer Youth Employment Training Program, Summers 1989 and 1990

EDUCATION AND MATH DEGREES

University of Washington, Seattle, WA

M.S. in Secondary Education and Curriculum and Instruction, with Mathematics Specialization, 1996

University of the Pacific, Stockton, CA

B.S. in Mathematics, with Mathematics Education major, Single Subject Credential, Fall 1994

San Joaquin Delta Community College, Stockton, CA

Associate of Arts in Mathematics, June 1992

Jamie Brown

123 Main St. • Apt. 13 • Hometown, MD 00000 • (555) 555-9821 • jb@company.com

Social Work Experience

Baltimore Central School District, Baltimore, MD
District Social Worker, 2000–present
- Provide direct social work services to elementary, middle, and high school students and families.
- As member of interdisciplinary team, establish, implement, and monitor effectiveness of Independent Educational Programs.
- Regularly communicate with parents, teachers, and special-education professionals regarding individual students.
- Conduct group discussions with students and parents pertaining to developmental, behavioral, and medical issues.

Johns Hopkins University Children and Teen Clinic, Baltimore, MD
Clinical Social Worker, 1998–2000
- Diagnosed, evaluated, and treated children, adolescents, adults, and families living within the guidelines of Care and Protection Petitions.
- Interacted with legal, medical, and psychological professionals.
- Provided individualized social work services for children and adolescents, including pregnant teens, foster-home residents, and those meeting court-mandated criteria.
- Maintained accurate and thorough documentation via case records.

Baltimore County Juvenile Court Clinic, Baltimore, MD
Field Placement Intern, 1997–1998
- Diagnosed, evaluated, and treated children, adolescents, adults, and families.
- Conducted evaluations and supported.

Johns Hopkins University Hospital, Baltimore, MD
Pediatric Social Work Intern, 1996–1997
- Provided clinical services, family counseling, and referrals for patients and families.
- Conducted home visits and completed follow-up evaluations.
- Participated in classroom-based education program for potential kidney transplant patients.

Education

Social Work and Psychology Studies
Johns Hopkins University, Baltimore, MD
Master of Social Work, May 1998

Colby College, Waterville, ME
Bachelor of Arts, Psychology and Bachelor of Arts, Sociology, cum laude, June 1996

Qualification and Capabilities

- Capabilities to serve within comprehensive social work capacities in school or health care settings.
- Experience creating and implementing treatment plans for clients with psychosocial, behavioral, and health-related disorders.
- Capacity to manage cases, maintain accurate case records, and create detailed reports.

Speech Pathologist

CHRIS SMITH

123 Main Street, Apartment 13 • Hometown, UT 00000 • (555) 555-1234 • csmith@company.com

OBJECTIVE Speech and Language Pathology Position with Clinical Fellowship Year.

QUALIFICATION

- Experience diagnosing and treating children displaying apraxia, language delay, hearing impairment, and articulation disorders and adult-exhibiting motor speech disorders and aphasia.
- Ability to accurately administer hearing screenings and tympanometry readings.
- Perspectives and skills required to effectively work on diagnostic evaluation team.
- Skills to document cases, communicate with colleagues, and correspond with clients and families.
- Fluency using Visual Phonics and American Sign Language.

GRADUATE AND UNDERGRADUATE PROFESSIONAL DEGREES

Brigham Young University, Salt Lake City, UT
Master of Arts in Communicative Disorders, anticipated December 2002
Bachelor of Arts in Communicative Disorders, magna cum laude, May 2000
- Graduate Overall GPA 3.98 and Undergraduate Major GPA 3.91 (out of 4.0)
- Outstanding Senior Award in Communicative Disorders Department, May 2000
- Phi Kappa Phi Honor Society Member and Utah Speech and Hearing Association Member

CLINICAL AND RESEARCH EXPERIENCE

Elmwood Elementary School, Salt Lake City, UT
Language, Speech, and Hearing Intern, February - May 2002
- Administered group therapy to Preschool-6th grade students with articulation and language disorders.
- Worked with students in classroom and independently outside of the classroom.
- Involved in Individualized Education Plan (IEP) assessments and meetings.

Brigham Young University Speech and Hearing Center, Salt Lake City, UT
Student Clinician, September 2000 - Present
- Diagnosed, then planned and administered therapy to children with apraxia, language delay, hearing impairment, and articulation disorders.
- Used Visual Phonics and American Sign Language with hearing-impaired child client.
- Diagnosed, then administered therapy to adult displaying motor speech disorders and aphasia.
- Established home programs to effectively train and motivate parents, spouses, and others.
- Wrote case summaries documenting clinical goals, approaches, and achievements.
Clinical Diagnostic Team Member, 1998 - 2000
- Interviewed, assessed, and wrote reports on stuttering, articulation, and language delay disorder cases.

Brigham Young University Language Disorders Department, Salt Lake City, UT
Visual Phonics and Down's Syndrome Researcher, 2000 - 2002

Bret Harte High School, Salt Lake City, UT
Special Education Classroom Volunteer and ASL Tutor, Summers 1999 and 2000

Jamie Brown

123 Main Street • Hometown, NC 00000 • (555) 555-1234 • jbrown@company.com

Systems Engineering Profile

- Extensive and diversified hardware and software knowledge.
- Expertise in prototype computer testing.
- Comprehensive investigative and research skills.
- Knowledge of programming languages, operating systems, as well as word processing, database, and spreadsheet software applications including: DOS, Windows, Macintosh, UNIX, Assembler Natural, Cs, Java, Pascal, COBOL, Visual Basic, Word, WordPerfect, Excel, Lotus 1-2-3 Access, Oracle, and RoboHELP.

Systems Engineering and Programming Experience

Maximilian Data and Computer Systems   **Charlotte, NC**

Systems Engineer   *1997-present*

Co-authored software test plan for computer prototypes. Researched, wrote, and edited test procedures. Developed computer engineering test tools. Wrote database application to track and generate reports on problems found during development. Organized preproduction testing of prototypes. Analyzed requirements for new processes to improve product testing. Created software that automated work-related processes, such as generating status- and engineering-change request reports.

Systems Programmer   *1994-1997*

Maintained over 300 assembler modules and developed 75. Formulated screen manager program to trace input and output to the VTAM buffer. Developed program to monitor complete security control blocks. Produced a standalone IPL and created a backrest on IBM 3380 DASD.

University of Georgia School of Law   **Atlanta, GA**

Systems Programmer   *Summers 1990-1992 and Full-time 1992-1994*

Initiated start-up and implemented operations. Designed and managed implementation of a network providing the legal community with a direct line to Supreme Court cases. Developed a system that catalogued entire library's inventory. Used Cs to create a registration system for a university registrar.

Engineering and Technical Education

Georgia Tech University   **Atlanta, GA**

B.S. in Computer Science   *May 1992*

Georgia Tech University   **Atlanta, GA**

Post-baccalaureate coursework   *1992-present*

Courses included: Advanced IBM 370 Assembler, SNA Fundamentals, MVS/ESA Architecture, Natural 2 Programming Language, MVS/XA Concepts and Facilities, MVS/XA Job Control Language, MVS/XA System Problem Determination, ACFNTAM Concepts, MVS/XA Using Utility Programs, MVS/XA Using and Creating Procedures.

Dana Johnson

123 Main Street • Hometown, FL 00000 • (555) 555-1234 • djohnson@company.com

TECHNICAL WRITING EXPERIENCE

1999-present   RIZZO ASSOCIATES, Melrose, FL
Technical Writer and Senior Project Administrator
- Research data and accurately describe the installation, removal, erection, and maintenance of all military hardware.
- Outline wiring diagrams, draw part breakdowns for illustrators, draft and finalize all descriptions associated with use of and training to use military hardware.
- Serve as overall program lead for specific projects in A-3, EA-3, and EP-3E programs.
- Work on IPB, MIM, and IFMM for all maintenance levels.
- Transform various source materials, including engineering drawings and wiring diagrams into user targeted written and disc-driven documentation and illustrations.

1994-1999   CAPABIANCO PUBLISHING, Winter Park, FL
Technical Writer
- Supported efforts to develop and finalize illustrations and documentation associated with military hardware.
- Served as project lead, including editing, layout, and corrections.

1990-1994   DARK WILLOW ENGINEERING CORPORATION, Killarney, FL
Editor/Writer
- Edited and wrote large proposals for government contracts.
- Designed format and coordinated production.
- Organized and maintained up-to-date dummy book through several revision cycles.
- Interpreted client requirements and determined applicability of proposal responses.

EDUCATION UNIVERSITY OF FLORIDA, Gainesville, FL

B.S. in Civil Engineering, 1994
Additional coursework in Computer Science, Mathematics, English Literature, and Journalism.

TECHNICAL WRITING AND PROJECT MANAGEMENT QUALIFICATIONS

- Proven abilities to structure technical writing projects and motivate others to complete components accurately and on time.
- Capacities to transform technical information into detailed illustrations and documentation.
- Sensitivities related to creation of classified training and support materials for military hardware.
- Security Clearance Level IA.
- Project and team management skills nurtured via observation and experience.
- Capacities to identify specific task components, set realistic deadlines, then monitor and motivate others.
- Expertise associated with the use of Word, WordPerfect, PowerPoint, Lotus 1-2-3, Excel, and CAD.

Francis Williams

123 Main Street • Hometown, FL 00000 • (555) 555-1234 • Cell (555) 555-5678 • fwilliams@company.com

TELEMARKETING QUALIFICATIONS

- Outstanding selling and closing capabilities illustrated by a proven track record of exceeding goals.
- Well-versed in active listening techniques, nurturing conversations through appropriate questioning.
- Drive and focus required to meet contact and sales quotas, meeting self and other established deadlines.
- Confidence in cold calling and direct sales roles, marketing services and products to businesses and clients.
- Pride associated with using earnings as telemarketer to pay for college tuition and expenses.
- Business Administration, Public Speaking, Persuasive Writing, and Marketing courses.

ACHIEVEMENT SUMMARY

- Induction into national club of Top Ten Percent 2000, 2001, and 2002.
- Awarded Golden Ring Award for meeting sales goals throughout Fiscal Years 2000 and 2001.
- Personally responsible for over $500,000 FY 2001-2002 annual sales as a result of accounts gained.
- Record of consistently reaching or exceeding established goals for over 4 years.

TELEMARKETING EXPERIENCE

2000-present ESP TELECOMMUNICATIONS, Saint Petersburg, FL
Telemarketing Professional
- Cold-called residential and commercial consumers, assessing domestic and international calling needs, and then recommending and marketing long-distance programs.
- Consistently achieved at least 125% of sales goals.
- Landed largest commercial accounts during 2001-2002 and 2000-2001 Fiscal Years.

1998-2000 TEST REVIEW EDUCATION GROUP, Miami, FL
Marketing Assistant
- Cold-called high school and college students and parents, marketing college and graduate school entrance exam preparation courses.
- Yielded 35% attendance at seminars and simulations used to market services.

RETAIL SALES EXPERIENCE

1995-1998 KAYBEE TOYS, Miami, FL
Sales Associate
- Addressed inquiries of customers, maintained inventory levels, and trained salespersons.

EDUCATION ROLLINS COLLEGE, Winter Park, FL
Bachelor of Arts, English, anticipated May 2004

MIAMI DADE JUNIOR COLLEGE, Miami, FL
Associate of Arts, Liberal Studies, August 2002

COREY DAVIS

123 Main Street • Hometown, MA 00000 • (555) 555-1234 • cdavis@company.com

SPORTS MEDICINE STUDIES

ITHACA COLLEGE, Ithaca, NY
BA Sports Medicine, May 1997

ATHLETIC TRAINING EXPERIENCE

ITHACA COLLEGE, Ithaca, NY
Senior Trainer, 1997–present
Conduct hydrostatic weighing and skin-fold body fat tests. Set up individual rehab and strengthening programs, and serve as nutrition and fitness consultant to all teams. Oversee all student trainers.
Rehabilitation Trainer, 1995–1997
Student Trainer, 1994–1997

WORLD WRESTLING FEDERATION, Syracuse, NY
Athletic Trainer for Syracuse and Rochester Appearances, 1996–present

FITNESS EXPERIENCE

MIDTOWN RACQUETBALL CLUB, Milford, MA
Aerobic Instructor, Summers 1993–1996

TOTAL HEALTH AND FITNESS STOP, Hopedale, MA
Aerobic Instructor, Summer and Part-time 1992

FOCUS ON FITNESS, Ashland, MA
Aerobic Instructor, Summers and Part-time 1990–1992

WORLD GYM, Framingham, MA
Aerobic Instructor, Part-time 1990–1994

CERTIFICATIONS AND AFFILIATIONS

A.C.E. (American Council on Exercise) Personal Trainer Certification and Fitness Instructor Certification Basic Life Saving and Cardiac Care Certified, American Heart Association. Standard First Aid Certified, American Red Cross. Member N.A.T.A. (National Athletic Trainers Association).

QUALIFICATIONS

- Experience implementing programs designed to prevent and treat injuries of athletes in variety of sports including football, wrestling, volleyball, basketball, swimming, water polo, and tennis.
- Taught a variety of weekly classes including hi-lo, low impact, body sculpting, and step. Introduced funk aerobics to participants age 15–65.
- Taught "FITKIDS" classes for ages 3–6 and ages 7–11. Also taught adult funk classes combining street and dance moves to accompany dance and rap music.

Travel Agent

Chris Smith

123 Main Street • Hometown, IL 00000 • (555) 555-1234 • csmith@company.com

Travel Industry Qualifications

- Four years of experience acquired via travel industry employment and training.
- Thorough knowledge of various reservation transactions, including booking, bursting, ticketing, sales, customer service, and dealing with contracted vendors to ensure customer reservation specifications.
- Expertise assisting individuals, groups, and corporate accounts with specialized knowledge of cruise industry and Disney packages.

Professional Experience and Achievements

SURGE AND SIEGE TRAVEL, INC.   Joliet, IL
Air and Sea Coordinator   1999-present
- Coordinate air ticketing requests and tour departures using APOLLO and SABRE systems.
- Serve as agency specialized for cruise industry.
- Regularly attend sessions hosted by cruise and air carriers, educating regarding options and plans.
- Track international and domestic fares, sharing data with colleagues daily.
- Issue tickets and final itineraries for air and cruise customers.
- Maintain and file pertinent materials and assist with updating of website (www.surgetravel.com).
- Assist with projects associated with marketing of Disney World, Disneyland, and Disney Cruises.
- Serve as group leader for numerous cruise and resort familiarization trips.
- Prepare detailed financial reports and assist senior management with development of strategic goals.

QUICK TRIP TRAVEL   Evanston, IL
Travel Consultant   1997-1999
- Arranged individual and group travel, regularly yielding monthly billings in excess of $10,000.
- Promoted agency via weekly visits to senior residences as well as college campuses.
- Regularly attended training sessions related to airline offerings and reservation systems updates.

GOTTA FLY TOURS   Wheaton, IL
Computer Operator/Intern   1995-1997
- Trained to use SABRE and other airline as well as cruise and resort reservation systems.
- Administered ARC ticket stock and accountable documents.
- Rotated through specialty areas and assisted with accounting activities.

Professional Training and Education

MIDWEST TRAVEL SCHOOL, Chicago, IL
Certificate, 1997

DEPAUL UNIVERSITY, Chicago, IL
Bachelor of Arts, History, 1995

WINDY CITY COMMUNITY COLLEGE, Chicago, IL
Associate of Arts, Geography, 1993

Jamie Brown

123 Main Street • Hometown, MD 00000 • (555) 555-1234 • jbrown@company.com

Tutorial and Teaching Qualifications

- Capacities to teach and tutor various high school subjects, including English, Literature, Creative Writing, US and World History, and self-paced SAT Preparation and GED curriculum.
- Tutored and taught English as a Second Language to university students in the US and abroad.
- Experience as tutor, instructor, and teaching assistant addressing needs of college and high school students with varied backgrounds, abilities, and motivations.
- Multicultural sensitivities gained through overseas studies and successes within ESL roles.

Undergraduate and Overseas Studies

Loyola College, Baltimore, MD
Bachelor of Arts in English, emphasis in Professional Writing, May 2002
- Overall GPA: 3.6; English GPA 3.8 and Dean's List 6 of 6 Eligible Semesters

Josef Eotvos Kollegium, Budapest, HUNGARY
Hungarian Language, Literature, and Politics courses, Fall 2001

University of Koln, Koln, GERMANY
German Language, History, Government, and Literature courses, Spring-Summer 2001

University of Edinburgh, Edinburgh, SCOTLAND
Took Scottish History course, Summer 2000

Tutorial and Teaching Experience

Loyola College, Baltimore, MD

Summer 2002 — Summer Enrichment Program Advisor and Tutor: Advised, tutored, and taught specialized courses to selected group of High School students. Planned and implemented 10-week Study Skills, SAT Preparation, and Writing Skills seminars, focusing on at-risk students with the potential to succeed in college. Created assignments based "Reality Academy," an ideal high school.

1998-2002 — International Students Association Tutor: Taught and tutored English as a Second Language to Japanese, German, and Russian students.

2000-2002 — Writing Center Tutor and Persuasive Paper Writing Seminar Instructor

1998-2002 — Study Skills Center English and History Tutor

St. Luke's School, Baltimore, MD

2001-present — Substitute Teacher and Tutor Grades 8-12

Baltimore County Women's Facility, Baltimore, MD

2001-present — GED Student Teacher, Fall 1993

Private English Tutoring, Budapest, HUNGARY and Koln, GERMANY

1990-1991 — English as a Second Language Tutor

DANA JOHNSON

123 Main Street • Hometown, OR 00000 • (555) 555-1234 • djohnson@company.com

CERTIFICATIONS AND QUALIFICATIONS

- State of Oregon Licensed Animal Health Technician.
- 7 years of progressively responsible clinical, research, and supervisory experience.
- Generalist experience with all species and varied procedures in private practices and state-affiliated research and treatment facility.
- Specialist skills and competencies associated with surgery.

ANIMAL CARE EDUCATION

UNIVERSITY OF OREGON, Eugene, OR
B.A. in Animal Health Technology, 1999

UNIVERSITY OF PORTLAND, Portland, OR
A.S. in Animal Health Technology, 1995

VETERINARY AND ANIMAL CARE EXPERIENCE

UPPER VALLEY ANIMAL CARE CLINIC, Marylhurst, OR
Senior Surgical Assistant, 1999-present
- Perform pre- and postoperative care and emergency care.
- Monitor ventilation and vital statistics of premature and critically ill animals.
- Collect and ship blood samples, perform intravenous and arterial catheterization, intubation of endotracheal and nasogastric tubes.
- Organize labs for and oversee veterinary students and clinical instruction sessions.

Surgical Assistant, 1997-99
- Assisted clinicians and students treating patients, and provided room pre- and post-operative care.

NEWMAN ANIMAL CARE CLINIC, Medford, OR
Surgery Intern, Part-time 1997-99

CHRIS SMITH, D.V.M., Portland, OR
Veterinary Assistant, Part-time 1993-95
- Assisted with daily diagnosis and treatment, and served as ICU specialist, completing oral, IV, IM, SQ, fluid therapy, radiology, hematology, immunology, chemotherapy-related tasks.
- Administered, assisted, and maintained anesthesia during surgery.

UNIVERSITY OF OREGON RESEARCH CENTER, Eugene, OR
Animal Technician/Research Assistant, Part-time 1993-95
- Directed hygienic procedures on 300 animals, including surgery and necropsies.
- Conducted research on pet food products and analyzed studies on nutrition, zinc, urine, feces, fluid therapy, medication, breeding, and artificial insemination.
- Collaborated in testing new vaccine for feline leukemia, submitting reports for FDA approval.
- Supervised and scheduled 20 center and union employees in conducting research.

Francis Williams

123 Main Street • Apartment 13 • Hometown, HI 00000
(555) 555-0988 • fwilliams@company.com

FOOD SERVICES EXPERIENCE

THE PALMS   Kaneohe, HI
Head Waiter   *2000-present*
- Manage, open, and close high-volume four-star restaurant.
- Hire, train, schedule, and supervise wait staff.
- Lead weekly quality assurance and menu discussion sessions.
- Oversee special catering events held on-site and at residences of patrons.
- Address concerns and special requests.
- Reconcile gratuity intake in accordance with tax regulations.

PALUA SAILS RESTAURANT   Kaneohe, HI
Head Waiter   *1998-2000*
- Provided efficient service to full bar, serving area, and catered affairs.
- Trained new wait staff.

CANDLE IN THE WIND   Honolulu, HI
Barback   *Part-time 1996-1998*
- Handled customer service and cash intake.
- Assisted with liquor inventory.
- Performed security services.

BLUE HAWAII RESTAURANT   Honolulu, HI
Busboy   *Part-time 1994-1996*
- Set and cleared about 20 tables per evening of large dining room.
- Trained new bus people.

SPECIALIZED TRAINING AND RECOGNITION

- Completed Palms Patron Services Training offered to Head Waiters and tenured servers.
- Regularly rated "superior" in all weekly, monthly, and annual performance reviews.
- Certified in the SIPS program for responsibly serving alcohol.
- Attended Restaurant Association training sessions: "Customer Satisfaction Is in Your Hands" and "Teaching Others to Service."

EDUCATION

HAWAII LOA COLLEGE   Kaneohe, HI
B.A. in Liberal Arts   *expected 2003*

Before-and-After Resumes

The following resume samples are under very tight space requirements. On a normal sheet of paper you could fit more lines and have wider margins, thus allowing for more content. A good rule of thumb is to allow half-inch margins on the top, bottom, left, and right.

Advertising Account Executive (Before)

CHRIS SMITH

csmith@company.com

123 Main Street
Hometown, NY 00000
(555) 555-1234

987 Centre Avenue
Hometown, NY 10001
(555) 555-5678

EDUCATION

1999-2002	**UNIVERSITY OF ROCHESTER**, Rochester, NY **Bachelor of Arts, French,** with a major GPA of 3.5, May 2002. **Bachelor of Arts, Psychology,** with a major GPA of 3.3, May 2001. Minor: **Economics,** with a minor GPA of 3.4. • **Management Studies Certificate,** for completion of courses taught by faculty of College and the William E. Simon School of Business Administration. • Economics Council, Activity Board, and Campus Times Staff Writer.
1998-1999	HOBART AND WILLIAM SMITH COLLEGES, Geneva, NY

EXPERIENCE

Spring 2001	THE FINANCIAL GROUP DISCOUNT BROKERAGE, Pittsford, NY **Intern/Assistant to Operations Manager:** Used computerized financial transactions and market tracking systems. Updated customer databases using Excel. Interacted with and completed administrative projects for licensed representatives and addressed client inquiries from throughout the United States.
Summer 2001	DAYS ADVERTISING, INC., Pittsford, NY **Intern/Assistant to an Account Manager:** Assisted with design of television and radio ads and proposals for varied products and clients, including Wegmans and Bausch & Lomb. Developed customer database.
2000-2001	ADEFFECTS, Rochester, NY **Intern/Assistant to an Account Manager:** Researched and developed promotional materials for local retail, manufacturing, and restaurant clients. Gained knowledge of small business marketing. Recommended changes in client advertising materials, consumer outreach strategies, and marketing literature.
Summer 2001	PEARLE VISION CENTER, Pittsford, NY **Sales Representative:** Implement strategy targeting upscale markets.
Summer 1999	IT HAPPENS, Antwerp, Belgium **Marketing Intern:** Determined target markets and developed ad budget for concert, event planning, and entertainment agency. Conducted market penetration surveys. Assisted graphic artists producing ads, posters, brochures, and reports.

Before

Advertising Account Executive (After)

CHRIS SMITH

123 Main Street • Hometown, NY 00000 • (555) 555-1234 • csmith@company.com
987 Centre Avenue, Apartment 13 • Rochester, NY 00000 • (555) 555-5678

ADVERTISING ACCOUNT MANAGEMENT QUALIFICATIONS

- Marketing research, strategic planning, promotions, customer service, and sales talents nurtured by diverse advertising, promotions, and retail internships and employment.
- Skills gained via courses including: Marketing, Marketing Projects and Cases, Motivation, Public Relations Writing, Advertising, and Consumer Behavior.
- German, French, Dutch, and Farsi fluency, and conversational Spanish capabilities.
- UNIX, HTML, Word, WordPerfect, Excel, PageMaker, PhotoShop, and Internet skills.

ADVERTISING AND MARKETING EXPERIENCE

DAYS ADVERTISING, INC., Pittsford, NY
Account Management Intern: Assisted with design of TV and radio ads and proposals for clients, including Wegmans and Bausch & Lomb. Developed client database. Summer 2001

ADEFFECTS, Rochester, NY
Account Management Intern: Researched and developed promotional materials for retail, manufacturing, and restaurant clients, using knowledge of small business marketing. Suggested client changes in outreach strategies, and marketing literature. 2000-2001

PEARLE VISION CENTER, Pittsford, NY
Sales Representative: Implemented strategy targeting upscale markets. Summer 2001

IT HAPPENS, Antwerp, Belgium
Marketing Intern: Determined target markets and developed advertisement budget for concert, event planning, and entertainment agency. Conducted surveys to determine market penetration. Assisted graphic artists with ads, posters, brochures, and reports. Summer 1998

BUSINESS, ECONOMICS, AND LANGUAGE STUDIES

UNIVERSITY OF ROCHESTER, Rochester, NY
Bachelor of Arts, French, with a major GPA of 3.5, May 2002.
Bachelor of Arts, Psychology, with a major GPA of 3.3, May 2002.
Minor: **Economics,** with a minor GPA of 3.4.

WILLIAM E. SIMON SCHOOL OF BUSINESS ADMINISTRATION, Rochester, NY
Management Studies Certificate, Marketing and Finance/Accounting Tracks, May 2002.

FINANCE EXPERIENCE

THE FINANCIAL GROUP, INC. DISCOUNT BROKERAGE FIRM, Pittsford, NY
Intern/Assistant to Operations Manager, Spring 2001

- Identifying information uses only two lines.

- Left-justified block text format is e-friendly; can be uploaded to Web sites and copied and pasted into e-mail.

- Experience presented under targeted "headline."

- Education presented under targeted headline to highlight specialized studies.

- Courses presented in Qualification Summary to highlight significance.

- Chris is a focused yet typical soon-to-be graduate. His "before" resume is multipurpose. Chris's strategy of having a multipurpose and a targeted resume is sound.

- Both possess qualities worthy of modeling.

- Think about the "headlines" used in the after version and about changes in the order of presentation.

- How did the qualification summary change your reaction to this resume?

- Courier font appears typewritten, not typeset.

- Education presented first, without dates, under general "header" in confusing format.

- Experience under basic and generic header in confusing format.

- Difficult to see chronological or functional progress year to year or job to job.

Jamie Brown

123 Main Street
Home (555) 555-5555

Hometown, CO 00000
Cell (555) 555-9999

EDUCATION
30 Education credits, with day care emphasis, and English minor.
Metropolitan State College, Denver, CO

EXPERIENCE
1999-present   NANNY
Care for twin boys from the age of two months through two years. Assist in selecting toys and equipment, provide environmental stimulation, personal care, and play.
Private residence, Livermore, CO

1997-99   TEACHER
Taught infant, preschool, and after-school programs. Planned curriculum, organized activities, communicated with parents and staff regarding growth and development. Suggested equipment to enrich children's experiences and helped create a stimulating environment.
Baby Bear Preschool, Keystone, CO

1995-97   TEACHER
Planned and implemented curriculum for infants. Communicated with parents and other staff regarding daily progress of children.
This Little Piggy Daycare Center, Dove Creek, CO

1993-95   TEACHER
Planned and implemented curriculum for toddler program. Enriched children's experiences through play, music, and art.
The Kid Corral, Wild Horse, CO

1991-93   CAREGIVER
Provided care in clients' homes, administering physical therapy when necessary. Planned activities to stimulate and improve children's skills and environment.
Residences, Dove Creek, and Keystone, CO

1995-present   VOLUNTEER
Ivywild Coalition for Retarded Citizens, Ivywild, CO

SKILLS AND INTERESTS
Valid driver's license; perfect driving record. CPR/first aid certified. Skiing, reading, music, arts and crafts.

Day Care Worker (After)

Jamie Brown
123 Main Street • Hometown, CO 00000 • (555) 555-1234 • Cell: (555) 555-9999

DAY CARE QUALIFICATIONS AND COMPETENCIES
- Over 9 years of diverse experience within home and school settings, teaching and caring for children ranging in ages from 2 months to 7 years.
- Commitment to the needs of infants, preschoolers, and kindergarteners.
- Academic background including courses in: Childhood Development, Early Childhood Education, Educational Psychology, and Assessments.

DAY CARE, TEACHING, AND CHILD CARE EXPERIENCE

1999-present   PRIVATE RESIDENCE, Livermore, CO
Nanny: Care for twin boys from the age of two months through two years. Provide environmental enrichment, personal care, and play supervision.
- Accompanied family on trips and cared for children during illnesses.

1997-1999   BABY BEAR PRESCHOOL, Keystone, CO
Teacher: Taught infant, preschool, and after-school programs. Planned curriculum, organized activities, communicated with parents and staff regarding children's growth and development.
- Responded to annual increase in students and move to new facility.
- Worked collegially with owner on goal development.
- Assisted with annual licensing documentation and visitation.

1995-1997   THIS LITTLE PIGGY DAYCARE CENTER, Dove Creek, CO
Teacher: Planned and implemented infant program, blending developmental and custodial needs. Communicated with parents regarding student progress.
- Enhanced skills development through interactive play and song.

1993-1995   THE KID CORRAL, Wild Horse, CO
Teacher: Planned and implemented curriculum for toddler program. Enriched children's experiences through play, music, and art.

1993-1999   PRIVATE CAREGIVER, Wild Horse, Dove Creek, and Keystone, CO

1995-present   COALITION FOR RETARDED CITIZENS VOLUNTEER, Ivywild, CO

EDUCATION
1990-1993   METROPOLITAN STATE COLLEGE, Denver, CO
- 30 credits in Education, with an emphasis on day care.

REFERENCES
William and Sarah Smithers, (555) 555-4444, reference@company.com
Sue Bear, Owner, Baby Bear Preschool, (555) 555-1234, bbear@company.com

---

- Professional and e-friendly Garamond font.
- Qualifications and competencies appearing first serve as objective and preview of assets.
- Experience under targeted "headline" in easy-to-review format.
- Date timeline shows chronological and functional progress.
- One of the few fields where references should appear.
- Jamie is an experienced nanny and day care professional. Her current employer has informed her that she will no longer be needed full-time. For the increasingly professional worlds of day care, private child-care, and preschools, she created a very professional resume.
- This version is targeted toward upscale day care facilities and parents.

Financial Planner (Before)

Dana Johnson

123 Main Street
Hometown, New Jersey 00000

(555) 555-1234
djohnson@company.com

Experience

ABC FINANCIAL CONSULTANTS, Princeton, NJ
July 1990-present
Financial Consultant/Financial Planner
- Developed $210 million client base via prospecting.
- Build portfolio that includes stock, bonds, options, and insurance products for more than 450 clients.
- Implemented financial plans and operations through account development and growth.

October 1988-July 1990
Sales Associate
- Worked directly with firm's top producer, profiling high net worth individuals for future business.
- Generated $90,000 for top producer via new accounts.
- Analyzed portfolios to expand account performance.

September 1987-October 1988
Account Executive Trainee/Intern
- Supervised about 35,000 accounts in the area of trade settlement, NASD regulations, and customer inquiries.
- Reported recommendations to upper management.
- Acted as liaison with New York operations.

MAPLEWOOD INVESTMENTS, Maplewood, NJ
Summers 1986 and 1987
Prospecting Intern
- Planned, created documents for, and oversaw invitations and confirmations for 3 annual Summer Financial Seminars.
- Researched stock and updated transactions.

Related Training

Successfully completed ABC Financial Consultant Sales Training and Advanced Training program in Princeton, NJ, headquarters. Licensed in Series 6,7,63 and health and life insurance.

Education

IONA COLLEGE, Iona, New York
Bachelor of Arts degree in Economics, 1988

Before

Financial Planner (After)

Dana Johnson

123 Main Street • Hometown, NJ 00000 • (555) 555-1234 • djohnson@company.com

Financial Planning Qualifications and Credentials

- Over a decade of progressively significant roles and achievements in planning, portfolio management, and client services.
- Personal responsibilities for more than $210 million client assets.
- Recognized for asset-based performance and customer service.
- Served as trainer and curriculum developer.

Financial Planning Accomplishments

1990-present

ABC FINANCIAL CONSULTANTS, Princeton, NJ
Financial Consultant/Financial Planner
Serve in comprehensive financial planning roles. Oversee individual and group portfolios. Serve as senior manager, supervisor, and trainer within corporate headquarters of firm responsible for over $800 million in client assets.

- Developed $210 million client asset base through aggressive prospecting and targeting campaign.
- Successfully built portfolio that includes stock, bonds, options and insurance products for more than 450 clients.
- Implemented financial plans and operations through account development and growth.
- Gained expertise associated with estate planning, asset allocation, and wealth succession.
- Completed ABC Financial Consultant Sales Training and Advanced Training Program. Licensed in Series 6, 7, 63, and health and life insurance.

1988-1990

Sales Associate
- Worked directly with firm's top producer, profiling high net worth individuals for future business.
- Generated $90,000 through new account openings.
- Analyzed portfolios to expand account performance.

1987-1988

Account Executive Trainee/Intern
- Completed about 35,000 account transactions annually.
- Completed comprehensive training related to trade settlement, NASD regulations, and customer service.

Summers 1986 and 1987

MAPLEWOOD INVESTMENTS, Maplewood, NJ
Prospecting Intern

Education

IONA COLLEGE, Iona, New York
Bachelor of Arts degree in Economics, 1988

Francis Williams

123 Main Street   987 Centre Ave.
Hometown, NY 00000   Homeville, NY 10001
(555) 555-1234   fwilliams@company.com   (555) 555-5678

EDUCATION

UNIVERSITY OF ROCHESTER, Rochester, NY
Bachelor of Arts, Health and Society, anticipated May 2003
Management Certificate in Public Sector Analysis, anticipated May 2002
Completed Language and Cultural Studies in Rome, Italy Spring 2001

ACTIVITIES AND LEADERSHIP

SIGMA DELTA FRATERNITY
President, 2002-2003, *Secretary,* 2000-2001, and *Member,* 1999-present

STUDENT HEALTH ADVISORY COMMITTEE
Member, 2002-2003

EXPERIENCE

CHECK YOUR PULSE AMERICA RESEARCH STUDY, Rochester, NY
Research Assistant: Helped design aspects of nationwide research study dealing with stroke prevention. Responsibilities included distribution of questionnaire, data entry, and report writing and editing. Fall 2001

NYS VETERANS NURSING HOME, Wood Cliff, NY
Human Resource Assistant: Supported various recruiting, payroll, and benefits activities. Collected, reviewed, and rated resumes. Communicated with candidates by phone and e-mail. Summer 2002

THE CARDIOLOGY GROUP, Wood Cliff, NY
Administrative Assistant: Greeted and scheduled patients, maintained files, assisted with billing, communicated with insurance carriers and pharmacies, and completed special tasks as assigned. 1998-present

YOUR INSURANCE GROUP, White Plains, NY
Office Assistant, Summer 2001

COMPUTER AND OFFICE SKILLS

Word, Excel, PowerPoint, Access, and Internet capabilities.
- Abilities to serve in receptionist, billing, and human resource roles.

Before

Francis Williams

123 Main St. • Hometown, NY 00000 • (555) 555-1234 • fwill@company.com
987 Centre Ave. • Homeville, NY 10001 • (555) 555-5678

MEDICAL PRODUCT SALES QUALIFICATIONS

- Knowledge of health care, business, and economics-related topics gained from courses including: Accounting, Microeconomics, Business Administration, Changing Concepts of Disease, Medical Sociology, Domestic Social Policy, Organizational Psychology, and Statistics.
- Confidence and experience communicating with physicians, health care practitioners, patients, and others associated with medical devices.
- Research, project management, time management, writing, and oral communication skills gained from employment, education, and activities.
- Capacities to conduct topic-specific research, identify trends or key issues, and document findings in reports as well as presentations.
- Persuasive communication style, required to educate regarding protocols and studies specific to medical products and treatment techniques.
- Word, Excel, PowerPoint, Access, and Internet capabilities.

HEALTH AND SOCIETY AND BUSINESS EDUCATION

UNIVERSITY OF ROCHESTER, Rochester, NY
Bachelor of Arts, Health and Society, anticipated May 2003
- Health and Society Major focused on study of Community and Preventive Medicine, as well as history and economics of health care delivery.
- Sigma Delta Fraternity President, Secretary, and Member.
- Student Health Advisory Committee, Member **and** Class of 2002 Senator.

WILLIAM E. SIMON SCHOOL OF BUSINESS ADMINISTRATION, Rochester, NY
Management Certificate in Public Sector Analysis, anticipated May 2003
- Certificate for completion of business, economics, and policy-focused courses taught by faculty of the College and of the Simon School.

TEMPLE UNIVERSITY ROME, Rome, Italy
Completed Language and Cultural Studies, Spring Semester 2001

HEALTH CARE, BUSINESS, AND RESEARCH EXPERIENCE

CHECK YOUR PULSE AMERICA RESEARCH STUDY, Rochester, NY
Research Assistant: Helped design aspects of nationwide research study dealing with stroke prevention. Fall 2001

NYS VETERANS NURSING HOME, Wood Cliff, NY
Human Resource Assistant: Supported recruiting, payroll, and benefits activities. Summer 2002

THE CARDIOLOGY GROUP, Wood Cliff, NY
Administrative Assistant, Summers and Part-time 1997-present

YOUR INSURANCE GROUP, White Plains, NY
Office Assistant, Summer 2001

- Left-justified block text format can be uploaded to sites and copy-and-pasted into e-mail.
- Objective presented via qualification summary.
- Marketing, business, and health-care courses presented first in qualification section, highlighting significance.
- A goal-targeted summary of qualifications is first, immediately followed by detailed education presentation. This "top loads" the most important information first.
- Summary of qualification, supplemented by a cover letter, shows commitment and the capabilities to succeed.

COREY DAVIS

123 Main Street • Santa Fe, NM 00000 • (555) 555-5555

EXPERIENCE

BRENDAN ELLIS CIVIL LITIGATION SPECIALIST/OFFICE MANAGER
Santa Fe, NM 1998-present
- Manage office and staff of 3 secretaries, ensuring smooth operation of firm.
- Interview clients; prepare files and discovery.
- Request and review medical documentation; ascertain evidence information and process all with the appropriate parties.
- Negotiate and settle cases with defense attorney and insurance companies.
- Attend mediations and conciliations.
- Prepare clients for depositions and trials.
- Control and maintain law office accounts.

BROWNINGTON, INC. ADMINISTRATIVE ASSISTANT
Albuquerque, NM 1993-98
- Confirmed all manpower hours and prepared logs to bill various sites.
- Provided clerical support to 24 software engineers.
- Recognized for "Excellence in Customer Satisfaction Southwest Region."

WILD RAIN EXOTIC GIFTS MANAGER/SALESPERSON
Silver City, NM 1990-93
- Sold art and memorabilia on consignment.
- Hired, trained, and supervised 8 sales personnel.
- Handled accounts, managed orders, and created promotions.

SANTA FE DISTRICT ATTORNEY'S DOMESTIC VIOLENCE WITNESS ADVOCATE
Santa Fe, NM Spring-Summer 1990
- Interviewed victims and witnesses, prepared documents, and organized information for court appearances.
- Assisted attorneys during trials.

NEW MEXICO PUBLIC DEFENDER'S LEGAL INTERN
Santa Fe, NM Summers 1988 and 1989
- Researched and drafted motions on criminal law and procedural issues.
- Interviewed clients at Illinois correctional institutions.
- Negotiated plea and bail agreements for defendants.

ATTORNEY DANIEL GALL LEGAL SECRETARY/LEGAL ASSISTANT
Santa Fe, NM 1986-90

EDUCATION

SAINT JOHN'S COLLEGE B.S., HUMAN RESOURCE MANAGEMENT
Santa Fe, NM 1990

Before

COREY DAVIS

123 Main Street • Hometown, NM 00000 • (555) 555-5555 • cdavis@company.com
987 Centre Avenue • Hometown, CA 00000 • (555) 555-1234

After

PARALEGAL QUALIFICATIONS AND ACHIEVEMENTS

- Case research, client relations, document management, and writing skills gained in progressively responsible positions over a 12-year period.
- Expertise as law office manager, compiling training manual, supervising support personnel, revamping accounting, debit, and credit systems.
- Trained and accomplished interviewer, negotiation, and mediation.
- LexisNexis, WestLaw, Word, FileMaker, Excel, QuickBooks, and Internet skills.

PARALEGAL AND MANAGEMENT EXPERIENCE

LAW OFFICES OF BRENDAN ELLIS   Santa Fe, NM
Civil Litigation Specialist/Office Manager   1990-present
- Manage office and staff of 3 secretaries, ensuring operation of firm with 3 attorneys and billings of $1.5 million and awards over $10 million annually.
- Interview clients; prepare files and discovery; handle multiple cases.
- Request and review medical documentation; ascertain evidence information and process all with the appropriate parties.
- Negotiate and settle cases with defense attorney and insurance companies.
- Attend mediations and conciliations.
- Prepare clients for depositions and trials.
- Control and maintain office accounts, using accounting and billing software.

SANTE FE DISTRICT ATTORNEY'S DOMESTIC VIOLENCE UNIT   Santa Fe, NM
Witness Advocate   Spring-Summer 1990
- Interviewed victims and witnesses, prepared documents and organized information for court appearances.
- Assisted attorneys during trials, taking notes and facilitating access to evidentiary documents.

NEW MEXICO PUBLIC DEFENDER'S OFFICE   Santa Fe, NM
Legal Intern   Summers 1988 and 1989
- Researched and drafted motions on criminal law and procedural issues. Interviewed clients at Illinois correctional institutions.
- Negotiated plea and bail agreements for defendants accused of misdemeanors. Attended criminal trials and depositions.

ATTORNEY DANIEL GALL   Santa Fe, NM
Legal Secretary/Legal Assistant   1986-1990

EDUCATION

SAINT JOHN'S COLLEGE   Santa Fe, NM
B.S., Human Resource Management, with Honors   1990
- Completed degree part-time while employed.

- Qualification and achievement summary support objective and previews experience.

- Experience under specialized headline, only presenting law background.

- Capitalization, italics, and bullets used as effective highlighting techniques.

- Education last, but notes achievement of receiving degree as returning student while working.

- Corey is an experienced paralegal who is relocating to the San Francisco Bay Area. She notes a local address to reinforce the reality of this relocation.

- Objective appearing as a qualifications and achievement section. Bullets show career progression and strong background appropriate for stated job-search target. Core of the document is the headline-focused "Paralegal and Management Experience" section. Bulleted achievements are cited under easy-to-identify locations and dates.

Pharmaceutical Sales (Before)

- Courier font appears bland and difficult to read.

- Lengthy objective contains unnecessary wording.

- Experience and education under basic and generic header.

- Titles use less-than-creative underline highlighting.

- Paragraph presentation of experience descriptions difficult to peruse quickly or read thoroughly.

- Internship presented as honors appears as college candidate rather than experienced candidate.

Chris Smith

123 Main St., Hometown, CA 00000, (555)555-1234, cs@company.com

CAREER OBJECTIVE
Challenging pharmaceutical sales position with a progressive organization seeking dynamic and driven sales professional.

EXPERIENCE
Pearls and Gemstones Corporation, San Francisco, California 6/01-Present
Sales Associate: Sell and market polished gemstones for the San Francisco office of international gemstone and pearl distributor and jewelry manufacturer.

Bank of Hong Kong, Hong Kong 6/00-8/00
Trader: International Securities Dealing Room: Responded to customers' executing orders in the areas of American and foreign equities, bonds, and options. Received training in and gained working knowledge of Bloomberg and Reuters information systems.

Bank of Hong Kong, San Francisco, California 11/97-10/99
Credit Analyst: International Lending Department: Prepared proposals on prospective customers and renewals and reaffirmations of existing facilities for credit committee. Performed financial statement, cash flow, and projection analysis. Conducted research using Bloomberg, Moody's, and S&P analysts and publications.

Computer Associates International, San Jose, California 1/97-9/97
Quality Assurance Analyst: Implemented quality assurance for inter/intranet-enabled, multiplatform, enterprise management solution used worldwide.

EDUCATION
University of California, Berkeley, California
Bachelor of Arts — Class of 1997
Major: Political Science. Minor: Economics.
Dean's List Fall 1996 and Spring 1995 and Overall GPA: 3.34/4.0

University of New South Wales, Sydney, Australia — Spring 1996

HONORS
International Internships, London, England
Gordon McMaster, MP: British Parliament 9/95-12/95
Performed research, assisted in speech writing, aided constituents.

IPA Political Internships, Washington, DC
Senator Barbara Boxer: U.S. Senate 6/95-8/95
Wrote research briefs on pending legislation.

Before

Chris Smith

123 Main Street • Hometown, California 00000 • (555) 555-1234 • csmith@company.com

OBJECTIVE

Pharmaceutical Sales Position using and expanding upon ...
- Record of success within direct marketing and information-driven sales roles.
- Confidence nurturing relationships via direct calls using information dissemination strategies.
- Capacity to understand and share knowledge of pharmaceutical products and protocols.
- Abilities to set goals, document efforts and outcomes, and maximize achievements.
- Bilingual English-Mandarin abilities and cross-cultural sensitivities.

SALES AND SALES SUPPORT ACHIEVEMENTS

PEARLS AND GEMSTONES CORPORATION, San Francisco, California   2001-Present
Sales Associate for Loose Diamond Division: Sell gemstones for international distributor and manufacturer. Sales methods include appointments onsite, telemarketing, trade show exhibiting, and Internet. Customers include manufacturers, retail and department stores, and catalogues.
- *Directly involved in sales to house accounts totaling $2.5 million in 2001.*
- *Indirectly involved in sales to salespersons accounts totaling $3 million in 2001.*

COMPUTER ASSOCIATES INTERNATIONAL, San Jose, California   1997
Quality Assurance Analyst: Analyzed business applications for functionality and marketability. Reviewed RFPs (Request For Proposal) and identified key marketing leverage points. Implemented quality assurance for worldwide projects and software products.
- *Supported customer service and sales representatives in refining product to match customer needs.*

BUSINESS AND FINANCE EXPERIENCE

BANK OF HONG KONG, Hong Kong   Spring 2000
Securities Trader: Executed American and foreign equities, bonds, and option orders.

BANK OF HONG KONG, San Francisco, California   1997-2000
Department Credit Analyst: Prepared proposals on prospective customers and renewals for credit committee. Researched using Bloomberg, Moody's, and S&P analysts and publications.

BUSINESS, ECONOMICS, AND LIBERAL ARTS EDUCATION

UNIVERSITY OF CALIFORNIA, BERKELEY, Berkeley, California   1993-1997
Bachelor of Arts Political Science, with minor in Economics,
- Intern for Member of British Parliament, Fall 1995, and Senator Boxer, Summer 1995.

HAAS SCHOOL OF BUSINESS ADMINISTRATION, Berkeley, California   1993-1997
- Management Certificate for completion of Marketing and Business courses.

- Garamond font is professional and space efficient.
- Qualifications, summarizing assets, and showing field knowledge are blended with brief objective.
- Experience uses two "headlines" with the first matching objective.
- Education uses headline related to objective.
- Courses presented to highlight significance.
- Bilingual abilities cited.
- Sales experience is presented first, using a format that highlights achievements.
- Education, using targeted "headline," is near the bottom.

JAMIE BROWN

123 Main Street, Hometown, NY 00000, (555) 555-1234

EXPERIENCE

SYRACUSE HEART ASSOCIATION, Syracuse, NY
Public Relations Manager, 2000-present
Organizing: Serve as consultant to the 7 state chapters. Organize statewide and regional campaign meetings; speak at campaign conferences. *Lobbying:* Review legislation regarding the Society and bring specific bills to attention of proper committee or individual. Staff the Legislative Advisory Committee and follow through on specific bills. *Fundraising:* Develop fundraising programs. Conducted two annual campaigns for newly merged Central Chapter. Serve as chair for New York Independent Health Agency Committee and secretary for Combined Federal Campaign. *Training:* Developed orientation courses held for new employees; acted as training coordinator.
Directorial Assistant for Greater Syracuse Chapter, 1995-1997
Assisted the Executive Director with administrative responsibilities, such as personnel and budget.

BIG APPLE NATURAL FOODS, Syracuse, NY
Special Events Coordinator, 1998-2000
Created and coordinated special events and promotions. Selected and wrote event advertising and promotional materials. Managed $425,000 marketing budget. Handled charity fundraising, corporate image positioning, and community outreach activities.
Assistant to the Director of Public Relations, 1997-1998
Assisted in promotion and publicity of special events. Drafted press releases. Developed press kits; maintained media relations. Compiled publicity files. Researched prospective consumer markets.

SYRACUSE UNIVERSITY, Syracuse, NY
Teacher's Assistant, Fall and Spring 1998
Assisted professor in editing book. Developed lesson plans. Graded midterm exams for class of 18.

ABC KID KAMP, Syracuse, NY
Coordinator, Summers 1997 and 1996
Organized daily activities program for 45 children. Developed promotional strategies for potential markets.

COMPUTER SKILLS

Word, WordPerfect, PageMaker, FileMaker Pro

EDUCATION

SYRACUSE UNIVERSITY, Syracuse, NY
Bachelor of Arts in Public Relations, *magna cum laude*, June 1998

Before

Public Relations Account Executive (After)

JAMIE BROWN   123 Main Street • Hometown, NY 00000 • (555) 555-1234 • jbrown@company.com

PUBLIC RELATIONS ACHIEVEMENTS

SYRACUSE HEART ASSOCIATION, Syracuse, NY
Public Relations Manager, *2000-present*
- Serve as consultant to 7 state chapters regarding campaign problems and activities.
- Organize statewide and regional campaign meetings; and speak at several campaign conferences.
- Review related state legislation activities and bring specific bills to the attention of proper committee or individual.
- Staff the Legislative Advisory Committee and follow through on specific bills.
- Develop fundraising programs and conducted two annual campaigns for newly merged Central Chapter.
- Serve as chair for New York Independent Health Agency Committee and secretary for Federal Campaign.
- Assisted with developing and teaching new employee orientation courses.

Campaign Assistant for Greater Syracuse Chapter, *1995-1997*
- Supervised chapter campaigns and assisted Executive Director with campaign personnel and budget.

BIG APPLE NATURAL FOODS, Syracuse, NY
Special Events Coordinator, *1998-2000*
- Managed $425,000 budget to coordinate special events and create advertising and promotional materials.
- Handled charity fundraising, corporate image positioning, and community outreach efforts.

Assistant to the Director of Public Relations, *1997-1998*
- Assisted in promotion and publicity of special events.
- Drafted, edited, finalized, and distributed press releases and kits to initiate and maximize media relations efforts.
- Researched prospective consumer markets using Internet and direct contact techniques.
- Created direct-mail lists, updated media lists, and maintained task priority lists.

SYRACUSE UNIVERSITY, Syracuse, NY
Teacher's Assistant and Proofreader for "Working with the Media" Class and Text, *Fall and Spring 1998*

PUBLIC RELATIONS AND COMMUNICATION EDUCATION

SYRACUSE UNIVERSITY, Syracuse, NY
Bachelor of Arts in Public Relations, magna cum laude, *June 1998*

QUALIFICATIONS AND CAPABILITIES

- Campaign development and implementation experience with major health agency.
- Supervisory experience with both professional and nonprofessional staffs.
- Ability to plan and direct successful programs for fundraising, public relations, and promotions-oriented clients.
- Extensive volunteer recruitment experience and success motivating diverse teams.
- Experience representing agency interests to legislators and lobbyists.
- Capacity to use Word, WordPerfect, Lotus 123, and PageMaker for drafting and editing features and promotional materials, budgeting and financial tasks, and graphics projects.

- Arial Narrow is a bit more creative.
- Identifying information uses one line.
- Headlines use descriptive phrases and creative style.
- Creative bullets replace functional subheadings and paragraph presentations.
- Qualifications and capabilities section is closing overview.
- Targeted achievements section is first, using a format that shows promotions within each of his first two work settings.
- Summer position omitted.
- Subtle, yet creative design is appropriate for this field.

Real Estate Professional (Before)

- Identifying information uses three lines.

- Experienced candidate's multipurpose resume does not inform reader of goals.

- Education presented first.

- Experience under basic and generic header.

- Bullet presentation of experience descriptions easy to peruse or read thoroughly.

Dana Johnson

123 Main Street
(555) 555-1234

Hometown, CA 00000
djohnson@company.com

EDUCATION
SANTA CLARA UNIVERSITY, Santa Clara, CA
Bachelor of Science in Business Administration, 1980

EXPERIENCE
SAN JOSE AND SANTA CLARA HOME LOANS, San Jose, CA
Real Estate Loan Officer, 2001-present
- Originated real estate loans, developed marketing plan to expand business.
- Conducted cold calls, created individualized mortgage broker packets, completed individual and group presentations designed to generate Conventional, FHA/VA, PERS, JUMBO, Community Home Buyer, and CHAFA loan business.

BAY AREA BANK, Santa Clara, CA
Real Estate Loan Officer, 1998-2001
- Originated real estate loans, developed marketing plan to expand business.
- Conducted cold calls, created individualized mortgage broker packets, completed individual and group presentations designed to generate loan business.
- Planned and implemented first-ever real estate expo promotional event.

HOUSING LENDING, Fresno, CA
Wholesale Account Executive, 1996-1998
- Marketed loan and financing programs to financial institutions and mortgage brokers in San Joaquin, Merced, Fresno, and Stanislaus counties.
- Conducted cold calls, created customer specific material packets, completed individual and group presentations designed to generate loan business.
- Train mortgage brokers, loan officers, and real estate agents in Conventional, Jumbo, FHA/VA, PERS, Community Home Buyer, and other niche programs.

CALIFORNIA MORTGAGE SPECIALISTS, INC., San Mateo, CA
Professional Real Estate Loan Auditor, 1992-1996
- Audited loans determining FHLMC/FNMA, FSLIC, or private investor marketability.
- Reviewed notes and deeds of trust to determine accuracy and legality.
- Interacted with Savings and Loan and Mortgage professionals in Western US.

SANTA CLARA SAVINGS, Santa Clara, CA
Loan Officer in Residential Lending Department, 1986-1992
- Responsible for residential and commercial loans in California and throughout US.
- Managed loan processing and underwriting staff of 10.
- Evaluated residential loans for approval or denial and FHLMC/FNMA conformance.
- Coordinated loan closing with production, closing, and with legal staffs.
- Traveled to project sites to establish positive relations with builders and sales representatives and outline financing and efficient loan procedures.

Loan Underwriter/Processor of Residential and Government Loans, 1982-1986
Loan Underwriter in Secondary Market Department, 1980-1982
Loan Packager in Loan Processing Department, 1978-1980

Before

Real Estate Professional (After)

Dana Johnson

123 Main Street • Hometown, CA 00000 • (555) 555-1234 • djohnson@company.com

REAL ESTATE LENDING ACHIEVEMENTS

SAN JOSE AND SANTA CLARA HOME LOANS, San Jose, CA
Real Estate Loan Officer, 2001-present
- Originated real estate loans, developed marketing plan to expand business in Santa Clara County.
- Conducted cold calls, created broker packets, completed presentations to generate Conventional, FHA/VA, PERS, JUMBO, and CHAFA loans.

BAY AREA BANK, Santa Clara, CA
Real Estate Loan Officer, 1998-2001
- Conducted cold calls, created individualized mortgage broker packets, completed individual and group presentations designed to generate loan business.
- Planned and implemented first-ever real estate expo promotional event.

HOUSING LENDING, Fresno, CA
Wholesale Account Executive, 1996-1998
- Marketed loan and financing programs in San Joaquin, Merced, Fresno, and Stanislaus counties.
- Conducted cold calls, created customer-specific material packets, completed individual and group presentations designed to generate loan business.

CALIFORNIA MORTGAGE SPECIALISTS, INC., San Mateo, CA
Professional Real Estate Loan Auditor, 1992-1996
- Audited loans to determine marketability to FHLMC/FNMA, FSLIC, or private investors.
- Interacted with Savings and Loan and Mortgage professionals in Western US.

SANTA CLARA SAVINGS, Santa Clara, CA
Loan Officer in Residential Lending Department, 1986-1992
- Evaluated residential loans for approval or denial and FHLMC/FNMA conformance.
- Traveled to project sites to establish positive relations with builders and sales representatives.

Loan Underwriter/Processor in Residential and Government Loan Departments, 1982-1986
Loan Underwriter in Secondary Market Department, 1980-1982
Loan Packager in Loan Processing Department, 1978-1980

PROFESSIONAL PROFILE

- Over 15 years in mortgage banking, customer service, finance, loan qualifications, and risk analysis.
- Expertise with Conventional, FHA/VA, PERS, JUMBO, and CHAFA loans.
- B.S. in Business, from Santa Clara University, in 1980 and continuing professional studies.

- Century Schoolbook font is professional.
- Identifying information uses only two lines.
- Clearly headlined achievement section, with detailed descriptions and highlight accomplishments.
- Dana is a professional with more than twenty years of experience. Her career has progressed nicely. Because of the fluid nature of her field, she is always ready to share an updated resume and talk about possibilities.
- Achievements are presented first, using a format that shows promotions and accomplishments.
- Profile is last, summarizing all qualifications offered and including education.

- Times New Roman font is traditional.

- Identifying information uses four lines and may not format well once e-mailed.

- Multipurpose resume generally good, but does not project focus.

- Education and work experience under basic and generic header.

- Dates, titles, and all first-line items highlighted via italics.

- Two-column and paragraph presentation of experience descriptions difficult to peruse quickly or read thoroughly.

- Zip code and street address included for experiences.

- All experience presented under one header.

Francis Williams

123 Main Street	PO Box 987
Hometown, Ohio 00000-0000	Homeville, Ohio 00001-0000
555. 555.1234	fwilliams@college.edu

EDUCATION

The Ohio State University	*Degree: BSBA*
Columbus, Ohio 43210	Major: Business, Marketing
GPA: 3.30/4.0	Expected Graduation Date: 2003

WORK EXPERIENCE

February 2002-April 2002   *Intern, Birthright Israel*
46 East Sixteenth Avenue   Columbus, Ohio 43201
Recruited and interviewed candidates for national Birthright Israel program. Recruitment included campus-wide telephone and marketing campaign.

July 2001-August 2001   *Intern, NetAds, Inc.*
2880 San Thomas Expressway   Santa Clara, California 95051
Designed database tracking sales leads and developments. Initiated and developed early stages of contact with potential clientele. Marketed product to more than 400 potential clients, including Visa, DreamWorks Inc. and Knight-Ridder Press.

October 2000-January 2002   *Server, World Cuisine Café*
106 West Vine Street   Columbus, Ohio 43215
Used thorough knowledge of varied food menu and over 75 different fine wines and spirits to guide guests through fine-dining experience. Demonstrated prompt, accurate service.

October 1998-December 1998   *Intern, Abercrombie and Fitch Co.*
4 Limited Parkway   Columbus, Ohio 43068
Analyzed sales and presented findings to supervisors. Photographed students at local college campuses for research and development. Designed men's garment for Spring line.

October 1996-September 2000   *Receptionist, Worthington Realtors*
882 High Street   Worthington, Ohio 43085

INTERESTS, ACTIVITIES, AND HONORS

Alpha Phi Women's Fraternity Alumni Relations Director: January 2002-present
American Business Women's Association Fundraising Chair: April 2002-present
Ohio State University Community Commitment Volunteer: September 1999-present
Project Open Hand Columbus, Volunteer: April 2000-present
Susan G. Komen Breast Cancer Foundation, Fundraiser: 1997-present
America Israel Public Affairs Committee Member: February 2002-present
The Ohio State University Trustees Scholar: 2001

Before

Student Seeking Internship (After)

FRANCIS WILLIAMS Home State University • PO Box 987 • Hometown, Ohio 00000

LOBBYING AND FUNDRAISING INTERNSHIP QUALIFICATIONS

- Experienced as fundraiser and program recruiter for campus organizations.
- Confidence in event planning, marketing strategy development, and outreach.
- Capacity to draft and finalize correspondence, promotional materials, and brochures.
- Research, analytical, and presentation skills associated with lobbying and topical reports.
- Business knowledge gained from courses including: Accounting, Finance, and Marketing.

BUSINESS AND MARKETING EDUCATION

THE HOME STATE UNIVERSITY, Columbus, Ohio
Bachelor of Science, Business Administration, anticipated May 2003
- Major: *Business, Marketing* and Secondary Major: *Business, Transportation Logistics*
- Overall GPA: 3.30, Trustees Scholar, and National Dean's List Scholar
- University of Dreams Internship and Professional Development Program, 2002

FUNDRAISING, OUTREACH, AND LEADERSHIP ACHIEVEMENTS

- Susan G. Komen Breast Cancer Foundation, Fundraiser, 1997-present
- America Israel Public Affairs Committee, Member, February 2002-present
- Alpha Phi International Fraternity, Director, Alumni Relations, January 2002-present
- American Business Women's Association, Chairperson, Fundraising, April 2002-present
- The Ohio State University Community Commitment, Volunteer, September 1999-present
- Project Open Hand Columbus, Volunteer, April 2000-present

OUTREACH, MARKETING, AND ADMINISTRATIVE ACHIEVEMENTS

BIRTHRIGHT ISRAEL, Columbus, Ohio
Recruiting and Marketing Intern, Spring 2002
- Recruited and interviewed candidates for national program providing free travel to Israel.
- Recruitment included campus-wide telephone and marketing campaign.

NETADS, INC., Santa Clara, California
Marketing Intern, Summer 2001
- Designed database tracking sales leads and initiated contact with potential clientele.
- Marketed to 400 potential clients, including Visa, DreamWorks Inc., and Knight-Ridder Press.

ABERCROMBIE AND FITCH CO., Columbus, Ohio 43068
Marketing Intern, Fall 1998
- Analyzed sales and presented findings to supervisors.

WORTHINGTON REALTORS, Worthington, Ohio
Receptionist, Summers and Part-time 1996-2000

- Book Antiqua font.
- Identifying information uses one line.
- Qualifications section serves as objective and overview.
- Headlines highlight significant entries and qualifications for cited goal.
- Bullets for all entries allows for quick perusal.
- Most important entries appear first.
- Francis's strategy of having one multipurpose and one targeted resume is good for those seeking internships. Both possess qualities worthy of modeling as you create or update resumes.

- Courier font is clear, yet bland.

- Experience appears first, under basic and generic header.

- Education, courses, and certification presented last.

Corey Davis

123 Main Street • Hometown, NJ 00000 • (555) 555-1234 • cd@company.com

Experience

EDISON TECHNICAL AND VOCATIONAL HIGH SCHOOL, Edison, NJ
9th Grade General Science Teacher, September 2001 – present

EDISON TECHNICAL AND VOCATIONAL HIGH SCHOOL, Edison, NJ
Biology Teacher (Contract Substitute), January – June 2001

MAPLEWOOD-SOUTH ORANGE SCHOOL DISTRICT, Rochester, NY
Substitute Teacher K-12, October – December 2001

NEWARK ACADEMY, Rochester, NY
Substitute Teacher K-5, October – December 2001

Education

FAIRLEIGH DICKINSON UNIVERSITY, Madison, NJ
M.S., Math/Science/Technology Education, expected August 2003
- Received Eisenhower Grant to study critical thinking in classrooms
- Researched and wrote thesis: Problem Based Learning to Increase Engagement in an Urban Science Classroom
- Created Interdisciplinary Biology, English and Social Studies unit
- Developed and used problem-based learning projects as well as inquiry-based learning units within classroom settings

DREW UNIVERSITY, Madison, NJ
B.S., Ecology and Evolutionary Biology, May 2000

Selected Courses

Human Genetics & Evolution, Biochemistry, Ecology, Evolution, Cell Biology, Mammalian Anatomy, Evolution of the Earth (geology), Calculus I and II, Statistics for Biologists, Probability, History and Philosophy of Education, Foundations of Math/Science/Technology, Teaching Math/Science, Inquiry in the Classroom, Classroom Dynamics, Differentiating Instruction, Developing Literacy Skills, Literacy through Math/Science/Technology, Assessment, Problem-Based Learning

Teaching Certifications and Qualifications

NJ STATE CERTIFICATION IN BIOLOGY, 7TH THROUGH 12TH GRADES, June 2002
NJ STATE CERTIFICATION IN GENERAL SCIENCE, June 2002

Before

Corey Davis

123 Main Street · Hometown, NJ 00000 · (555) 555-1234 · cdavis@company.com

Teaching Certifications and Qualifications

- NJ State Certification in Biology, 7th through 12th grades, received June 2002
- NJ State Certification in General Science, received June 2002
- Creativity and knowledge to create lessons for students at various readiness levels
- Interest in teaching science, mathematics, as well as Spanish
- Experience co-teaching in an inclusion classroom

Science, Mathematics, and Education Studies

FAIRLEIGH DICKINSON UNIVERSITY, Madison, NJ
Master of Science, Math/Science/Technology Education, anticipated August 2003
- Received Eisenhower Grant to study how to bring critical thinking into classrooms
- Thesis: Problem Based Learning to Increase Engagement in an Urban Science Classroom
- Created a unit incorporating literacy building strategies into science
- Developed and used problem-based and inquiry-based learning units within classroom settings
- Developed unit differentiated for three different readiness levels

DREW UNIVERSITY, Madison, NJ
Bachelor of Science, Ecology and Evolutionary Biology, Psychology minor,
May 2000

Science, Mathematics, and Education Coursework

- Human Genetics & Evolution, Genetics, Biochemistry, Ecology, Evolution, Cell Biology, Principles of Experimental Biology Lab, Animal Behavior, Mammalian Anatomy, Evolution of the Earth
- Calculus I and II, Statistics for the Sciences, Statistics for Biologists, Probability
- Foundations of Math/Science/Technology, Teaching Math/Science, Inquiry in the Classroom, Classroom Dynamics, Differentiating Instruction, Literacy through Math/Science/Technology, Assessment, Problem Based Learning

Teaching Experience

EDISON TECHNICAL AND VOCATIONAL HIGH SCHOOL, Edison, NJ
9th Grade General Science Teacher, September 2001 – present
Biology Teacher (Contract Substitute), January – June 2001

MAPLEWOOD-SOUTH ORANGE SCHOOL DISTRICT, Rochester, NY
Substitute Teacher K-12, October – December 2001

NEWARK ACADEMY, Rochester, NY
Substitute Teacher K-5, October – December 2001

- Century Schoolbook is a professional and appropriately titled font.
- Identifying information uses two lines.
- Qualification summary appears first as objective and overview.
- Summary entries replace individual job descriptions.
- Headlines highlight significant education and courses, the strengths of his candidacy.
- Corey is about to complete his master's degree, so he is searching for a new position.
- Corey determined that his education and courses were the central core of his candidacy, so they were highlighted appropriately.
- Think about the "headlines" used in this version and about changes in the order of presentation.

Resources, Publications, and Helpful Web Sites

Not too long ago reference librarians were characterized as the best and least utilized job-search resources. Today, Internet search engines are powerful but perhaps the most overused tool. This section identifies some additional obvious and not-so-obvious research and job-search support tools.

Resources, Publications, and Helpful Web Sites

Printed and Web-based resources are critical because job seekers and resume writers have a lot to do. They must conduct pre-research (research before job search) to set goals; to enhance field-focused vocabulary used in resumes, correspondence, and during interviews; to develop a hit list of prospective employers; and to prepare for interviews. Also, interactions with others, including mentors, role models, and advocates are crucial to success.

The following listing of publications and Web sites is offered to facilitate your efforts to complete the seven steps to job-search success. Identify those that address your needs, and use those that are appropriate to your strategies and goals.

Publications

America's Top Internships (The Princeton Review)

An extremely valuable annually published work that identifies options for those seeking pre- and post-graduation internships. Used creatively, it can offer insights into potential career employers. Indexing by geographic, field, and special criteria makes it an easy to use and, for some, a pre-research as well as job-search tool. In fact, you can use the indexes of this book, combined with its companion piece, *The Internship Bible,* as goal-setting assessment devices. By reviewing the indexes, then identifying and prioritizing your top five fields of interests, you can gain focus and identify potential employers.

The Back-Door Guide to Short-Term Job Adventures (Ten Speed Press)

This publication addresses the needs of those seeking pre- or post-graduation internship, extern-ship, and related experiences. Readers can use post-graduation experiences like those indexed and described in this book to "bridge" from commencement to first jobs. It contains creative and nonbusiness-oriented, fun, community service, and meaningful skill-building opportunities.

Book of Lists (Crain Communication and/or your local business journal)

Annual publications listing "top twenty-five" firms in specific cities or regions. A-through-Z listings of top firms include fields such as the following: Accounting, Advertising, Airlines, Architecture, BioTech, Commercial Banking, Computer Networking, Computer Training, Venture Capital, and Video Production, to name just a few. They often include listings of "fastest growing public and private firms" as well as "highest paid CEOs." Clearly, these are among the best resources to use when seeking up-to-date information needed to create a hit list of potential employers and, of course, when networking.

Career Opportunities In (Checkmark Books/ Facts on File)

Titles and topics include the following: Health Care, Newspaper, Magazines, Mental Health and Social Work, Marketing and Sales, Medical Technologies and Technicians, Radio and Television, Public Administration, Education, Public Relations, Film and Video, Performing Arts, Therapy and Allied Health Professionals, Environmental, and Physical Sciences. This is one of the best "if you can describe a job, you can get a job" collection of publications. Books contain concise descriptions of field and functional options. Like many books of this kind, appendices list potential employers, professional associations, as well as educational options. These too-often-ignored final sections can be "hidden gems" for career explorers and job seekers.

The *Careers For* series (VGM Career Horizons, a division of NTC Publishing Group)

Intriguing titles include "Careers for" the following groups: Animal Lovers, Bookworms, Caring People, Computer Buffs, Crafty People, Culture Lovers, Environmental Types, Fashion Plates, Film Buffs, Foreign Language Aficionados, Good Samaritans, Gourmets, Health Nuts, History Buffs, Kids at Heart, Music Lovers, Mystery

Buffs, Nature Lovers, Night Owls, Numbers Crunchers, Plant Lovers, Shutterbugs, Sports Nuts, Travel Buffs, and Writers. This is a creative and ever-expanding "what can I do with a set of skills and interest in" collection. Each book uses metaphor-linked titles to connect readers with career options. Each books contains brief descriptions of fields and functions, intended to stimulate additional pre-research.

The *Careers In* series (VGM Career Horizons, a division of NTC Publishing Group)

Titles and topics include "Careers in" the following areas: Accounting, Advertising, Business, Child Care, Communications, Computers, Education, Engineering, Environment, Finance, Government, Health Care, High Tech, Journalism, Law, Marketing, Medicine, Science, Social & Rehabilitation Services. One of the most used and easiest-to-read sets of "jobs-within-fields" publications. Each book contains brief descriptions of functional options within fields noted in the titles. Information regarding fields and employment options should inspire continued pre-research and facilitate development of the career focus required of effective job search. Listings of professional associations are very useful. Reviewing these publications will most definitely instill within readers the vocabulary required to state goals and, later, resume-writing and job-search efforts.

The *Directory of Executive Recruiters* (Kennedy Information)

A comprehensive listing of contingency and retainer firms, indexed via industries and recruiter specialties. This publication is particularly valuable for experienced job seekers and those with technical and specialized backgrounds.

The *Executive Recruiters Almanac* (Adams Media)

A user-friendly listing of search firms and other third-party organizations. It contains discussions of how to use these organizations most effectively as well as listings of numerous firms indexed by fields, functions, and industries. While exceptionally valuable for experienced candidates, this publication can facilitate the efforts of almost all candidates.

The *Great Jobs For* series (VGM Career Horizons, a division of NTC Publishing Group)

Majors included in the series include the following: Psychology, History, English, Communication, Business, Sociology, Foreign Language, and Engineering. This is an excellent "what can I do with a major in" collection of publications. Each easy-to-read and quickly reviewed book contains recommended fields listed by majors. These books naturally stimulate pre-research efforts that facilitate goal-setting. Even if your particular major does not appear in a title, reading a few of the books in the collection should inspire you to complete field-focused research.

The *Harvard Business School Career Guide* series (Harvard Business School Publishing)

Subjects include the following: Management Consulting, Finance, Not-For Profit, and Marketing. These books are written for MBAs, but, if used creatively, they can provide exceptional support for undergraduates and others interested in "Ivy League-caliber jobs." Each begins with general discussions of investment banking, finance, and consulting, followed by comprehensive listings of organizations within these fields, and ending with extremely powerful annotated bibliographies.

The *Internship Bible* (Princeton Review/ Random House Inc.)

Another of the annually published internship directories that, if used creatively, offers insights into post-graduation opportunities. It also offers indexing by geographic, field, and special criteria.

Internships (Peterson's)

Another annually published book that identifies pre- and post-graduation "internships" that, if used creatively, offer insights into potential externship and post-graduation opportunities. Indexing by geographic, field, and special criteria makes it an easy to use and, for some, a pre-research as well as job-search tool.

The *JobBank Guide To* series and *The JobBank* series (Adams Media)

JobBank guides list companies by industry, including Health Care, Computer, and High Tech. JobBank books list companies as well as other job-search related organizations within specific cities and regions. Regional titles cover cities and regions such as the following: Atlanta, Austin/San Antonio, Carolina, Chicago, Connecticut, Dallas/Fort Worth, Denver, Detroit, Florida, Houston, Indiana, Las Vegas, Los Angeles, Minneapolis/St. Paul, Missouri, Ohio, Greater Philadelphia, Phoenix, Pittsburgh, Portland, San Francisco Bay Area, Seattle, Tennessee, Virginia, and Metro Washington, D.C. These publications also contain brief discussions regarding general job search.

The Knock 'em Dead series (Adams Media)

These general job-search, resume, and interview guides target experienced as well as first-time job seekers. Each is comprehensive in content, yet easy to read and inspirational. They educate and motivate people in all phases of job search.

Making a Mil-Yen Teaching English in Japan (Stone Bridge Press)

This specialty publication highlights an increasingly popular post-graduation option. For those who wish to use opportunities to "test teaching as a career," "begin an international career," or "bridge from commencement to first jobs," this an excellent resource. Once in Japan, you can explore education, business, travel, tourism, and varied other careers.

Naked at the Interview (John Wiley & Sons)

Immodestly speaking, one of the best comprehensive goal-setting, job-search, and interview resources for soon-to-be and recent college grads. Don't let the title fool you. It is not X-rated, nor is it just for those seeking to improve interview skills. It is a humorous and easy to use pre-research as well as job-search tool. Many of the resumes and correspondence examples offered illustrate effective approaches applicable to all job seekers.

The *Opportunities In* series (VGM Career Horizons)

Another of the often-used and easy-to-read set of "if you can describe a job, you can get a job" collection of publications. Each book contains brief descriptions of functional options within fields noted in the titles. The information regarding fields and employment options should inspire continued pre-research and, ultimately, facilitate development of the career focus required to begin effective job search.

Peterson's Job Opportunities series (Peterson's)

Titles include opportunities for the following concentrations: Business Majors, Engineering and Computer Science Majors, and Health and Science. This is an exceptional series of employer directories that, if used effectively, facilitates internship, externship, and post-graduation job-search efforts. Like others, it offers indexing by geographic, field, and other special criteria. Indexes refer readers to brief profiles with names, addresses, and basic identifying information for potential employers.

Plunkett's Industry Almanacs (Plunkett Research, Ltd.)

Collection of publications including industries such as the following: Biotech and Genetics, Health Care, Retail, and E-Commerce, to name a few. This is an excellent resource for those seeking internships, externships, or entry-level opportunities within any of the fields covered. These books also offer geographic and functional indexes and Web page citations. They are very expensive, so they are best used as library resources.

US Directory of Entertainment Employers (EEJ Publishing)

An annual specialized publication that can be used as a comprehensive employer listing for those seeking internships, externships, or entry-level opportunities within the entertainment field. Lists advertising agencies, television and film production houses, lawyers, public relations firms, agents, recording studios, film studios, and many other prospective employers.

Vacation Work's Teaching English Abroad: Talk Your Way Around the World! (Peterson's)

This comprehensive guide offers information for those seeking this increasingly popular option. Teaching overseas can be a "wonderful experience," as well as a "springboard to an international career."

The *Vault Guides* series (Vault Reports, Inc.)

Another collection of publications that begins with detailed field and functional descriptions and ends with employer listings. In addition to name, address, phone, and URL for each employer, these publications offer good "getting started" and "pre-interview" information. The one-page-for-each-employer format is easy to use and offers quick photocopying options, which facilitates employer research. It is an excellent first resource to use to start developing a "hit list" once goals are focused. Also, more comprehensive industry and employer reports can be ordered as desired.

Wet Feet Press Guides (Wet Feet Press)

This is another series of printed as well as Web-accessible publications focusing on specialized fields including Advertising and PR, Biotechnology, Consulting, Entertainment and Sports, Finance Services, and Technology. These publications offer field and function information, as well as firm and industry specific profiles. Specialized resources targeting particular companies and addressing issues related to interviewing are accessible via the Web.

Web Sites

As you progress on your own research, you will find your own valuable sources of information on the Internet. Here are a few places to begin:

www.ipl.org/ref/AON

The Internet Public Library Associations on the Net provides access to professional associations. Resources available through professional associations are often the most valuable. Membership directories facilitate networking for goal-setting as well as job-search efforts. Journals and other publications enhance the vocabulary needed to enhance specialized field-focused vocabulary. By joining associations, attending seminars, reading literature, and networking with members, you will truly talk the talk and walk the walk.

www.yahoo.com

Allows you to navigate your way to much pertinent information, including offerings on information including the following: Resume Builder, My Career Center, Salary Wizard, Executive Center, Career Communities, and Company Research. The site also provides information about associations, company information, and additional data that can be used for goal-setting, networking, as well as direct job-search efforts.

www.careerbuilder.com

One of many multiple industry and national posting, resume-collection, and job-search information sites. It promotes the capabilities of a "personal search agent" that allows you to identify job-search criteria and then be contacted whenever new postings come up. Categories for postings include the following: Admin/Corporate, Accounting, Banking and Finance, College, Contract/Freelance, Customer Service, Engineering, Executive, Health Care, Human Resources, Information Technology, Manufacturing, Nonprofit, Retail, Sales and Marketing, and

www.careers.wsj.com

The *Wall Street Journal's* Career Journal is a multifaceted site. It contains articles, postings, resume collections, links to other sites, resume critiquing, and general advice regarding job search and careers. It is a high tech, online version of what would have been career- and job-search-focused periodicals or newspaper sections just a few years ago. It is an inspirational as well as educational and logistical support site of value for experienced candidates.

www.flipdog.com

Another multifaceted site that contains articles, postings, resume banks, resume critiquing, and general advice. While the over 300,000 jobs within the system should motivate some, others will find additional resources quite valuable. You can get expert advice from the Resource Center, have employers look for your resume, enhance your career via a semimonthly newsletter, use the search agent, and reach employers via job banks and employer links.

www.hotjobs.com

This site, a Yahoo! service, boasts over 400,000 jobs, internships, and career-oriented positions. It also offers industry information, job-search advice, and a relocation center. Postings are accessed by categories including these: Company, Staffing Firm, U.S. Location, Int'l Location, HotJobs Canada, Accounting and Finance, Advertising and PR, Arts and Entertainment, Publishing, Banking and Mortgage, Clerical and Administrative, College, Construction and Facilities, Customer Service, Education and Training, Engineering and Architecture, Entrepreneurial and Start-up, Entry Level, Government, Health Care, Hospitality and Travel, Human Resources, Insurance, Internet and New Media, Law Enforcement and Security, Legal, Management Consulting, Manufacturing and Operations, Marketing, Nonprofit and Volunteer, Pharmaceutical and Biotech, Real Estate, Restaurant and Food Service, Retail, Sales, Tech Contract, Technology, Telecommunications, Temp Jobs, and Transportation and Logistics.

www.WorkTree.com

The self-proclaimed largest job-search portal in the world, this site offers access to over 50,000 links to all types of job and career resources. Information-laden links are categorized under headings including the following: National Jobsites, HotJobs, HeadHunter, Government Jobsites, Federal, State, Local, Industry Jobsites, Advertising, Healthcare, IT, City/State Jobsites (Atlanta, Boston, Texas, etc.), International Jobsites (Australia, Canada, India, etc.), Salary Calculator, Compare Salaries, Living Cost, Resume Services, Resumes, Cover Letters, Power Job Search, Recruiter Link (Banking, Engineering, etc.), Employer Links (Biotech, Oil & Gas, etc.), College Graduates, Entry-Level and MBA, Newspaper Links (Austin, New York, Seattle, etc.), *Fortune* 1000 Jobs, Airlines, Health Care, Job Tips, and Articles. It also boasts user access to 3,000,000-plus jobs. Boasting aside, it is a comprehensive portal that eases access to information that can maximize efforts of many.

www.monster.com

Literally and figuratively, the monster of all posting, resume-collection, and career-advice sites. This creatively advertised and most recognized posting, resume-bank, employer-research, search-agent, and job-search advice site isn't scary at all. It is very user-friendly, and their cute corporate logo is rather inviting. This site promotes with great pride that it contains over 17 million resumes and 1 million postings for job seekers of all stages and ages, including internship candidates, soon-to-be and recent college grads, and experienced professionals. While too many use this resource passively for reactive efforts only, it can be a very, very powerful proactive tool.

www.google.com

A user-friendly and all-encompassing search engine that can be used for goal-setting, job search, interview preparation, and other critical job-search efforts. Simply type in a keyword to identify sites noted in this book. Navigating through sites identified will enhance your knowledge of fields, functions, and companies.

www.metacrawler.com

Another easy-to-use and comprehensive search engine that uses keyword searches to identify valuable sites. Searches can be inspired by simple words or complete phrases. As examples, you can enter "resume," "advertising careers," "consulting firms," "interview skills," "behavioral interviews," or "salary negotiation," just to name a few, into the engine. These seven phrases alone yielded over 400 hits from this engine.

www.wetfeet.com

Do research, get advice, find a job are the first three major headings you will see when you access this site. Research is broken down into links including the following: Companies, Careers and Industries, Newsletters, Salary and Perks, City Profiles, International, Insider Guides, and Self-Assessment. Get Advice includes Resumes, Interviewing, Managing Your Career, Internships, Diversity, Discussion Groups, Career Changers, MBAs, and Undergrads. Find a Job has two basic links: Job Listings and Internship Listings. As you navigate through the varied links, you will be provided general information and offered opportunities to buy some of the varied and valuable publications created by this group.

www.vault.com

Major headings you will see when you access this site include the following: Employers, Job Seekers, Community, Industries, Career Topics, Companies, and Hot Links. Employers are encouraged to post jobs and internships, access the resume database, and complete surveys so data on the firm might be included in future publications. Job Seekers are linked to Find a Job, Find an Internship, Get a Graduate Degree, Featured Employers, Post Your Resume, Resume Review, Career Coaching, Job-Search Survival, and Student Center options. Community users are granted access to Message Boards, Ask Our Experts, and How's My Resume links. Industry options include Consulting, Finance, Law, TV News, and more, with Career Topics offering information on Career Change, Compensation, Job Search, and other issues. Like other sites, basic information is offered, and you will be given opportunities to purchase publications created by this particular group.

www.fortune.com

Grants you access to information and the annual lists generated by the venerable periodical *Fortune*. Lists include: *Fortune* 500, Global 100, 100 Best Companies to Work For, and 100 Fastest Growing Companies. Topical career advice as well as "Q&A" exchanges are also offered. This is a useful resource to use when developing hit lists of prospective employers.

www.thomasregister.com

A comprehensive resource for finding companies and products manufactured in North America. Simply enter one or more words into the search box after selecting the product, company, or brand name you're looking for to search from over 72,000 product headings and more than 170,000 company listings.

www.net-temps.com

Net-Temps is the self-proclaimed number-one destination of job seekers looking for contract, temporary, or direct employment through a staffing agency. Employers can post a job; candidates can find a job, gain career advice, post a resume, or create a search agent. This site is unique in that it addresses needs of those seeking part-time, temp, or contract situations, and it highlights various agencies. Over 45,000 total jobs are advertised.

www.rileyguide.com

A directory of employment and career information sources and services on the Internet, this site provides instruction for job seekers and recruiters on how to use the Internet to their best advantage. Originally a comprehensive printed reference, then a rather passive, yet thorough listing, and now an interactive site, this is an excellent resource.

www.idealist.com

Lists over 29,000 nonprofit and community organizations in 153 countries, which you can search or browse by name, location, or mission. It contains thousands of volunteer opportunities in your community and around the world and a list of organizations that can help you volunteer abroad. It is characterized by many as the best Nonprofit Career Center on the Web, with thousands of job and internship listings.

Industry-Specific Sites

- *www.association.org* (Association of Internet Professionals)
- *www.adage.com* (Advertising Age)
- *www.bio.com* (Biotechnology and Pharmaceutical)
- *www.chronicle.com* (Chronicle of Higher Education)
- *www.fjn.com* (Financial Job Network)
- *www.gamasutra.com* (Gamasutra for Computer Animation and Video Games)
- *www.lawjobs.com* (Law Jobs)
- *www.medzilla.com* (Biotechnology, Pharmaceutical, and Medical)
- *www.pmi.org* (Project Management Institute)
- *www.prsa.org* (Public Relations Society of America)
- *www.starchefs.com* (Food Services)

Information Technology Sites

- *www.brainbuzz.com*
- *www.computerjobstore.com*
- *www.dice.com*
- *www.techies.com*

Soon-to-Be and Recent College Graduate Sites

- *www.bestjobcollegecentral.com*
- *www.collegecentral.com*
- *www.collegegrad.com*
- *www.idealist.com*
- *www.internships.com*
- *www.monstertrak.com*

Federal Government Sites

- *www.fedworld.gov* (FedWorld Information Network)

Additional Listings

The following are more search engines, resume banks, and other sites to get you started on your Internet research efforts.

- *www.brassring.com*
- *www.careermosaic.com*
- *www.careerpath.com*
- *www.altavista.com*
- *www.freeality.com*
- *www.excite.com*
- *www.infosek.com*
- *www.lycos.com*
- *www.recruitusa.com*
- *www.worktree.com*

Index

THE EVERYTHING GET-A-JOB BOOK

By Steven Graber

Find a great job without going crazy!
THE EVERYTHING GET-A-JOB BOOK
From resume writing to interviewing to finding tons of job openings
Steven Graber

Whether you're looking for your first job or just trying to find a better one, *The Everything® Get-a-Job Book* will give you the practical job search advice you need. From creating a polished resume that effectively presents and sells your candidacy, to job hunting strategies on the Internet, to handling stressful interview questions smoothly, *The Everything® Get-a-Job Book* will help you stand out in the crowd. You'll find real-life examples of what not to do, as well as job search tips that can really make a difference.

Trade paperback,
$12.95 ($19.95 CAN)
1-58062-223-2, 304 pages

OTHER *EVERYTHING*® BOOKS BY ADAMS MEDIA CORPORATION

BUSINESS

Everything® **Business Planning Book**
Everything® **Coaching & Mentoring Book**
Everything® **Home-Based Business Book**
Everything® **Leadership Book**
Everything® **Managing People Book**
Everything® **Network Marketing Book**
Everything® **Online Business Book**
Everything® **Project Management Book**
Everything® **Selling Book**
Everything® **Start Your Own Business Book**
Everything® **Time Management Book**

COMPUTERS

Everything® **Build Your Own Home Page Book**
Everything® **Computer Book**

Everything® **Internet Book**
Everything® **Microsoft® Word 2000 Book**

COOKING

Everything® **Barbecue Cookbook**
Everything® **Bartender's Book, $9.95**
Everything® **Chocolate Cookbook**
Everything® **Cookbook**
Everything® **Dessert Cookbook**
Everything® **Diabetes Cookbook**
Everything® **Low-Carb Cookbook**
Everything® **Low-Fat High-Flavor Cookbook**
Everything® **Mediterranean Cookbook**
Everything® **One-Pot Cookbook**
Everything® **Pasta Book**
Everything® **Quick Meals Cookbook**
Everything® **Slow Cooker Cookbook**

Everything® **Soup Cookbook**
Everything® **Thai Cookbook**
Everything® **Vegetarian Cookbook**
Everything® **Wine Book**

HEALTH

Everything® **Anti-Aging Book**
Everything® **Dieting Book**
Everything® **Herbal Remedies Book**
Everything® **Hypnosis Book**
Everything® **Menopause Book**
Everything® **Stress Management Book**
Everything® **Nutrition Book**
Everything®**Vitamins, Minerals, and Nutritional Supplements Book**

HISTORY

Everything® **American History Book**

All Everything® books are priced at $12.95 or $14.95, unless otherwise stated. Prices subject to change without notice.
Canadian prices range from $11.95–$22.95 and are subject to change without notice.

Everything® **Civil War Book**
Everything® **World War II Book**

HOBBIES

Everything® **Bridge Book**
Everything® **Candlemaking Book**
Everything® **Casino Gambling Book**
Everything® **Chess Basics Book**
Everything® **Collectibles Book**
Everything® **Crossword and Puzzle Book**
Everything® **Digital Photography Book**
Everything® **Drums Book (with CD),** **$19.95, ($31.95 CAN)**
Everything® **Family Tree Book**
Everything® **Games Book**
Everything® **Guitar Book**
Everything® **Knitting Book**
Everything® **Magic Book**
Everything® **Motorcycle Book**
Everything® **Online Genealogy Book**
Everything® **Playing Piano and Keyboards Book**
Everything® **Rock & Blues Guitar Book (with CD), $19.95, ($31.95 CAN)**
Everything® **Scrapbooking Book**

HOME IMPROVEMENT

Everything® **Feng Shui Book**
Everything® **Gardening Book**
Everything® **Home Decorating Book**
Everything® **Landscaping Book**
Everything® **Lawn Care Book**
Everything® **Organize Your Home Book**

KIDS' STORY BOOKS

Everything® **Bedtime Story Book**
Everything® **Bible Stories Book**
Everything® **Fairy Tales Book**
Everything® **Mother Goose Book**

NEW AGE

Everything® **Astrology Book**

Everything® **Divining the Future Book**
Everything® **Dreams Book**
Everything® **Ghost Book**
Everything® **Meditation Book**
Everything® **Numerology Book**
Everything® **Palmistry Book**
Everything® **Spells and Charms Book**
Everything® **Tarot Book**
Everything® **Wicca and Witchcraft Book**

PARENTING

Everything® **Baby Names Book**
Everything® **Baby Shower Book**
Everything® **Baby's First Food Book**
Everything® **Baby's First Year Book**
Everything® **Breastfeeding Book**
Everything® **Get Ready for Baby Book**
Everything® **Homeschooling Book**
Everything® **Potty Training Book,** **$9.95, ($15.95 CAN)**
Everything® **Pregnancy Book**
Everything® **Pregnancy Organizer,** **$15.00, ($22.95 CAN)**
Everything® **Toddler Book**
Everything® **Tween Book**

PERSONAL FINANCE

Everything® **Budgeting Book**
Everything® **Get Out of Debt Book**
Everything® **Get Rich Book**
Everything® **Investing Book**
Everything® **Homebuying Book, 2nd Ed.**
Everything® **Homeselling Book**
Everything® **Money Book**
Everything® **Mutual Funds Book**
Everything® **Online Investing Book**
Everything® **Personal Finance Book**

PETS

Everything® **Cat Book**
Everything® **Dog Book**
Everything® **Dog Training and Tricks Book**
Everything® **Horse Book**
Everything® **Puppy Book**
Everything® **Tropical Fish Book**

REFERENCE

Everything® **Astronomy Book**
Everything® **Car Care Book**
Everything® **Christmas Book, $15.00,** **($21.95 CAN)**
Everything® **Classical Mythology Book**
Everything® **Divorce Book**
Everything® **Etiquette Book**
Everything® **Great Thinkers Book**
Everything® **Learning French Book**
Everything® **Learning German Book**
Everything® **Learning Italian Book**
Everything® **Learning Latin Book**
Everything® **Learning Spanish Book**
Everything® **Mafia Book**
Everything® **Philosophy Book**
Everything® **Shakespeare Book**
Everything® **Tall Tales, Legends, & Other Outrageous Lies Book**
Everything® **Toasts Book**
Everything® **Trivia Book**
Everything® **Weather Book**
Everything® **Wills & Estate Planning Book**

RELIGION

Everything® **Angels Book**
Everything® **Buddhism Book**
Everything® **Catholicism Book**
Everything® **Judaism Book**
Everything® **Saints Book**
Everything® **World's Religions Book**
Everything® **Understanding Islam Book**

SCHOOL & CAREERS

Everything® **After College Book**
Everything® **College Survival Book**
Everything® **Cover Letter Book**
Everything® **Get-a-Job Book**
Everything® **Hot Careers Book**
Everything® **Job Interview Book**
Everything® **Online Job Search Book**
Everything® **Resume Book, 2nd Ed.**
Everything® **Study Book**

All Everything® books are priced at $12.95 or $14.95, unless otherwise stated. Prices subject to change without notice.
Canadian prices range from $11.95–$22.95 and are subject to change without notice.

WE HAVE EVERYTHING . . . .

SPORTS/FITNESS

Everything® **Bicycle Book**
Everything® **Fishing Book**
Everything® **Fly-Fishing Book**
Everything® **Golf Book**
Everything® **Golf Instruction Book**
Everything® **Pilates Book**
Everything® **Running Book**
Everything® **Sailing Book, 2nd Ed.**
Everything® **T'ai Chi and QiGong Book**
Everything® **Total Fitness Book**
Everything® **Weight Training Book**
Everything® **Yoga Book**

TRAVEL

Everything® **Guide to Las Vegas**
Everything® **Guide to New England**
Everything® **Guide to New York City**
Everything® **Guide to Washington D.C.**

Everything® **Travel Guide to The Disneyland Resort®, California Adventure®, Universal Studios®, and the Anaheim Area**
Everything® **Travel Guide to the Walt Disney World® Resort, Universal Studios®, and Greater Orlando, 3rd Ed.**

WEDDINGS & ROMANCE

Everything® **Creative Wedding Ideas Book**
Everything® **Dating Book**
Everything® **Jewish Wedding Book**
Everything® **Romance Book**
Everything® **Wedding Book, 2nd Ed.**
Everything® **Wedding Organizer, $15.00** ($22.95 CAN)

Everything® **Wedding Checklist, $7.95** ($11.95 CAN)
Everything® **Wedding Etiquette Book, $7.95** ($11.95 CAN)
Everything® **Wedding Shower Book, $7.95** ($12.95 CAN)
Everything® **Wedding Vows Book, $7.95** ($11.95 CAN)
Everything® **Weddings on a Budget Book, $9.95** ($15.95 CAN)

WRITING

Everything® **Creative Writing Book**
Everything® **Get Published Book**
Everything® **Grammar and Style Book**
Everything® **Grant Writing Book**
Everything® **Guide to Writing Children's Books**
Everything® **Writing Well Book**

ALSO AVAILABLE:
THE EVERYTHING® KIDS' SERIES!

Each book is 8" x 9¼", 144 pages, and two-color throughout.

Everything® **Kids' Baseball Book, 2nd Edition, $6.95** ($11.95 CAN)
Everything® **Kids' Bugs Book, $6.95** ($10.95 CAN)
Everything® **Kids' Cookbook, $6.95** ($10.95 CAN)
Everything® **Kids' Joke Book, $6.95** ($10.95 CAN)
Everything® **Kids' Math Puzzles Book, $6.95** ($10.95 CAN)
Everything® **Kids' Mazes Book, $6.95** ($10.95 CAN)
Everything® **Kids' Money Book, $6.95** ($11.95 CAN)

Everything® **Kids' Monsters Book, $6.95** ($10.95 CAN)
Everything® **Kids' Nature Book, $6.95** ($11.95 CAN)
Everything® **Kids' Puzzle Book $6.95,** ($10.95 CAN)
Everything® **Kids' Science Experiments Book, $6.95** ($10.95 CAN)
Everything® **Kids' Soccer Book, $6.95** ($11.95 CAN)
Everything® **Kids' Travel Activity Book, $6.95** ($10.95 CAN)

Available wherever books are sold!
To order, call 800-872-5627, or visit us at everything.com

Everything® is a registered trademark of Adams Media Corporation.